ONLINE
PROFESSIONAL
DEVELOPMENT

ONLINE
PROFESSIONAL
DEVELOPMENT

Design, Deliver, Succeed!

John D. Ross

A Joint Publication

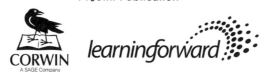

CORWIN
A SAGE Company

learning forward

CORWIN
A SAGE Company

FOR INFORMATION:

Corwin
A SAGE Company
2455 Teller Road
Thousand Oaks, California 91320
(800) 233-9936
Fax: (800) 417-2466
www.corwin.com

SAGE Ltd.
1 Oliver's Yard
55 City Road
London EC1Y 1SP
United Kingdom

SAGE India Pvt. Ltd.
B 1/I 1 Mohan Cooperative Industrial Area
Mathura Road, New Delhi 110 044
India

SAGE Asia-Pacific Pte. Ltd.
33 Pekin Street #02-01
Far East Square
Singapore 048763

Acquisitions Editor: Dan Alpert
Associate Editor: Megan Bedell
Editorial Assistant: Sarah Bartlett
Production Editor: Amy Schroller
Copy Editor: Matthew Adams
Typesetter: C&M Digitals (P) Ltd.
Proofreader: Eleni Maria Georgiou
Indexer: Michael Ferreira
Cover Designer: Rose Storey
Permissions Editor: Karen Ehrmann

Copyright © 2011 by Corwin

Printed in the United States of America

Library of Congress Cataloging-in-Publication Data

Ross, John D. (John Douglas)

Online professional development : design, deliver, succeed! / John D. Ross.

p. cm.
A Joint Publication with Learning Forward.

Includes bibliographical references and index.

ISBN 978-1-4129-8712-7 (pbk.)

1. Teachers—In-service training. 2. Career development—Computer-assisted instruction. I. Title.

LB1731.R615 2011
371.1—dc22   2011012968

This book is printed on acid-free paper.

11 12 13 14 15 10 9 8 7 6 5 4 3 2 1

Contents

Additional materials and resources related to *Online Professional Development* can be found at **www.corwin.com/rossonlinepd**

Preface

WHY THIS BOOK?

In July 2004, I attended the Secretary's No Child Left Behind Leadership Summit in Orlando. The meeting drew together state and national leaders to explore technology's potential to support the implementation of NCLB, especially through e-learning options. Earlier that year, I had launched an online learning portal for the nonprofit educational lab I worked for and had delivered online professional development to more than 1,200 educators in Tennessee. I was developing a follow-up course for the fall, and the future looked bright for our growing online professional development efforts, so the topic was of special interest to me.

At one of the sessions, a panel of K–12 distance learning experts related their experiences. They all agreed that students who participate in distance learning programs had to have certain qualities. They had to be motivated, manage time well, and be independent learners. They had to be focused, have good study skills, and should be able to find and evaluate information. I thought to myself, I wanted *all* of my students to have those skills! I commented to the panel that when I was a classroom teacher, I didn't have the luxury of working just with those students who were motivated or resourceful. The characteristics they were describing were important characteristics for all learners. I proposed that a teacher's job is to reach all students, despite the strengths they do or don't bring to the classroom. The same is true in e-learning, including professional development. One of the panelists responded that essentially what I said was true—in spirit—but we just weren't there yet. I think we're there now.

This book presents a framework you can use to design and deliver online professional development to meet the needs of the educators with whom you work. It's a framework based on my experiences developing and delivering online professional development for multiple state and regional organizations for more than a decade. The framework combines what we know about designing effective professional development—across many modes of delivery—and the resources available to deliver it online. It will help you make decisions and answer critical questions every step of the process, including determining why you want to deliver professional development online, policies and practices to support your efforts, the technologies that are right for you, and whether it worked.

I field requests for developing and delivering online professional development from staff at state departments of education, school districts, and other education providers. The number of requests has definitely increased over the past several years, especially with the hope of cutting costs for providing high-quality professional development using online technologies. When I started, I didn't have a process to follow, nor did many of the people I worked with, so I hope that the framework will help you make better decisions, uncover and deal with hidden costs and considerations, and ultimately find or develop a solution that best matches your needs. The book is the result of concern—concern that too much online professional development is following in the footsteps of previous distance learning efforts—efforts that have been far from successful, for some, dismally so. In the 1990s, many colleges and universities tried putting their course offerings online, asking college professors to not only become instructional designers but also web programmers. Many of these efforts failed, some with significant price tags and glaring scrutiny in the media. I see schools, districts, and others following along these same misguided paths as they consider online learning and professional development, but they don't have to! They *can* be successful! *You* can be successful.

As an education community, we know many things about how people learn. We know how to provide successful instruction that addresses different learning preferences, styles, and needs. We know what we want learners to know and be able to do in different domains, and we can identify activities and resources that not only help promote learning but demonstrate mastery of learning. Unfortunately, much of that knowledge seems to be forgotten when technology comes into the picture. In my experience, technology has a blinding effect. Just because you *can* use something doesn't mean it's effective.

The access to powerful digital technologies pervades our lives. We can take digital pictures of our family and share them with friends and relatives across the globe in just a few seconds. We can plan our vacations online, seeing movies and pictures of the places we want to stay, and then book tickets from the comfort of our living rooms. We don't even need to enter a single store to successfully complete our birthday or holiday shopping lists and have all our gifts show up on the doorsteps of our loved ones—on time, wrapped, and with a personal greeting. Unfortunately, our familiarity with these technologies often encourages this blinding effect when it comes to education. The spurious logic somehow follows that since we have e-mail, websites, and other online technologies, we must be able to put professional development online. In homage to the movie *Field of Dreams*, I describe this logic as the "if we build it, they will come" philosophy about technology, and I run into it time and time again. Unfortunately, unlike the movie, the adage is rarely true.

The answer to whether you can use ubiquitous and common technologies to provide effective online professional development is a resounding "Yes, you can!" I have some successful experiences doing this, as have other organizations across the country. But the idea that if you just put something online you'll change professional practice ignores that critical knowledge we have about how people learn, how we can support different learning preferences and needs, and how technologies best match those needs. It's not impossible, but it takes some planning and maybe broadening your understanding of what online professional development is or can be.

I worked in an educational research lab for more than 10 ten years. I'm used to finding, using, and conducting research, especially related to educational technology and how it supports teaching and learning. Unfortunately, there's not a lot of conclusive research about online professional development available. If you're an educator, you understand how difficult it can be to implement a rigorous research experiment in the dynamic setting of a school, and very few studies provide conclusive evidence in relation to online professional development practices. The field is growing, and I've addressed this young body of work when it's present, but in order to get you started I've also turned to experts who are developing and delivering online professional development— including some, like me, who have evaluated their own work and conducted their own research. Their stories are shared throughout this book, with longer profiles on the book's companion website, **www.corwin.com/rossonlinepd.** I also encourage you to share your own stories and resources on the book's companion website. You can combine what we have learned with what you already know about designing effective learning to design and deliver online professional development successfully.

Perhaps the most compelling lesson I've learned in writing this book, confirmed by interviewing these experts, is that what you consider online professional development may be different from what I envision, and both may change 3 or even 5 years from now, yet all can be effective. There are fundamental decisions to be made and steps to take to effectively provide online professional development regardless of the technologies you use. Those technologies are going to change over time, sometimes very quickly, so focusing on specific technologies up front is often a losing proposition. Any online professional development effort can both be effective and meet the needs of the educators you work with if you make some key decisions that will capitalize on good instruction and match it to the capacity of existing or even new and emerging technologies. This book can show you how.

MY BACKGROUND

My career in developing and delivering online professional development in its many forms evolved over time, often serendipitously. I haven't kept track of how many educators I've worked with through my online professional development efforts. There have been more than a thousand principals in Florida, many thousands of reading teachers in Tennessee and Georgia, leadership teams from schools across the state of Alabama, technology specialists in West Virginia, coaches who work with English language learners in North Carolina . . . and the number keeps growing. Being an "online professional developer" wasn't a career path option when I was growing up, but being a teacher was. I became a teacher and still look upon myself first and foremost as a teacher. As the world of online professional development has grown and this career opportunity became an option, I believe being a teacher first has helped me to be successful in this growing field.

When I went back to school to study instructional design and technology, I spent time researching how students and teachers could use technology to support their learning. In the late 1990s, digital technologies were becoming more prevalent and showing up more often in classrooms across the country. In elementary and secondary schools, most of the new personal computers were grouped in labs, and many weren't even connected to the Internet. But college campuses were moving into the world of distance learning, putting material online, and trying to expand their reach through web-based courses. Blacksburg, Virginia, is the home of Virginia Tech, where I was going to school, and was what *Reader's Digest* deemed at that time as "the most wired town in America." The growing power of the Internet was of specific interest at the university, and efforts were under way on campus to create online courses and degree programs. An instructional technology masters program was developed while I was there, and I was asked to create some online grade reporting systems for it, since I had created some during my dissertation research. It was exciting work, though very crude by today's standards, just 10 years later. But it started me along this path towards designing and developing online professional development.

While I've had an interest in computers and technology since I was first introduced to the Mac Classic back in 1986, I maintain what may be considered a sense of "healthy skepticism" about technology. That's important to know as you read this book. I encouraged my students to consider the source of any information so they can determine what biases may exist. I continue that effort now with graduate students or when I present workshops or speak at conferences. I want you to know where I'm coming from. People who work in technology are often accused of pushing the latest and greatest. I admit that can be exciting, but I temper that enthusiasm with a bit of a reality check. I hope my background in instructional design helps temper my technology enthusiasm to a reasonable degree. The newest technology is of no value if no one uses it. And one of the ways we can do a reality check is to ask some of what I call the *why* questions. Why do you want to do this? Why online professional development? From reading this book, I hope you not only figure out why, but how.

Acknowledgments

With my experiences in online learning now extending beyond a decade, I've had the privilege of working with many different people who have helped shaped my thinking, worked by my side, and offered a hand or a shoulder along the way. Thanks go to Tammy McGraw, who provided an entryway into this field early in my career, and to Jane Copley, who really saw the potential of online professional development and who taught me it's not always a bad thing to argue. I owe a great deal to my former colleague Carol Thigpin and our collaborators James Herman and Linda Stachera in the Tennessee Department of Education and the thousands of educators I worked with online, many of whom I feel I've built rapport with even though we've never met in person. I have to thank my collaborators in other state departments of education, including Henry Pollock in Florida; John Bell, Chris Wilson, Telena Madison, and their colleagues in Alabama; Julie Morrill, Sallie Mills, and Lisa Wells-Davis in Georgia; and Joanne Marino and Ivanna Mann-Thrower in North Carolina. While some have moved to new positions, I'm also deeply indebted to my ever-patient and helpful friends at Alchemy in Austin, especially Sean Ramsey, Martin Mascarenas, and Kem Phillips. I've had many tremendous colleagues who have helped me stay sane (I hope) and shouldered the burden along the way, including Jonathan Caldwell, Nathan Davis, and Amber Henderson. A special thanks to Laurene Johnson; and, for the ongoing personal and professional support and encouragement I've received, to Sharon Harsh. Thanks go to Marlene Johnshoy, one of the participants in my crowdsourcing experiment who came up with the winning name for the book. Finally, thanks to Dan Alpert, for encouraging me to undergo this project, and Jeff Mann, who saw me through it.

I'd also like to thank all those who agreed to be interviewed for this book and who shared their stories and ideas. You will find brief descriptions of their work throughout the book, with longer profiles on the book's companion website. Their experiences provide valuable context and detail far greater than any single person's experience.

Steve Baxendale, Project Coordinator
Pacific Open Learning Health Net, World Health Organization

Al Byers, Assistant Executive Director for e-Learning and Government Partnerships
National Science Teachers Association

Sandy Fivecoat, CEO
WeAreTeachers

Stan Freeda, Project Coordinator
OPEN NH

Melinda George, Senior Director, and Elizabeth Wolzak, former Senior Manager, Instructional Design
PBS TeacherLine

Liz Glowa, Educational Consultant

Stew Harris
New Media Mill

Matt Huston, Director of Online Learning
Peer-Ed

Joellen Killion, Deputy Executive Director
Learning Forward

Howard Lurie, Director
Teachers' Domain

Dan Meyer, CEO
Atomic Learning

Liz Pape, President
Virtual High School

Henry Pollock, former Director of Education Retention Programs
Florida School Leaders

Lauren Thurman and Lori Weedo
Second Life Educators of Escambia County

Christine Terry, Missouri Program Director
eMints Program: e-Learning for Educators

Barbara Treacy, Director
EdTech Leaders Online, Educational Development Center, Inc.

Ross White, Associate Director
LEARN NC

PUBLISHER'S ACKNOWLEDGMENTS

Corwin gratefully acknowledges the contributions of the following reviewers:

Jennifer Borgioli, Consultant
Learner-Centered Initiatives
Floral Park, NY

Linda Z. Carling, Program Director for Teaching and Learning Online
Johns Hopkins University School of Education
Center for Technology in Education
Columbia, MD

Tammy Evans, Director of Professional Development
Manatee, SD

Barbara Frank, Senior Policy Analyst
NEA Academy
National Education Association
Washington, DC

Theresa Gray, Professional Developer
Erie 2-Chautauqua-Cattaraugus
BOCES
Fredonia, NY

Catherine Huber, Principal
Northwood Elementary School
West Seneca Central School District
West Seneca, NY

Jill Montoya, Coordinator of Online Professional Development
Jefferson County Public Schools
Golden, CO

Rosetta Riddle, Coordinator of Professional Learning Teams
Professional Learning Department
Henry County Schools
McDonough, GA

About the Author

 **John D. Ross** has been helping educators from the classroom to the state board room better understand how technology integration enhances school improvement efforts for more than a decade. Spearheading the 2004 launch of an online professional development environment for an educational nonprofit, Dr. Ross has since designed and delivered online professional development that has gone to many thousands of educators in Alabama, Florida, Georgia, North Carolina, Tennessee, and Virginia. He has connected with educators across the nation through podcasts, webcasts, webconferences, social networks, dabbling in Second Life, and his blog.

Dr. Ross is the subject-matter expert for *Principal Connections Online*, an expanded, web-based version of the popular training on technology integration for K–12 leaders. He worked with the Council of Chief State School Officers (CCSSO) to design and develop the free, web-based, *Data-Based Decision Making Tool: A Resource for Teachers* a comprehensive guide for developing and implementing school improvement efforts; and he also developed the web-based version of the K–12 Total Cost of Ownership, or TCO, Calculator, which is based on the work of the Integrated Technology in Education Group. He served as the director of the Institute for the Advancement of Emerging Technologies in Education and as the director of technology for the Appalachia Regional Comprehensive Center (ARCC), both funded by the U.S. Department of Education, where he helped educators at all levels investigate and incorporate new and emerging technologies in support of their work.

Dr. Ross is a frequent presenter in the field of educational technology at state and national conferences and has served as a consultant and trainer for teachers, administrators, and policy makers. He teaches an online graduate class he created about technology integration for Bethel University based on the textbook he coauthored with Dr. Katherine Cennamo from Virginia Tech and Dr. Peg Ertmer from Purdue. The textbook, *Technology Integration for Meaningful Classroom Use: A Standards-Based Approach* (Wadsworth, Cengage Learning, 2010), is the first to address the revised National Educational Technology Standards for Teachers (NETS-T) developed by the International Society for Technology in Education (ISTE). Dr. Ross was a classroom teacher for 10 years and holds a PhD in curriculum and instruction and instructional technology from Virginia Tech. You can find out more about him at www.TeachLearnTech .com.

For Jane Copley and Sharon Harsh

for their vision and their trust

Why *Online* Professional Development? 1

THE OPD FRAMEWORK

When I started designing and delivering online professional development, I didn't have a process to follow. Neither did most of the experts I interviewed. Instead we learned as we went along, sometimes through some difficult lessons. What was remarkable about sharing our experiences was how similar they were. It's not that we all followed exactly the same path, but we did build on what we knew about designing instruction, effective teaching, professional development, and the skills and knowledge from related areas to harness the growing number of online technologies to support online professional development.

If you've picked up this book hoping to find a list of technologies and tutorials on how to use them, you might be disappointed. There is a lot of information about different technologies and how they support the many different forms of online professional development you might consider, from formal facilitated courses to incorporating social media and virtual environments to build and sustain an online community. But while the technologies you use are a major component of online professional development, there are other factors you need to consider to design and deliver a successful program. Too many projects focus so much on the technologies up front that the end result is over budget, underutilized, and—all too often—ineffective.

Now when I go in to consult with organizations that want to develop online professional development, I've got a few tools to use to help them think about the bigger picture. Those tools are presented in this book and should be helpful whether you're planning to find, purchase, or develop all or parts of your online professional development program. They're organized around a cyclical framework I developed and have used with several clients, who ultimately helped me to refine it (see Figure 1.1). It's a great conversation starter, and I use it to help them grasp the scope of their project, determine what resources they may already have, and better understand what they'll need to find the best solution for them. It's an easy way to see it's not just about the technology. In the best of situations, the framework helps them understand many related parameters required to put a successful program into place that can grow over time. It's flexible and can address new professional development needs that arise, incorporating relevant new technologies as they become available. But if you're focused too much on a specific technology, one that may be obsolete by the end of your project, you're not going to have that kind of success.

You may be in a different place in the framework than the district next door or the organization across the street. It's also an iterative process, so you may return to some of the steps each year as your program grows and expands. It should be flexible enough to inform you about parameters to consider and strategies to address them, should you need them, when and where you need them most. Your solution can and will likely look different from mine or those profiled in this book. And that's okay. The framework is a checkpoint to make sure that your solution is the most successful it can be for your given circumstances, the resources you have, and the outcomes you hope to obtain.

Each chapter addresses one section of the framework, along with suggested strategies, research when available, and best practices from other experts. I propose a tangible outcome for each step, but the degree to which you create these things, like a vision statement, gap analysis, technology specifications, or others is up to you. I encourage you, however, to consider each of the components in the framework and determine the most appropriate outcomes for your own project. If ignored, some of them can really come back to haunt you and can delay or derail your project.

I start with one of the most important components, yet one that is often not considered: determining your need. I approach this through the question, Why *online* professional development? It's surprising to find so many groups that have not considered this crucial question. Don't be one of them.

ASKING THE RIGHT QUESTIONS

Why is a part of the famous "Five Ws"—who, what, where, when, why—that most students are encouraged to consider when conducting research and presenting information. The Five Ws offer a simple way to monitor whether you've covered your bases. But in this familiar list, Why usually comes last. While I'll get to all of these questions, and even some How questions—which is what most people are interested in—I believe that Why is best addressed up front.

Why questions are the hard questions. Why questions are the ones teachers use in classrooms to push students to higher levels of thinking and to help students and teachers monitor their own understanding. Margaret Heritage from UCLA, an expert on formative assessment, once said at a conference I attended that the Why questions are the essential questions to ask when assessing learning. They make students think, and they can help teachers better understand what students do or don't know, going beyond just getting the answer correct. Why questions make adults think, too, and I wanted to begin with a little reflection before charging into the How questions.

Figure 1.1 Online Professional Development Framework

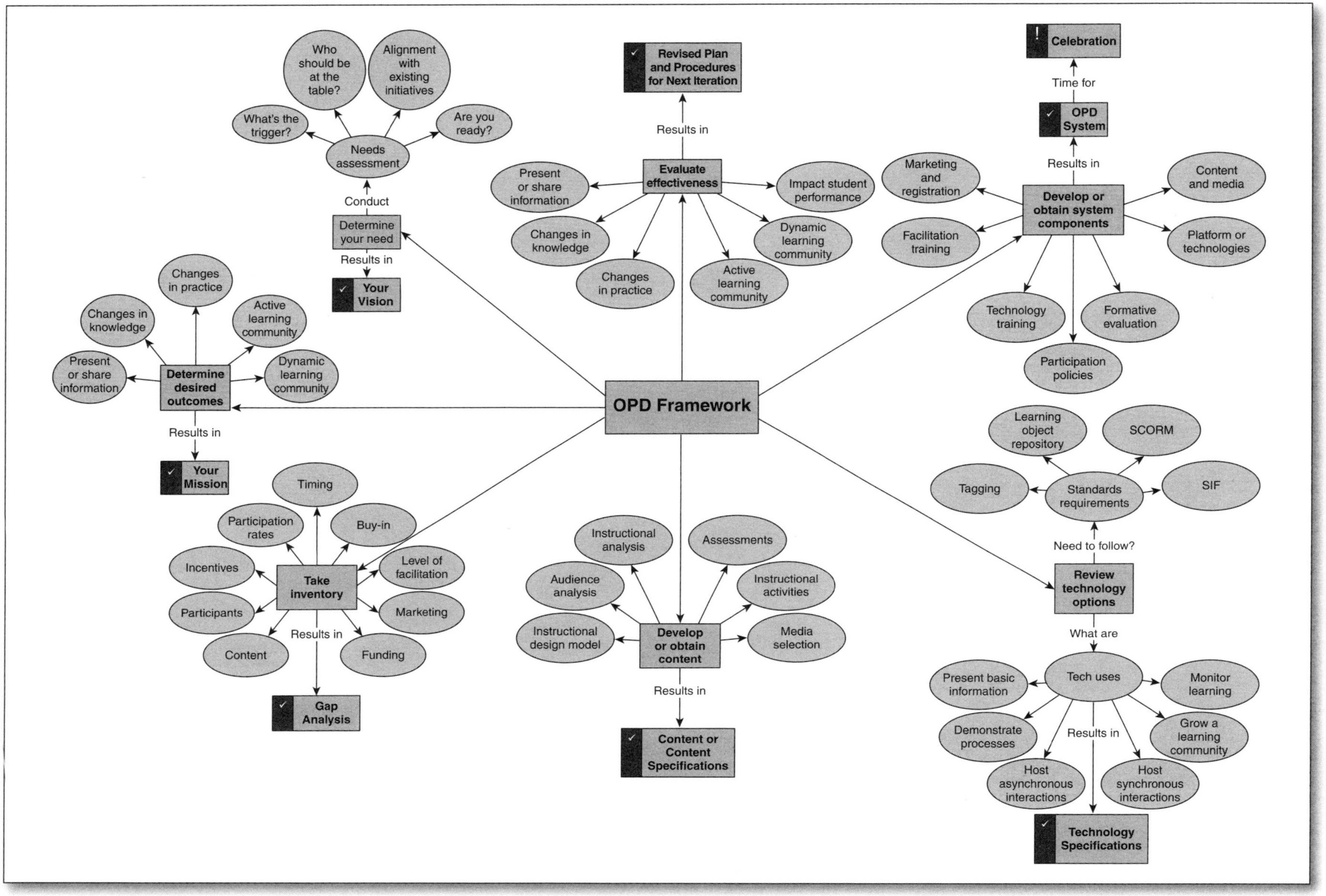

You may frame your need for online professional development from different perspectives. You may want to develop your own system from the bottom up while others are trying to purchase parts or an entire system—whether just delivery technologies, or content, or the whole shebang. Up until just a few years ago, there was much more activity in the development range, but now there are many providers who offer solutions for purchase, with some free materials also available. These include learning management systems (LMS) that you can populate with your own content or entire hosted solutions that include the software, content, training, and facilitators. Throughout the book, I will address decisions from both perspectives. (The term *learning management system* or LMS is used to refer to systems that manage the data related to course content and users. These and related systems are explored in greater detail at the end of Chapter 5.) Activities will be included in each chapter to guide your thinking, whether you're developing or purchasing online professional development. Regardless of your perspective, Why is still an important question to answer first.

WHY ONLINE PROFESSIONAL DEVELOPMENT?

As educators, we know a good deal about professional development, or staff development as it's also called. (In this book, I'll use the term *professional development*.) We've studied professional development efforts for decades. Different models have evolved over time and have been evaluated and researched. The U.S. Department of Education sponsored the National Awards Program for Models of Professional Development in the late 1990s, whose findings were used to create a free toolkit for educators (Hassel, 1999). Seminal research conducted by experts such as Joyce and Showers (2002) has led to the development of different models of professional development that have proven effective over time. The topic of "what works" in professional development is a perennial one and is the focus of much research and publication (Birman, Desimone, Porter, & Garet, 2000; Gall & Vojtek, 1994; Guskey, 2003; Yoon, Duncan, Lee, Scarloss, & Shapley, 2007). The methods used to determine what works range from case studies, evaluations, and observations of programs through—albeit less often—rigorous research designs that can be considered experimental or quasi-experimental. Even the young field of online professional development, specifically, has received scrutiny (Dede, 2006).

Standards for professional development have been developed by state and local education agencies as well as national and international organizations such as Learning Forward (formerly called the National Staff Development Council [NSDC; 2001]). With the growing opportunities to use networked technologies to support teaching and learning, new standards for this medium have been introduced by the International Council for K–12 Online Learning (iNACOL) for online courses (2010b) and online teaching (2010a). The Southern Regional Educational Board (SREB; 2004) developed standards for online professional development specifically, while Learning Forward published guidance for using e-learning to support its own standards (NSDC, 2004).

If you're considering online professional development, you likely have models that you currently use or are considering. You're also likely to be aware of standards for professional development and may even have your own. One of the reasons to consider online professional development is that it meets many of the criteria of what researchers and practitioners consider critical for effective professional development. In fact, I've found in my own work that online professional development may be better able to meet more of those criteria than more common models of professional development. As online technologies have become commonplace in our homes and schools, they provide greater opportunities to reach more educators through high-quality professional development opportunities that are sustained over time. Let's consider one list of criteria as a point of reference.

In 2005, as the director of part of a large contract from the U.S. Department of Education for the nonprofit educational lab I was then working with, our team conducted a review of professional development studies to identify components of effective professional development (Larson, 2005) with the aim of describing effective *online* professional development. The lab had conducted professional development for more than 40 years and had entered into the realm of online professional development a couple of years earlier. The review was conducted to inform the education community about the components of effective professional development and to help implement and improve our own efforts.

After reviewing over 100 abstracts, articles, reports, and dissertations published between 1985 and 2005, 21 studies were identified that met established criteria of rigorous research. The studies had to have research designs that could be considered experimental or quasi-experimental with a matched control group. Each had to use and describe strong research designs and good data measures. From reviewing the 21 studies, nine components of effective professional development were identified. Some of the components had more evidence than others, being found across more studies, but the list looks similar to many that might be found in the literature or published in standards. From this report, effective professional development

- is linked to student learning outcomes;
- is job-embedded;
- is ongoing and sustained with follow-up;
- incorporates authentic, active learning experiences;
- includes subject-matter content;
- encourages reflection on pedagogy, content, and beliefs;
- incorporates collaboration with colleagues and/or experts;
- provides support for teachers; and
- measures impact on student achievement.

In my estimation, our online professional development met *more* of these criteria than more traditional delivery modes. It held more opportunities to provide ongoing, job-embedded professional development with resources available anytime, anyplace. Not only were activities authentic, participants often had the opportunity to practice the activities or implement new strategies within the context of working with students or other colleagues and then reflect on their actual practice—in real time. That's not to say that face-to-face professional development opportunities cannot meet these criteria. Some do. However, the technologies used to support online professional development proved to be powerful tools that made it easier—and ultimately more cost-effective—to provide high-quality professional development opportunities to the educators served.

Some of the identified components are commonly incorporated in most models of professional development regardless of the mode of delivery. These include incorporating authentic, active learning experiences; including subject-matter content; and—hopefully—linking to student learning outcomes. Following are those components that I believe were *better* met by online professional development than face-to-face efforts. These are presented as some reasons why you might consider *online* professional development.

Effective Professional Development is Job-Embedded

There are certainly job-embedded models of professional development that are not delivered online. Technical, peer, collegial, challenge, or team coaching are examples. There are also mentoring programs that use exemplary educators to guide new principals and their staff and programs that connect new teachers with veteran teachers. But more traditional forms of job-embedded professional development such as these are time-consuming and costly. A coach can only work with a limited number of colleagues and can find it difficult to schedule preobservation and postobservation conferences and classroom visits within teachers' busy schedules.

Instead of completing training in 2 or 3 days during the summer or during other inservice days, online technologies provide educators the flexibility to work through material over a period of weeks or even months during the school year. The groups may be able to determine their own timelines, set benchmarks and deadlines, and set the expectations for participation. By dividing course content up into smaller chunks of information delivered during the school year, participants are able to learn and practice new material during relatively short periods of time that better fit into their busy schedules and then go apply it—sometimes the next day! They could then come back to their group and provide real data from their experiences highly specific to the content and skills being studied. Even aspects of coaching and mentoring, mentioned earlier, can be augmented by online technologies. This potential for job-embedded learning is a powerful reason why you might consider online professional development.

Ongoing and Sustained With Follow-Up

The one-shot workshop has been much maligned. Adjectives used to describe it are often linked to the concept of "one-size-fits-all." What is usually lacking in these models is ongoing and sustained follow-up. A recent review of empirical research (Yoon et al., 2007) found that while some workshop-based professional development can have a positive impact on student learning, a more important finding is that the time spent in the professional development and the subsequent follow-up were critical factors leading to improved student learning. Workshops that contained more than 30 contact hours proved to positively impact student learning, and eight of the nine studies in the sample included significant structured follow-up activities.

It is hard to provide follow-up in more traditional face-to-face settings. Sometimes, a multiday workshop in the summer is paired with half- or full-day workshops during the school year as a form of follow-up. It is this follow-up, however, that is most often cut in negotiations with clients. Many districts or schools are willing to bring in a trainer for an initial workshop, but the costs begin to mount when you consider bringing that trainer back during the school year. Travel costs still exist whether you bring someone in for one day or several days, although there may be some savings in terms of lodging and actual contract time for a single-day visit.

With online professional development, participants are provided greater opportunity to receive follow-up feedback and support throughout the year, from peers and experts. After attending a workshop, faculty members can participate in an online learning community with other participants from the workshop. E-mail, discussion lists, and social networking tools all provide opportunities for continued dialogue, reflection, and collegial interaction around new skills and knowledge. These and similar digital technologies also provide a record of personal and community growth, documenting efforts to implement new methods, barriers and challenges faced, and how they were overcome.

The result is a string of connections, not just back to the original workshop, but forward to monitor implementation and identify future professional development needs. New staff can also access artifacts from past professional development efforts they could not attend and can benefit from those work products—lesson plans, classroom videos, instructional activities, curriculum guides, policies, observation protocols, and more—developed by previous participants and providing an opportunity to maintain organizational knowledge. While it's possible this can be accomplished through face-to-face professional development, the ability for digital technologies to provide a cost-effective means to deliver professional development and provide ongoing follow-up make this opportunity for ongoing and sustained professional growth much more of a reality, and it's a key reason why you might consider online professional development.

Encourages Reflection on Pedagogy, Content, and Beliefs

Professional development that aims to change educator practice often fails to achieve its goals if participants are not allowed to spend sufficient time considering and questioning their own values and beliefs about their roles and how new skills and knowledge align or conflict with those beliefs. Many more traditional forms of professional development can also encourage reflection, but the ongoing nature of many online professional development efforts provides opportunities for more mature reflections. Changing beliefs is a tall order—even more so if you expect to do it in a day or two far removed from actual practice.

The key here is time, and that is what online professional development can provide. It's not that online professional development can magically create time, but it can distribute time by providing periodic opportunities to develop deeper reflections over weeks or months. It can also shift time required for professional growth by embedding professional learning and reflection at the same time as actual practice. You can reflect after a 3- or 8-hour workshop, but a series of reflections over 3 or 8 weeks while you're implementing new strategies in your classroom is likely to have greater meaning.

Teachers participating in online professional development may be asked to reflect on their current practices, and then are required to collect data over a week or two to support and sometimes challenge those reflections. In one professional development course I designed, teachers at first self-reported they were already doing a good job helping their students read at or above grade level, which actually begged the question of why they even needed the professional development in the first place. There was more than a little grumbling from the participants about having to take this training. However, once they actually collected data about their students' performance and shared it with others, perceptions changed. It was not uncommon that as many as 40% of students in the participating schools were not reading at grade level (these were schools targeted for low student achievement in reading to begin with). Knowing this data was highly motivating to many of the teachers, and they were then more willing to engage in efforts to reflect on and change not only their classroom practice but school policies, as well. The reflections at the end of the course indicated a greater understanding of the need for the professional development and included descriptions of how the content and resources were actually incorporated into their practice (see Box 1.1: "Learning From Experience: Comprehensive Literacy Program" for more information about this program).

The previous story is an example of how online professional development can shift time for professional growth, by embedding reflection within practice. Whether taking a course, as described, participating in an online lesson study, or attending a series of webconferences with colleagues over a semester, online professional development provides greater opportunity to support reflection closer to actual practice. Summer workshops can promote reflection, but embedding reflection within practice and professional development at the same time is another reason to consider online professional development.

Box 1.1 Learning From Experience: Comprehensive Literacy Program

Project Title: Comprehensive Literacy Program

Organization: Edvantia, Inc. for the Tennessee Department of Education (TDOE)

Contact: John Ross, former Senior R&D Specialist

URL: www.epd.edvantia.org

Date First Implemented: 2004

Audience: K–3 teachers and principals; K–12 teachers of special education

Need: *What Was the Initial Trigger?*

The TDOE identified online professional development as a strategy for providing access to the same high-quality professional development to faculty in all 56 (later 75) schools that received Reading First funds and contracted with Edvantia to develop and deliver it.

Intended Outcomes:

The goal was to provide access to the same high-quality professional development content to all Reading First schools in Tennessee.

Incentives:

Faculty and administrators from schools that applied for Reading First funds were required to participate in one of the two 13-week courses per year and received 30 professional development hours for their participation.

Instructional Design Considerations:

Building on the expertise of internal staff in face-to-face professional development as well as multimedia and online instructional design, the course was designed to capitalize on the best available research for online professional development. Special attention was paid to the development of learning communities and the needs of adult learners. Reading-specific content and skill acquisition were emphasized over technology skills. Guidelines for content development included internally developed instructional design guidelines as well as application of Keller's (1987) ARCS model of motivational design.

Lessons Learned:

Two significant barriers to success identified by participants were time and technology. Teachers reported lack of time to complete the course and conflict with other school commitments. Strategies to address the barrier of time developed through consultation with participants include making sure there is buy-in for the program from the principal and that the school leadership places as much value on the online program as other professional development

(Continued)

(Continued)

programs. Most teachers completed the course at school, so it was encouraged that time be made available during or immediately before or after the school day to allow teachers to work on the course activities.

Several technology-specific problems were noted, including older computers or low-bandwidth Internet connections, although the most common problem faced by participants was forgotten passwords, so several automated password reminder options were developed. Because the course included videos, CDs containing all videos and handouts were mailed to each school to allow teachers to access these materials offline. Other technology problems included not being able to install software on school computers as well as pop-up blockers, spam filters, firewalls, and network caching software. These problems were addressed by including answers to Frequently Asked Questions on the website as well as including solutions to these topics in the facilitator training and supporting materials.

A "group self-paced" model was developed for the program based on the premise of developing an online learning community that has a designated leader with content expertise. The course included supports for this leader, such as a facilitator's notebook and companion CD, guidance on preparing for course modules at the beginning of each, additional tips and hints indicated by a leader icon throughout the content, administrative reports to monitor group progress, and a separate online leader community in which they could ask questions and share advice.

Evaluation:

Pretest and posttest scores of the participants were compared during the first semester and statistically significant gains were made by the participants, with posttest average scores above 80% for every module. When interviewed, a majority of the literacy leaders reported that the initial reaction to the program was not positive; however, by the end of the program, literacy leaders reported an overwhelming positive reaction to the program by their teachers, with an agreement at a rate of 2:1 that their teachers ended up liking the program.

Professional economists external to the organization conducted a cost-benefit analysis of the program that showed significant savings in terms of delivery as compared to having to deliver the same training face-to-face at each school in the program (see Chapter 7 for more information on the cost-benefit analysis).

See the book's companion website for more information about the profiled programs. **www.corwin.com/rossonlinepd**

Incorporates Collaboration With Colleagues and/or Experts

Social networking and Web 2.0 tools have changed the way we learn, work, play, and live. The very nature of these technologies implies collaboration. Certainly, you don't need to use these technologies to collaborate with colleagues or experts, but they do provide greater opportunities for collaboration within and beyond the walls of a school. Collaboration can occur between two colleagues, a small group, or an entire faculty.

A good example of peer collaboration is the mentoring relationship that many schools or districts create between new and veteran teachers. A well-structured mentoring program can certainly be considered professional development, especially for the new teacher. But problems occur when the mentor teams don't have corresponding periods of time to get together. Even worse is the new teacher who may be paired with someone out of his or her content area or with someone who teaches the same subject at a different school. I was one of those teachers. If it hadn't been for informal networking at Friday night football games, I might have floundered that first year. Later in my career I discovered online discussion boards where I could learn from and share ideas with other teachers across the globe. Now, some colleges of education routinely use technology to connect with student teachers and first-year graduates to facilitate collaboration once they are in the field.

There are many different kinds of collaborative groups that are formed in schools. Some groups may focus on specific issues, such as curriculum and instruction, lesson planning, analyzing student and program data, or considering issues related to school culture. Sometimes these teams are created out of convenience rather than purpose, with every teacher who happens to have the same planning period put on the same team whether they have the interest or skills to be on that team or not. Others may be organized around proximity, with all teachers having classrooms in the same part of the building being on a team. Certainly, there are excellent models of group collaboration at schools that don't require technology, but technology provides greater opportunity to connect those with similar needs or interests who can't connect during the school day because of scheduling or lack of proximity.

For example, not all of your math teachers may be able to meet at the same time during the day, but by using a file server and a discussion list or a more sophisticated LMS or social networking application, all of your math teachers can collaborate around instruction and assessment. They can create and revise lesson plans, post videos of classroom instruction for comment, or include digitized samples of student work for analysis. Using these technologies can allow grade-level teams, or content-specific teams—even those from both the middle and high school or middle and elementary schools—to collaborate and engage in relevant professional growth all year long.

One of the harder forms of collaboration to implement is that between educators (and students) with experts outside of schools. Educators and outside experts are pretty busy, after all, and few have the time to significantly engage with schools regardless of how much they want to, but there are some examples of collaboration that would not be feasible without online technologies. I helped organize an online book study where the authors of a book participated in a live webconference—providing deeper insight into concepts addressed in the book and answering questions directly to participants. The audio portion of the webconference was recorded and incorporated in a web-based facilitator's guide for future book study groups. Several conferences now incorporate web-conferencing or webcasting technologies to connect distant participants. I have even attended a conference in the virtual environment Second Life that drew speakers and participants from across the nation and beyond. The ways that online professional development can support and extend collaboration with colleagues and experts described in this section are certainly a reason for considering why online professional development might be right for you.

Provides Support for Teachers

Just as it's common to turn to the Internet for news, shopping, entertainment, and even teaching resources, it's easy to conceive the many ways that online professional development provides ongoing support for teachers. Educators can access high-quality content in a variety of formats—text, images, videos, simulations, and more—at any time of the day, sometimes as just-in-time training. They can also find content and pedagogical support from others, whether colleagues from across the hall or across the country. Even experts may be available for support, whether in real time or through an artifact such as the book study archive described earlier.

Online professional development also offers ongoing support for educators through personal reflection by creating online portfolios, blogs, journals, or websites related to professional growth opportunities. These artifacts can be used to document growth or to help educators determine the need for future growth opportunities. Individuals may organize their portfolios around a set of standards and can review which standards they might want to cultivate most. School leaders, including teacher leaders and master teachers, can provide ongoing support for their colleagues through formal and informal discussion and dialog around these artifacts conducted wholly or partly online. Policies and guidelines can be posted on a learning community website so that staff meetings can focus more on professional development activities. Online forums or webconferences can allow educators to deepen knowledge and skills learned during workshops or can provide one-on-one support for specific needs.

More traditional forms of professional development can offer support for teachers, but that support is often limited in terms of scope or time. Resources and technologies common to the many forms of online professional development described here provide ongoing support through a variety of means, and this is one more reason to consider online professional development.

Box 1.2 The Potential for Online Professional Development: One Perspective

Joellen Killion is the deputy executive director for Learning Forward (formerly the National Staff Development Council), which is arguably one of the most influential organizations that impacts professional development in the country. Their standards for professional development have been adopted or adapted by many professional development providers across the country, and their conferences and publications keep educators informed about new trends in professional development policy, practice, and research. In an interview, Killion described her perspective on the potential for online professional development as well as advice for how providers might reach that potential.

According to Killion, online professional development is a tremendous opportunity to access high-quality information to support professional learning. It can provide models of practice, and that information can be presented to just about everyone who wants it. She does caution, however, that it has to go further. Receiving information is not enough. Professional development requires supporting "transfer to practice," as she puts it, to "transform how people think."

She believes we're in a good place in time right now, but we have work to do. She's convinced that we now have technology that has the capacity to replicate anything we might normally do in a face-to-face environment, which may not always have been the case. She encourages online professional development providers to move beyond what was once possible, though, and use technology to not only do what can be accomplished in a face-to-face setting but to do more. Consider means for providing feedback and guidance during practice. Leverage technology's capacity to address social interaction and support deep learning, transform thinking and belief systems, and accommodate ongoing professional learning.

To do this, she echoes the sentiment that online professional development providers need to truly understand the learning process and that professional learning is intended to support ongoing implementation. It's not just the one-time presentation of information. It's changing practice by changing what educators think and believe—about content, pedagogy, and their own ability to truly help students reach their maximum academic potential. That takes interaction. It takes follow-up and support. It takes more than just thinking you're going to do something cheaper. Hopefully, through this book and the efforts of online professional development providers, including you, we can use technology to reach the potential that Killion describes.

Box 1.3 Caveat Emptor: Talking to Vendors

These research-based criteria make good questions to ask vendors when considering whether to purchase online professional development. After determining your need, use the following questions to interview or research online professional development providers.

Linked to student learning outcomes

- What student learning outcomes are addressed?
- Are they aligned to your local or state standards?

Job-embedded

- How does the professional development support the daily needs of the participants?
- What content or skills are addressed that are immediately applicable?

(Continued)

(Continued)

Ongoing and sustained with follow-up

- What is the duration of the professional development? Is it flexible?
- What kind of follow-up is provided?

Incorporates authentic, active learning experiences

- What kind of activities do the participants complete? Ask for examples or guest access.

Includes subject-matter content

- What subject-matter content is included? How is it used to leverage new skills and knowledge?
- Does the subject-matter content match the needs of all of your participants?
- Does the subject-matter content align with required content standards, or preferred pedagogies or philosophies?

Encourages reflection on pedagogy, content, and beliefs

- What kind of reflective activities are included? Who participates in them?
- Is a process for deep reflection nurtured in the professional development?

Incorporates collaboration with colleagues and/or experts

- How is collaboration supported? What technologies are used?
- Are your participants ready, both in terms of technical skills and process, to collaborate in the ways supported by the course?

Provides support for teachers

- What kind and degree of content, program, and technical support is provided? Does it match the needs of your participants?

Measures impact on student achievement

- What data indicates impact on student achievement as a result of participation in the program? How do those students compare to yours?

DETERMINING YOUR NEED FOR ONLINE PROFESSIONAL DEVELOPMENT

In the previous section, many reasons were given as to why online professional development can be worthwhile and effective, but there is no one such thing as "online professional development." It comes in many shapes and sizes and can look different from school to school. No matter how it's organized or which technologies you use, with planning and monitoring, you can develop online professional development that effectively meets your needs.

In this section, the first part of the planning and implementation framework is introduced, *Determining your need for online professional development* (see Figure 1.2). As you might have guessed, it addresses the Why question. Now it's your turn to consider why online professional development might be right for you. All too often there is an assumption that online professional development is needed. The decision has already been made, although there has rarely been significant discussion or analysis to really justify online professional development. Very often, the decision is not fueled by need, but by what one individual or a small group perceives is needed.

Figure 1.2   Once truly determined, your needs shape your vision for online professional development.

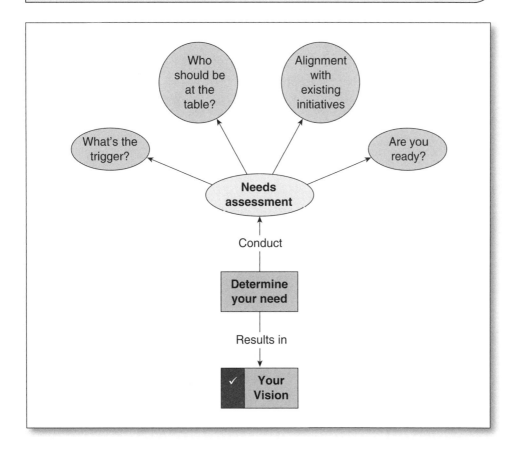

Presupposing that online professional development is needed without exploring the parameters of the need can derail a project. Too many organizations have bypassed this important step, and the results are usually higher costs, missed deadlines, poor quality, and frustration all around. You can turn that trend around. Take some time now to truly determine why online professional development is right for you. This is important whether you're going to build a system from scratch or plan to purchase parts or all of it.

I approach most projects from the perspective of an instructional designer, and from that perspective the most common method for answering the Why question is to conduct a *needs assessment*. There are many different models for conducting a needs assessment that have come from the fields of instructional design, organizational development, and even the military. You can conduct the needs assessment yourself or hire an expert from outside of your organization. It can be as detailed as you need it to be. Those decisions can depend on factors such as the scope of the proposed project, the resources (time, money, people, and material resources) you have available to conduct the needs assessment, and whether it would be beneficial for data to be gathered by internal staff or an impartial outsider. The important thing is that you truly determine whether you have a need or not.

A needs assessment usually involves collecting and analyzing data to determine if there really is a need and to describe that need if you find it. Steve Baxendale from the World Health Organization also notes that doing a needs assessment was one successful strategy he used for getting greater buy-in. Collect data from people who will be impacted by the project—such as the eventual users—through surveys, interviews, or focus groups. You can conduct brainstorming or group planning meetings. Bring in relevant data that can help to identify or clarify the need. These can be new policies or regulations, teacher certification and training data, or student performance data. Sometimes, current efforts aren't working, and this can be a reason to try online professional development. Use multiple methods; you may have to conduct several rounds of data collection and analysis until you've finally identified needs clearly. Your goal is to determine whether there's a gap between an expected outcome (e.g., number of highly qualified teachers, student performance levels, use of a desired pedagogy or resource) and your current practice. If so, there's a need. Regardless of how you conduct your needs assessment, there are a few factors to consider to inform the process. These factors are presented next.

What's the Trigger?

What prompted the decision? What happened that made you believe you need online professional development? Sometimes it's just the desire of an individual or group of individuals. It could be that someone at the central office or a school board member went to a conference and attended a good session on online professional development. It could be a pet project of someone with an interest in technology. Maybe the next district over has started providing online professional development, and you feel the need to keep up. Dig deeper to get beyond what one or a few people want versus what is needed.

There may be a change in policy, guidance, or regulations that requires training. A new policy that requires all paraprofessionals to have new qualifications can indicate a need for professional development. A new funding stream, such as a grant that is tied to specific resources and methods, may require professional development. Have you had changes in staffing? You may have significant growth in the number of educators in your district, or you could have had significant overturn in terms of new versus veteran employees, or your own professional development staff may have been significantly reduced. Your staff may have prompted the request in an effort to reap some of the benefits described earlier in this chapter, like flexible access to support and resources, job-embedded activities, or ongoing professional development with follow-up. Have there been changes in the student population? A new industry entering or leaving the community can significantly impact the makeup of your student population. The introduction of people from different cultures or backgrounds can be seen as a need for professional development across a district on several topics. These are all real needs I've encountered.

Ultimately, since the goal of schools is to help all students reach their academic potential, collect evidence from student performance that suggests the need for professional development. Has student performance changed recently? For any particular group of students? Have you implemented or do you plan to implement a new intervention, instructional strategy, or curricular resource across a group of teachers or schools? Perhaps you've already identified an intervention that has been shown to address the learning needs of students like yours, but it requires ongoing professional development to ensure it's implemented with fidelity.

For any of these reasons, bring in data that helps to explain or support why you believe online professional development is needed. Data is objective and helps you move beyond guessing, perceptions, and opinions. Share that data with others charged with making the decision to go forward or not.

Who Should Be at the Table?

Consider who can help determine if there's a need and who *has* to be present to make the decision that online professional development is the answer. If you're leaning towards online professional development, make sure you have people who will be impacted by it all along the planning, development, implementation, and monitoring phases. Too often, this type of decision is relegated to technology staff that may not have expertise in curriculum and instruction *or* professional development. While you'll certainly need to include your technology staff for some decisions, don't forget your curriculum and instruction personnel, staff developers, and potential facilitators and participants. Not all of these people need to actually sit at the table every time decisions are made, but data from these groups can be collected and used when planning and decision meetings occur so the needs of these groups are represented.

Too often, the people who will use the system the most, often teachers or administrators, are not consulted in the process. Providing your participants a say in the process is critical. It not only increases buy-in for your project but can better help determine what you will or won't be able to do. Melinda George from PBS TeacherLine notes that sometimes they have to do a "double sell" if the district leader has bought into the project but the teachers have not, perhaps by not being involved in the decision. As she says, "You can't impose it on the teachers or they'll see it as a requirement and not an opportunity." (For more information about PBS TeacherLine, see Box 1.4: "Learning From Experience: PBS TeacherLine.") Get the right people to the table from the beginning.

Box 1.4 Learning From Experience: PBS TeacherLine

Project Title: PBS TeacherLine

Organization: PBS

Contacts: Melinda George, Senior Director, and Elizabeth Wolzak, former Senior Manager, Instructional Design

URL: www.pbs.org/teacherline

Date First Implemented: 2000

Audience: K–12 educators

Need: *What Was the Initial Trigger?*

PBS launched MathLine in 1995 with funding from the U.S. Department of Education, then built on this work through a Ready to Teach grant to develop TeacherLine, which expanded into other content areas. TeacherLine now has more than 100 courses that are fully online and fully facilitated, as well as a new Peer Connection component that makes the learning objects in those courses searchable and usable in a more standalone fashion for coaches and mentors.

Intended Outcomes:

The initial courses were designed to address the needs of K–12 teachers in core content areas.

Incentives:

Continuing education units and graduate credit

Instructional Design Considerations:

TeacherLine has done a lot of work around determining what an effective online course looks like and how it is structured. Wolzak developed a course outline for TeacherLine called a Performance, Objective, Assessment, and Activity Chart (POAAC) that guides the development process and facilitates conversations with partners or content experts. TeacherLine provides a project manager and an instructional designer, and the institutions they partner with provide a project manager and a writer. TeacherLine courses have similar strands, so they are familiar to those who take more than one course, and they have a 33% rate of repeat learners (some who take multiple courses).

Wolzak notes that it's important when designing online instruction to know the needs of your learners. The audience for professional development is adults, and they have different needs than children. She suggests modeling what you want them to do in their classroom. They come with a wealth of prior knowledge, so she encourages reflection and incorporates peer review and sharing of experiences.

All TeacherLine courses are project-based and have a direct real-world application to the classroom. There are often fewer activities in a TeacherLine online course than more traditional face-to-face instruction, and courses result in something tangible and relevant. Language arts classes often incorporate case studies, and science courses model inquiry-based learning strategies. All courses have performance objectives, and every objective is assessed through the use of a rubric. Multiple-choice assessments are not used.

Lessons Learned:

One of the myths about online learning is that it's always the same, but in reality, there are so many flavors of professional development. Review what other people are offering and make sure you know what your audience wants.

TeacherLine created some self-paced learning opportunities in the past, but they were not very popular. Self-paced was a really tough way to get buy-in from teachers online, so everything they do now is facilitated. TeacherLine has a 94% completion rate, and George feels that facilitators make the biggest difference in whether a person completes successfully or not.

Much of the meat of the course occurs in the discussion area, so they think hard about discussion questions so that it can be manageable both for the learner and the facilitator. The discussion area can strengthen the development of community by connecting to and learning with peers. The facilitator is the "guide on the side" and does not necessarily direct the discussion.

TeacherLine uses metatagging (see Chapter 5 for more about metatagging, SCORM, and learning objects). They built the original database but engage an outside organization to actually tag the learning objects as they are put into the database. Schools or districts can also license TeacherLine content in a SCORM-compliant form.

Evaluation:

TeacherLine contracts with an outside evaluation organization to review the pre/post survey data, and data have been used to monitor what has gone well and how to offer new opportunities. Through evaluation of the first Ready to Teach grant, TeacherLine was able to determine what teachers wanted in terms of content and activities. The 100 courses were deconstructed and put into a searchable database embedded in a collaborative environment, called Peer Connection, intended to provide information to support coaches and mentors in a flexible environment.

See the book's companion website for more information about the profiled programs. www.corwin.com/rossonlinepd

How Will Online Professional Development Align With Existing Initiatives?

Make sure you consider the professional development efforts that are already in place and those that may be planned. Talk to more than just your professional development staff. In some departments, project staff in different content areas provide professional development. Will online professional development support existing initiatives? Will it conflict with existing initiatives? It may be possible that online professional development can fill gaps within existing initiatives, leveraging available resources.

Of course, consider whether online professional development can replace existing initiatives. It's very common to migrate a successful professional development program from face-to-face to online delivery. In this case, you may actually improve the existing program through some of the reasons described earlier in this chapter, such as providing ongoing support and follow-up in a job-embedded environment. You may also be able to get your successful program to more people by going online.

Are You Ready for Online Professional Development?

This "you" is the holistic you that includes everyone who will be impacted by the system. If you're working in a school or district, are the faculty and staff ready? Is there an organizational culture that will support online professional development? In a review of effective professional development models, Gall and Vojtek (1994) report that successful outcomes are more likely in schools that have norms of collegiality and experimentation. Determining readiness of this type can be difficult, but if your users aren't ready, the system won't be used, and you will waste your investment.

Schools also need to be ready to incorporate online professional development at a programmatic level. When will participants access the material? What computers will they use? Online professional development can be as rigorous as any model of professional development and shouldn't be seen as an add-on. Consider how online professional development will be incorporated into the daily operation of the school or district so that it's seen as valuable. Determine how you will support and reward participation.

Readiness also refers to technical readiness. Do you have the capacity to deliver online professional development, and can your participants receive it? Many district networks block streaming media, such as videos, or prohibit smartphones, social media, and other technologies. If you're planning to incorporate these now-common technologies, be sure they can be used. Schools and districts also often have very strong firewalls that may block e-mails or other communications from your system, especially if your system requires significant network resources.

After you've considered these parameters, try to determine your greatest area(s) of need. You may have several that you have to prioritize, because some may be more urgent than others. Some may not be possible in a year, or more. It's good to know what they are, though, because time for continued review of this and related data from your online professional development efforts is part of the framework (see Chapter 7). You need to know if your needs have been met, if they've changed, or whether new needs arise.

Take time to review the four questions in Box 1.5: "Take Action: Conduct a Needs Assessment and Create Your Vision." Consider the questions and examples presented in this section to help you determine why you need online professional development. These questions are the same no matter whether you're developing or purchasing online professional development. Use the answers from these questions to determine your greatest need(s). Finally, use the answers to these four questions to develop a vision to guide your online professional development system—your vision of where you want to be in 1 to 3 years.

I recommend you develop vision and mission statements for this work not just because I think they are useful but because they are common components in both education and commercial sectors. Educators are familiar with creating vision and mission statements for school improvement plans. The corporate sector incorporates them into business plans. When done well, they are a common means for guiding work in both arenas, so I encourage you to incorporate them into your own plan for providing online professional development. One of the principles of effective professional development, according to Guskey (2000), is "small changes guided by a grand vision" (p. 37). Regardless of the scope of your intended project, a clear vision will guide you.

Box 1.5 Take Action: Conduct a Needs Assessment and Create Your Vision

Take time to truly determine your needs and address the questions presented in this chapter. Record your needs and share them with all who will be working on or with your online professional development system. The needs you identify will also help you evaluate the success of your program.

Assess your needs using these four questions:

1. What's the trigger?

2. Who should be at the table?

3. How will online professional development align with existing initiatives?

4. Are you ready for online professional development?

List your greatest area(s) of need in priority order.

1.

2.

3.

Based on your needs, create your vision for online professional development. Describe where you want to be 1 to 3 years from now.

CONCLUSION

From your needs assessment process, you may determine there's a need that can be addressed by online professional development. The need itself doesn't imply that online professional development is the answer. In fact, sometimes you may discover that online professional development is not the solution to addressing a need. But because so many reasons why you might consider online professional development have been identified, I'm going to assume the affirmative.

After determining your needs, draft a vision for your online professional development system. The term *system* is used in a broad sense. It doesn't just mean hardware and software. Your system is going to impact policies, practices, personnel, and all the resources necessary to get and keep your online professional development up and running. This is true even if you're just planning on purchasing a course or two. There are too many stories of educators who enrolled and paid for outside online professional development but never took the steps to determine if they could use it for recertification or opportunities for advancement in their job. If you don't figure that out up front, it's rare to get credit after it's over. Describe why online professional development is the answer and how it can meet the needs you've identified. Describe the broad outcomes you have for your online professional development system.

I'm not going to tell you how to write a vision statement. I once attended a workshop led by noted education leadership expert Bob Eaker, who said that as educators, we have been "visioned to death." We know how to write vision statements, and it doesn't take a year or a month to do so. But do put your vision for your online professional development system down on paper so that as you and your team move forward, you're all on the same page about what you want to accomplish. You just need to create the long view of where you want to be in 1 to 3 years in terms of your online professional development efforts. Once you have that vision, the rest of this book will help you find or develop a system that is right for you.

How Much Does It Cost? 2

Asking about cost is a reasonable question, especially in an era when funding for education seems ever scarcer while demands on teachers and school leaders seem to be increasing exponentially. Teachers are charged to use the latest research- or evidence-based instructional methods and resources. School leaders have to be instructional leaders and experts with the growing amount of data schools generate. Shifting school populations and new policies require entire faculties to learn new procedures and implement new pedagogies. This constant need for growth and renewal is the foundational need for ongoing professional development. But *ongoing* relates not only to the professional growth opportunities but to the funds that support them.

Cost is often the question I'm first asked, but it's hard to determine actual costs until you've really figured out your needs. To determine your bottom line, you have to first articulate your vision. Then, to better determine what it's going to cost, you have to know what that vision's going to look like. You have to answer, "What do I want to achieve?" These are your outcomes, and this section of the framework is designed to help you better articulate your desired outcomes in the form of a mission statement (see Figure 2.1.), again following common school improvement and corporate development practices.

This chapter explores outcomes commonly sought from online professional development and encourages you to consider both known costs and some hidden costs that will influence your bottom line. Knowing both known and hidden costs is part of the concept of determining your total cost of ownership, or TCO, and will help you to answer even harder questions like, "Did it work?" or harder still, "Was it worth it?" Knowing if it worked or was worth the effort requires determining your return on investment (ROI). In education, though, that return isn't just measured in dollars and cents but in learning, so a critical consideration of identifying your desired outcomes is knowing how you will measure them. That's covered in more detail in Chapter 7, but keep it in mind

Figure 2.1 Determining your desired outcomes helps to describe your mission for online professional development.

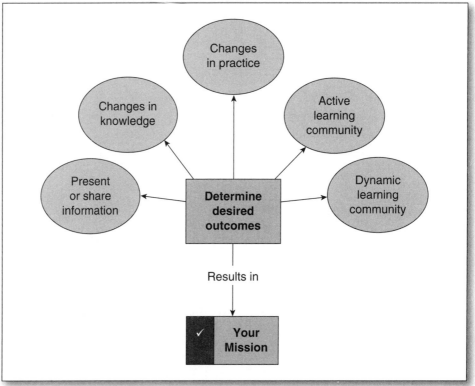

from the beginning so you put structures into place to adequately measure your outcomes. There's no simple formula for determining your costs, but being better informed about the TCO for your solution will help you project more reasonable costs as you develop an implementation plan composed of elements across chapters in the book.

Before going too far, review the OPD Decision Matrix (Figure 2.2). This is a matrix I developed and used with several clients to facilitate discussions around online professional development. It's a distillation of my experiences of developing several large-scale online professional development programs as well as consulting with others on their projects. It has proven to be a useful discussion tool, especially for those new to the idea of what needs online professional development might address. This chapter explores the categories listed in the matrix to better help you understand the range of parameters that will influence the TCO of your final solution.

When I was a child I owned a coin bank that was composed of a graded set of cylinders. When a coin was dropped in the bank, it rolled down a chute until it found the right-size cylinder and dropped in. You could see into the cylinder to quickly count up how much money you had in the bank based on indicators on the side. This matrix is like that bank. For each column of the matrix, the higher up you want to go, the more money you need

Figure 2.2 OPD Decision Matrix

Costs →	What are your desired outcomes?	How will your outcomes be measured?	What technical support do you have available?	What content and program support do you have available?	What is the level of security required?	What technology is required?	How easy is the technology to use?	What is the level of risk you are willing to accept?
	Active to dynamic learning community that supports continuous school improvement efforts through changes in beliefs and practices	Measure changes in student performance / Measure changes in schoolwide practice	Dedicated personnel, some availability "after hours" (depends on scale)	Dedicated personnel, some availability "after hours" (depends on scale)	Credit or recertification data; Personal contact information; Secure transactions required; Course artifacts stored	Dedicated server(s) for the learning management systems (LMS), user data, or for media; Increased network capacity to accommodate rich media and large volume of participants	Participants collaborate in an online environment, both synchronously and asynchronously (e.g., wikis, videoconferencing, or webconferencing)	No risk accepted
	Changes in teaching or leadership practices	Measure changes in educator practice	Personnel available for routine maintenance and support	Someone dedicated a few hours a day (depends on scale)	Directory information; Users have to be approved; Use is tracked	Significant storage space for user-generated content (e.g., portfolios, docs, other)	Participants create and share documents with some rich media (pictures, videos, etc.)	Some risk accepted
	Changes in teachers' or leaders' knowledge	Measure changes in participant knowledge	Can request tech support from tech department or other source with some wait time	A few hours dedicated each week	Some content is only available to registered users; Anyone can sign up	Need proprietary software (media players) or hardware (headsets, microphones)	Participants attach documents to e-mail or post to website	Fairly tolerant of risk
	Present or share information	Record and report usage and affective data	Some to get project started; Limited and sporadic	Just me in my spare time	No personal data stored; All content is open to all people	May have to download client software but generally operates on standard applications	Similar to sending e-mail or surfing the Web	Open to risk if issues can be resolved reasonably

in your bank. The most important column, of course, is your desired outcomes. Those outcomes are going to help you describe your mission for moving forward. As you move up the outcomes column, you'll also require higher levels in the other columns. You can present or share information with little technical and content support and commonly available technologies, but when you tackle changing knowledge and skills, you're going to need more support and security, and you will likely use additional technologies. These are factors that will influence your bottom line. You may have already considered some of these costs, but in my experience most projects do not consider all of these costs from the outset.

Your costs will increase even if you have only one or two decision points that are higher up the matrix. For example, even at lower outcomes, if you plan to securely store confidential user data, your costs will increase as you develop a system or purchase technologies that support secure transmissions. If you incorporate technologies that are novel or challenging to your participants, your training and support costs will likely increase. The OPD Decision Matrix is explained in detail in this chapter, beginning with outcomes for online professional development, so you can better consider the factors that will influence your TCO and what some reasonable outcomes might be for your project.

OUTCOMES

You've already begun to determine what your outcomes might be if you've answered why you need online professional development and have developed a vision statement. At this point, dig deeper and be more explicit. Clearly describe what you expect to happen. If I were to visit your campus (or district, or state, or whatever region your system serves) and observe your system in place, what would it do? What would you consider success? After a year? Or 3 to 5 years? Very often start-up costs are different from ongoing costs, so think about year one and then the benchmarks in the future that make the most sense for you.

Presenting or Sharing Information

While many of the clients I've worked with want to immediately jump to the outcome of dynamic learning communities, perhaps unknowingly envisioning a costly system to operate and maintain, many might benefit from considering outcomes lower on the matrix to begin with. There are areas where information presentation is a vital aspect of professional growth and can be a beneficial professional development experience. Consider many of the compliance training topics that schools have to address. These may include issues related to student health and safety, acceptable use of school resources, new employee orientation, or other school or district policies. Many of these topics are well suited to presentation at this level, and success is often based on whether the participant did or did not receive the training; or participants may take a forced-choice assessment that is also well suited for online presentation.

It's also valuable to present foundational information to learners before they're ready to incorporate new skills and knowledge into their practice. Providing opportunities for your audience to go online and review information before attending a more in-depth training, whether online or face-to-face, is a great way to make sure everyone who attends your training has the foundational knowledge necessary to get a larger ROI of your professional development dollars. Information can be shared online in many formats, including downloadable handouts, video, simulations, or other multimedia. This level of outcome is also consistent with just-in-time training that has been extremely popular with teachers implementing new tools or practices, especially new technologies (read about one example in Box 2.1). Perhaps a teacher implementing podcasting for the first time goes online one last time the day before to review the step-by-step tutorial she's used to prepare her podcasting lesson—just to make sure she is comfortable enough with the technology. Presenting information online also provides opportunities for your users to return to and review information at their leisure, which is a great strategy for supporting different learning preferences and providing opportunities for additional practice.

Box 2.1 Atomic Learning: Getting to the Heart of the Matter

Atomic Learning began in 2000 as an outgrowth from a group of technology coordinators in Minnesota who routinely met and discussed issues related to technology integration. A perennial topic was related to the routine requests from teachers for basic skills. They were often asked "how do I learn . . . ?" just about anything with the new software that was becoming more common in schools at the time. The group hoped that by providing media-based, just-in-time training in short segments to teachers in their schools, they'd be able to use technology to address those questions and spend more of their time focusing on the tougher concepts related to integrating technology in teaching and learning—the "how do I apply . . . ?" questions.

Despite the iconic 1950s Atomic-Age icon, the atom in Atomic Learning actually refers to the core idea that each 3-minute segment is designed to address. According to Dan Meyer, chief executive officer, the idea is that if you can't explain or demonstrate something in 3 minutes, you're probably trying to explain something else. The 3-minute limit on what is presented essentially by video also helped in the times of limited Internet bandwidth.

The initial idea was a success, because teachers found it helpful to learn one or two skills in the very limited time they had available during a typical school day, sometimes just a few minutes between classes. It also doesn't take long to review or rerun the lesson. And while Atomic Learning still provides "how do I learn . . . ?"

(Continued)

(Continued)

training on more than 150 software applications to educators in more than 47 countries, they now provide more support for the "how do I apply ...?" questions and even feature professional development on technology integration and 21st-century skills, including self-assessments that participants can take to guide their learning.

Meyer suggests that one reason for their success was focus. They didn't intend at the beginning to provide courseware. Instead, their learning atom-based model allowed them to quickly generate content that teachers really wanted to know in a format that they became comfortable with. He suggests, "Develop deep before you go wide." To learn more about this program, review Box 2.2: "Learning From Experience: Atomic Learning."

Box 2.2 Learning From Experience: Atomic Learning

Organization: Atomic Learning, Inc.

Contact: Dan Meyer, Chief Executive Officer

URL: www.atomiclearning.com/

Date First Implemented: 2000

Audience: The original target audience was K–12 teachers in the upper Midwest but now includes educators from more than 47 countries, plus a component for higher education.

Need: *What Was the Initial Trigger?*

In the late 1990s, a network of technology coordinators in Minnesota set out to use technology to answer common questions related to basic technology skills. Those short technology tutorials were later launched as the new company, Atomic Learning.

Intended Outcomes:

The original intent was to provide just-in-time training or to address a teachable moment related primarily to software that was finding its way into the classroom in the late 1990s.

Incentives:

Participants receive certificates of completion.

Instructional Design Considerations:

The original constraint was that the tutorial sessions had to be presented within a 3-minute timeframe. Bandwidth was originally an issue, but Meyer says that if it took longer than 3 minutes, you were probably trying to answer a different question. Designers include experts on the software as well as pedagogical experts, sometimes practicing teachers.

Lessons Learned:

The 3-minute "atom" of learning that has been the guiding principle for the development of learning objects provided by Atomic Learning has become its strength. During the school day, teachers often only have small blocks of time to conduct research or confirm a process, and that 3-minute opportunity filled important needs.

Customers wanted to be able to measure progress, with pressure for a quick and easy forced-choice assessment being a common request, but the short segments did not lend themselves well to such an assessment. Forced-choice assessments especially did not lend themselves well to the philosophy of the Atomic Learning staff. Meyer suggests you can assess mastery by reviewing the application of skills required by projects. Teachers requested and now can receive certificates of completion that shows that they have completed segments of training.

Meyer reports that starting out as educators helped because they felt they understood schools and their needs. But over time, needs change, and you have to be careful to listen to your customers to meet their needs.

Technology can change quickly. Meyer notes that you can build interest and get the word out through early adopters, but to build for sustainability, sometimes you have to slow down and let people catch up to you.

Evaluation:

Atomic Learning conducts a yearly customer survey of their large user base that helps them determine new features and enhancements. They also conduct focus groups in the product development process to provide formative feedback.

See the book's companion website for more information about the profiled programs. **www.corwin.com/rossonlinepd**

Changes in Participant Knowledge

I make the distinction between changes in participant knowledge versus practice because many people acquire knowledge but never put it into action. This is one of the great pitfalls associated with "one-shot" workshops—especially those separated in time from when the new knowledge and skills can be applied. Participants can score high on measures that report changes in knowledge at the end of a workshop, but if you never see the practices in place, your ROI at this outcome level is negligible.

Online professional development that has changing knowledge as its intended result can be addressed by a variety of settings but is more costly than presenting and sharing information, primarily because you've got more up-front development and tracking of participant data. Change requires multiple measures—before and after—and takes more effort than determining whether information was simply distributed. Self-paced instruction is a common goal of many of the clients I work with, and this is one outcome that self-paced instruction is useful for. Often, participants complete a "course" of study, a module, or other lesson assignment and take a quiz at the end that can be graded by technology. Taking existing face-to-face workshops and modifying them for online presentation was a common early practice for online professional development, and that content can serve as a basis for reaching this outcome. While you can achieve this outcome in both self-paced and facilitated environments, it's difficult to move to the higher outcome levels of changes in teaching or leadership practice in a completely self-paced environment. Therefore, costs are higher to reach those higher outcome levels.

Changes in Participant Practice

This is a commonly desired outcome. After all, if your professional development is related to a new teaching strategy you've identified or a curricular resource that you've invested a lot of money in, you want to see those things used. But as many who have conducted professional development will tell you, to reach the level of changing educator practice, you often first have to tackle participants' beliefs—their beliefs about content, pedagogy, and what it means to be an educator. This takes time and is challenging. This is not something a completely self-paced course may best be suited for, as that level of growth usually requires human interaction and discourse, although it could include some self-paced segments followed by interaction. This level of change often requires opportunities to view examples of success, to express one's feelings and thoughts, to debate and challenge ideas, to test new skills, and to receive feedback—all over time.

Fortunately, the technologies commonly available in many schools allow participants growth opportunities at this outcome level that can be job-embedded and sustained over time. More traditional face-to-face workshops, even week-long summer workshops, are often not as well suited for supporting this type of professional growth. Placing all or part of those workshops online or providing online follow-up improves the potential to reach this outcome. Increased costs for achieving this type of outcome are often due to the human capital you have to invest in terms of facilitators, coaches, or discussion leaders. Approaches can vary, however, and don't necessarily require a set course of study but can include a series of online discussions or interactive webconferences and can help prepare you for the highest outcome in the matrix: learning communities.

Active to Dynamic Learning Communities

A laudable goal for many schools is the development of a professional learning community or community of practice. There are several models that have been successfully employed in and outside of education (DuFour, DuFour,

& Eaker, 2008; Wenger, McDermott, & Snyder, 2002), but they take time and effort. I realize that both of the terms *professional learning communities* and *communities of practice* are used in schools today, that these terms usually have different meanings, but that they are not used consistently. I don't want to negate or contradict the valuable work conducted by proponents for either type of community, and since the focus of this book is online professional development and online technologies can support many different community models, I'm going to refer to them as *learning communities*. Successful learning communities, in any form, are often the most difficult outcome to obtain and have costs beyond setting up a social network.

As technologies that supported user groups and discussion lists evolved into social networking tools that were easier to use (e.g., blogs, wikis, Facebook, and Ning), online communities became commonplace around hobbies, sports, and other recreational areas and interests. You can find online groups of off-road auto racers who post the results of their latest meet, or find and contact local running groups online so you'll have new friends to jog with when you visit a new city. These are often self-formed and self-sustaining groups that have capitalized on the ease with which information can be shared online. Professions and organizations, too, have capitalized on these technologies, and it's perhaps from this genesis that online learning communities in education have evolved. Successful models of online learning communities in education exist (see the feature about WeAreTeachers in Chapter 5, Box 5.2, for one example), but successful communities require a lot of time—whether volunteering time for recreational networks or designated personnel and activities in professional networks—and time is going to cost you.

The technologies used to support learning communities online can be as simple as those described earlier or can include proprietary applications or even virtual reality environments such as Second Life. Even if using free or low-cost technologies, the additional costs stem from the need for purpose and organization that must be managed by people. People's time costs money. Unlike social networks, educators may not join a learning community out of sheer enjoyment or excitement for participation. It often takes more effort to get real sharing to occur. According to Ross White from LEARN NC, "The notion that if we just give teachers a place to share [they will], whether lessons plans, discussion forums, or other materials has not proven to be true." Barbara Treacy from EDC concurs. She notes, "Just because you set up another site to keep a conversation going, it may not last. There has to be a purpose to the community—a reason to keep people coming back to the community." (For more about EDC's online professional development efforts, review Box 2.3: "Learning From Experience: EdTech Leaders Online." A profile of LEARN NC can be found in Chapter 4, Box 4.2.) In White's experience, teachers need to feel they are getting back more from a community than what they contribute. You can prove there are benefits to belonging to your community, but "it takes a significant amount of effort and someone to champion that effort in order to be successful," says White.

Online learning communities require organization and facilitation to ensure that the activities of the users meet the needs you establish, as well as keeping the users engaged and motivated. And when those needs focus on improving student performance through changing practices and beliefs, it takes a lot of nurturing and monitoring to keep the community on task and to reach your goals. Elizabeth Wolzak, formerly from PBS TeacherLine, suggests keeping topics focused. For example, "The topic of assessment is too large, but using a particular type of assessment for a specific audience can focus a discussion."

Many schools would probably be happy with *active* learning communities in which the members focus on a particular topic for a limited period of time. They engage in structured activities that help them better understand and address the topic in their own setting, whether implementing new teaching strategies or monitoring school policies. The idea of a *dynamic* learning community that emulates the enthusiasm and activity of the interest-based communities described earlier could be the mature evolution of an active learning community, but it is the most difficult to achieve regardless of the technology supports you're using. It's dynamic because the community members themselves determine topics and activities and guide or nurture the evolution of the group. Whether wholly online or through a hybrid approach, a dynamic learning community can capitalize on a variety of online supports that can extend the activities of the community beyond in-house meetings and events and can become the centralized structure that supports all professional growth within a school—yielding significant returns on your investment.

You can reach the highest outcome levels on the decision matrix, but there's no one set path for getting there. A school that already has a well-established and successful learning community embedded in its culture might have the best opportunity to implement online professional development that is targeted at that higher outcome level. Similarly, a district that has a course catalog of successful face-to-face workshops may want to first consider supporting those courses with online technologies and begin at the level of changes in educator knowledge. But even if you are starting from scratch and building or purchasing a system, you can still expect to reach even the highest outcome levels, if you have the resources. It's unlikely, however, to expect to jump right in at the highest levels without significant and ongoing resources—people, time, money, and other material resources, like the technologies you select.

Take a moment to determine *your* desired outcomes. Review the needs you identified earlier and think about how they influenced the creation of your vision. The rest of the columns in the OPD Decision Matrix are inputs that will influence your cost, but it's important to keep your outcomes in mind. Outcomes higher up the continuum dictate higher inputs. Changes in knowledge and practice will encumber greater costs related to collecting evaluation data. Learning communities require facilitation and technologies that keep sensitive data secure. Review your vision and determine *your* outcomes a year from now, 3 years from now, and 5 years from now (or a period that's reasonable for you).

Box 2.3 Learning From Experience: EdTech Leaders Online

Organization: Educational Development Center, Inc. (EDC)

Contact: Barbara Treacy, Director

URL: http://edtechleaders.org

Date First Implemented: 2000

Audience: K–12 teachers and school administrators

Need: *What Was the Initial Trigger?*

This grant-funded program grew out of earlier research on experimenting with online learning in a collaborative effort between EDC and the Harvard Graduate School of Education originally funded by the AT&T foundation. In the fall of 2000, EDC took the challenge to build the EdTech Leaders Online (ETLO) program to scale high-quality professional development online. ETLO then became the core partner of the 10-state e-Learning for Educators Ready to Teach grant funded in 2005 by the U.S. Department of Education to Alabama Public Television.

Intended Outcomes:

EDC was intent on finding an effective way to provide professional development to educators. They experimented with technology as the medium, but the goal was high-quality professional development.

Incentives:

Participants get a certificate for the amount of hours in the course. Graduate credit is available for a fee from Antioch University. State programs may offer graduate credit or continuing education units according to state guidelines.

Instructional Design Considerations:

EDC uses a learning community model with discussion at its core. The program has required the use of a strong facilitated online discussion to help support a learning community model. Some synchronous webconferencing has been used, but sparingly because EDC wants to provide flexibility to allow participants to meet their weekly learning goals on their own schedules.

Courses are based on week-long sessions that include readings, online and offline activities, and a focused discussion prompt. Their design encourages carefully crafted prompts to engage participants and encourage them to be

(Continued)

(Continued)

reflective in their responses. There are goals for the week aligned to goals for the overall course. The discussions actually become one of the ways to determine what and whether the teachers are learning.

Project-based learning is another strategy EDC incorporates. Besides the weekly projects, there is often a culminating final project that is built through the progress of the course. Local courses include projects with outcomes that teachers or administrators can implement in their school, district, or organization. These projects are another way learning can be assessed.

According to Treacy, "Less is more." Limited funds help you learn to design tightly. Content must be aligned to the learning goals. Again, she discourages throwing media in just to have it. "Be judicious. Just because two readings are good, 25 aren't better." Stay focused on helping the learning to be better.

Lessons Learned:

EDC uses a capacity building approach in which the participants are not just signing up to take a course but are involved in a program in which they learn how to teach online as well as create online content. Learning to teach is the first part, but then participants deliver online courses in the year following the training. This has allowed EDC to develop a community of trained online designers and facilitators.

EDC has tried to build in addressing the Why question as a core aspect of the program. Common questions, reports Treacy, are, "Why are you interested in online learning? What goals are you trying to meet? What's the connection with other initiatives?" EDC really wants the leadership to understand what they're getting into and why they're getting into it, so they can really become engaged in the process.

Not every tool is appropriate, as different tools serve different learning goals and different learners. According to Treacy, "It's important not to throw in tools for the tool's sake. Participants will push back if the tool is not making it easier or better. It has to increase learning or make it more efficient to be useful."

Evaluation:

EDC uses pre- and post-surveys and conducts annual evaluation reports. Boston College recently completed an evaluation report over multiple years of participation titled *e-Learning for Educators: Effects of Online Professional Development on Teachers and Their Students* (O'Dwyer et al., 2010). It is available from the project website. Results show that teacher participants are learning and liked learning online. They report using what they learned online with their students. There is indication of retention of what they have learned, even after 6 months. The results are consistent across settings, such as rural, urban, novice, state-by-state, or different grade levels.

See the book's companion website for more information about the profiled programs.   **www.corwin.com/rossonlinepd**

Box 2.4 Take Action:
Determine *Your* Desired Outcomes

Based on your vision, describe the outcomes you would like to see 1, 3, and 5 years from now (or some period that is reasonable to your program). Use the matrix below to briefly describe those outcomes at the desired level. You may find that you include outcomes in more than one level, or that they change over time. For example, you may want to have a system to present basic compliance information for all teachers in a district within a year and that is available each subsequent year, but that adds online courses or supports an existing learning community within 3 to 5 years.

	One Year	Three Years	Five Years
Dynamic learning community			
Active learning community			
Changes in practice			
Changes in knowledge			
Present or share information			

MEASURING YOUR OUTCOMES

Once you have a better handle on your desired outcomes, there are some factors that you may or may not have considered that will definitely influence not only your costs but also whether your outcomes are actually feasible or reasonable. Being able to describe your desired outcomes is a critical step in determining whether it all worked in the end. Greater detail for measuring these outcomes is presented in Chapter 7, but do consider how you're going to measure your outcomes up front. Try to avoid the pitfall of relegating evaluation for the end of your project. Consider it throughout your development and delivery.

Presenting or Sharing Information

Measuring professional development at this lowest outcome level is usually the least costly and can be supported by many common technologies.

Usage data in terms of page hits, views, and visitors are common methods of determining online activity and are analytics that are inexpensive to obtain. At this outcome level it's also easy to survey users through forced-choice or open-ended response formats. While it may be difficult to link information presentation directly to increased student performance, presenting information can set up the conditions for making teachers and school leaders more effective at providing opportunities that do lead to increased student performance.

Changes in Participant Knowledge

I'm often asked whether participants can be tracked to see if they did indeed visit every page in a course or determine how long they spent on each. The answer is yes and that it will cost you. It's pretty useless data, though. Just because you open a page, it doesn't mean you read it or understood it. Yes, you can track time spent online, but it's of little value if you're interested in changes in skills or knowledge, and you may save yourself some time and money by not worrying about it.

Technologies that can be used to measure changes in your participants' knowledge include quizzing and survey tools, many of which are built into common learning management systems (LMS). An additional cost for these measures comes from developing items that truly measure changes in knowledge. Developing assessment items that validly address the content and determine user mastery take more time than creating a satisfaction or use survey that can be used over and over regardless of the content. And measuring *changes* implies gathering knowledge data up front, such as through a pretest, and then comparing changes in knowledge at the end of a session, usually through a posttest. There are many technologies that make this easy, but your human resource costs will increase with each component you add, especially when you move into open-ended responses that must be analyzed by a person.

Changes in Participant Practice

Much of the increased costs from this level of outcome are due to human resources. Again, people's time costs money. Measuring changes in educator practice means someone has to go into classrooms or schools and observe whether teachers or school leaders are actually using new skills and knowledge. Depending on the focus of the professional development, it may be possible to evaluate artifacts such as lesson plans, curriculum maps, school policies, minutes from staff meetings, or other documents—many of which can be generated and stored digitally. But ultimately, some type of observation is usually required. To save costs, consider existing observation processes, such as walkthroughs by principals or classroom visits by lead teachers, that can be customized to help gather data specific to your online professional development. This focused approach can not only save you money but will provide rich data that can support a more coherent personal and professional development plan that will benefit those with whom you work.

Active to Dynamic Learning Communities

Those who aim for this worthwhile outcome from their online professional development efforts will see additional costs due to the increased types of data required to evaluate success. Similar to the lower outcome levels, you may still incorporate surveys, use pretests and posttests of knowledge, and observe classrooms and documents, but it's at this level that there is greater effort to scrutinize the impact of your efforts on student performance. Indeed, student data may drive the activities pursued by community members. Summative tests that may be offered once a year, while important in the public eye, are but one source of student performance data to consider. And as you gather and analyze more and different types of data and compare trends across them, your costs will increase.

Schools and districts commonly participate in improvement planning processes, as most have to report these plans to the state or other governing bodies. While the approaches taken to analyze data and report strategies in improvement plans differ, these opportunities can include analyzing changes in schoolwide practice and student performance as they relate to the goals of your online professional development. In fact, if your online professional development is a component of your school's or district's coordinated professional development offerings, you may see a savings in costs—or a shared burden of costs—due to the direct relation it has to school improvement efforts.

Changes in Student Performance

Hopefully, student needs inform all professional growth opportunities in schools. They help individuals determine what areas to pursue for their own professional growth as well as form the basis for schoolwide or districtwide professional growth opportunities. Having said that, you can have an impact on student performance across the levels of the continuum, but it's the hardest outcome to link to your professional development. Teachers can deepen their content knowledge and apply that new knowledge by refining or honing lessons and activities or bringing in resources addressed in your online professional development. Administrators can change their practice to incorporate management practices, policies, or academic interventions you've addressed that can ultimately impact student performance by keeping students in class more often or providing targeted assistance. You can have all these things happen but find it hard to tie them directly to student performance, especially if you didn't identify how you might observe changes in student performance and focus your online professional development on student performance from the beginning. Guskey (2000) recommends that if you want to improve student learning as a result of your professional development, it must "focus specifically on learning and learners" (p. 208). Further suggestions for evaluating all of these outcomes, including impact on student performance, are presented in Chapter 7.

SUPPORT

One common motivation for considering online professional development for many projects I've worked on is that funds and/or staffing have been reduced.

This is an all-too-common occurrence in education. Funds become tighter, but you still have to provide professional development for everyone using that new reading series that was just adopted, or update everyone on changes in district policies, or make sure they know how to use the new software in your school. In situations like this, many people have turned to online professional development as a potential solution to address those needs.

The human resources required to develop, implement, and support online professional development can be significant. Once in place, technology can often offer an economy of scale in terms of delivery as there's little cost difference between allowing 10 people access your website versus 100—some, but little. But providing support to 100 people can become much more costly than 10, depending on the type of support you have to provide. Self-paced does not mean self-supporting. Many people forget to factor in the costs of content, program, and technical support when considering the total cost of their online professional development.

Technical Support

Technical support staff are in critical demand in schools and are often highly overburdened in terms of the number of technical support requests they receive. While business and industry reports ratios of 50 to 75 staff to every technical support person, few schools can reach this ratio. Consider a relatively small school of 600 students, 25 faculty, and 5 administrators and staff. Using a national average of 1 computer for approximately every 3 students (Gray, Thomas, & Lewis, 2010), plus a computer for each teacher and administrator, there can be 230 computers in that school. And that doesn't include printers, fax machines, phones, scanners, cameras, videoconferencing units, and all the other technologies that have to be supported, including the school's network. What is the chance that school has at least one dedicated technology support person? Or even a part-time support person? Only 31% of all public schools report a full-time staff member for technology support and/or integration (Gray, Thomas, & Lewis, 2010). Most schools are more likely to rely on a few technology support personnel at the district level who are also supporting every other school in the district plus the central office.

When you add online professional development into the mix, you have to consider how technical support will be provided. While many teachers take online courses towards degrees at home, data from my own offerings consistently indicates that most teachers access online professional development during the day from a school computer. This may be out of convenience, because the network is faster, they don't want to take their work home, or they have friends at their school they can discuss it with. Whatever the reason, when you implement online professional development in a school setting, you're going to incur some burden on the technology infrastructure in that school and, thus, the technology support staff.

If you work for a school or district, you can reduce your technical support costs by coordinating your efforts with your technology staff to determine the best strategies for providing support. Give them an opportunity to be in on the planning. Depending on the scope of your project, perhaps your project can fund part of or an entire support position. Or if your online professional development supports other initiatives, those budgets may cover the costs of support personnel for your project.

If you work for an outside entity, you will likely have to provide your own technical support. And if you're not local to those you work with, you'll need an easy way for your participants to receive that support, which may include costs associated with e-mail, a toll-free help line, or even extended office hours for support personnel. Regardless of how often these are used, you'll still have to pay salaries for the time support staff are on call. Support personnel may require some training of their own and access to tools to support users. Webconferencing tools that allow you to view and even operate a participant's computer have solved many distant technical support issues, but you have to pay for them. All of these factors impact your bottom line.

Content and Program Support

Besides technical support, you'll also have to provide support to your users concerning issues related to content. Adults are inquisitive people and often pose questions relating to the content or a specific activity. Is it accurate? Can we do the activity a different way? What if we got *this* outcome? There are also questions related to managing the process, what I refer to as *program support*. What if I don't complete this assignment? Can we extend the deadline? How do I get my certificate? How do we pay for the course? These are not issues your technical support staff should be concerned with, but someone has to answer, and the time spent has to be billed somewhere.

In a facilitated environment, you will have costs related to training your facilitators and providing ongoing support to them. Don't neglect refresher training. Some of the most rewarding conversations I've had have been with facilitators who asked to modify activities to better meet the needs of the participants. Those conversations helped me to better understand how the content was being used and how to improve courses. They were invigorating, but when new or different methods or activities were generated from that process, I had to find ways to inform my content development team and other facilitators. You may have to train facilitators every semester or year, or at least provide short refresher trainings periodically.

Consider the resources you have in place that you can leverage to reduce your content support costs. You may have access to a staff development department, which may be a logical unit to house your online professional development. Experienced staff developers can make excellent online facilitators once they are trained in the technology and online pedagogies. Folding your online professional development into an existing staff development department also helps with program questions, as you're likely to be able to follow established guidelines and processes and reduce duplication of effort. You may also have teachers who have taken other online coursework who could serve as a pool from which to draw for online facilitation, maybe receiving a course release to facilitate online activities.

As far as costs for support for your online professional development are concerned, you can't expect to just "put it online" and ignore it. Once there, your online professional development, regardless of the format you use, will need ongoing nurturing and support that will impact your TCO.

SECURITY

An often-overlooked concern is appropriately managing the data related to your participants and keeping that data secure. While many of us have our computers remember the many different passwords we have for our favorite websites, online professional development can involve data that is not only pertinent to individuals but must be protected by law. Some of that data is used to determine whether staff meet specific requirements for employment, such as being considered highly effective, obtaining tenure, or meeting recertification requirements. The more sensitive the data you collect, the greater your costs will be impacted as you ensure that it's collected and stored securely.

Once you start requiring users to log in or otherwise create an account to access your content, you have to provide a method to ensure that account information matches the user every time she or he logs in. These costs occur primarily during the development side and can be minimal, but they may mean the difference between a free or for-fee version of software. You want to make sure you develop a means for users to obtain information about their account, such as forgotten passwords, as quickly and easily as possible with little or no cost to you. Automation, when possible, saves money. You may also need to ensure the integrity of the data, so that when people log back in, they return to the appropriate content, perhaps even to the same page, screen, or media element they last viewed. This type of usage tracking is common to most LMS and even some websites that simply use cookies to track users.

When your participants have to be verified or approved before they can access your content, another layer of complexity is added to the data and, thus, a bit more cost. On many commercial websites, we often log in with just an e-mail address and a password and can opt out of providing any other information. When personal information is required, you need to take additional measures to ensure that that data is kept secure and cannot be accessed inappropriately. The most stringent data security requirements occur when the level of personal information can be used to track or identify individuals, contains credit card or other financial information, or contains data that impacts one's tenure. This level of security often requires purchasing a license for secure transactions and can be influenced by the number of users and transactions you have. It's also a renewable cost, usually annual, that must be budgeted for.

If you're purchasing online professional development, ask your provider to describe how data security and management are handled and any costs—optional or built in—associated with them. Secure transactions, such as allowing for credit card transactions to enroll in a course, are going to cost extra. Many LMS build in secure data storage as a function of their licensing fee, with some options for additional cost. Some providers include routine backup and redundancy options so that even if there are power outages, surges, or—in my own experience—a hurricane, you don't lose any of your data. That peace of mind can be worth the cost. Ask your provider for their "uptime" rate. It may even be provided on their product literature. Go for 99% or higher.

REQUIRED TECHNOLOGY

Inherently technology-centric, there are several technology-specific factors that impact the cost of developing and/or delivering your online professional development, not the least of which is that technology rapidly becomes outdated and has to be replaced. Schools often push replacement cycles to the limits, sometimes 5 years or more, but you're likely to start having to replace some of your technologies within 3 years, especially if you are serving a large number of participants. Different technologies will be explored in Chapter 5, and from those descriptions you will be better prepared to investigate costs for those you select. There are a couple of issues you may want to consider up front, however, before you hone in on any one solution.

Since you are considering delivering content online, you'll save costs if your participants can access your content using standard web browsers installed on their computers. It's becoming easier to access videos, streaming media, and even interactive webconferencing software through free software, but that is not always the case. Be cautious of proprietary media formats and try to use common cross-platform technologies. Flash-based technologies are one example. Flash is a free media player that comes installed on common web browsers and makes it easy to access media that is of high quality but smaller in file size and faster in transfer rate. If you're familiar with YouTube or TeacherTube videos, you're using Flash. There are also several applications that export to Flash, but the original version of the iPad, for example, does not support Flash.

Webconferencing tools are following the rapid evolution of media players, but many still require your end users to download client software, software that allows them to use the service on their own computer. While not directly a cost factor, some schools don't allow staff to install *any* software on school computers, not even to upgrade media players, so be cautious when selecting them and know your end user's technical capacity. If they can't download your software, you may have to develop alternative formats. Also, some interactive software is best accessed through the use of headphones or microphones or a headset with both. Consider who will bear the burden of those costs, you or the user. If you do need proprietary software or hardware, you just need to make sure you inform your users in plenty of time so it can be installed or purchased.

As your online professional development system grows, so may your need for storage space. The cost of storage has decreased dramatically, but weigh the number of expected users and the number of artifacts they might create and store on your system. Users may create lesson and unit plans, curriculum maps, personal and group reflections, drafts of policies, and presentation files. If your school or district requires a professional portfolio, find out whether you need to store portfolio artifacts on your system or can link to them elsewhere, which will save you storage costs.

Media, especially video, will quickly use up storage space and bandwidth. If you plan to incorporate a lot of rich media, you may want to consider a video hosting service. Prices will be based on the amount of total data you store on the host's server, not the number of videos, along with how much data you transfer to your users from its servers. So, as the number or size of your videos increase, your data *storage* costs increase. As your number of users increases, your data *transfer* costs increase.

If you're purchasing online professional development, determine how much storage and data transfer is covered in your licensing fee. Get your vendor to explain it in terms that make sense to you. Bits and bytes mean little in terms of visualizing capacity, but knowing that you can have 1,000 people each store the equivalent of one 10-page document and one 5-slide presentation for each week of your course, as well as unlimited e-mails, might indicate you're probably covered in terms of cost. It just depends on what your participants will need.

Ultimately, you may want to host your own LMS. This, of course, requires an initial investment in terms of hardware in the form of servers to host the software and personnel to manage the system. Don't skimp on the minimum hardware and network requirements. Like computers, servers may last an average of 3 to 5 years, so routinely incorporate replacement costs in your annual budget. Hosting your own LMS will also only be a cost-savings option if you have the tech support to run it. There are free LMS, but only the software is free, not hardware, networking, or support, and some free solutions have limited capabilities compared to their for-fee counterparts. Make sure you know what "free" is going to cost you and how that compares to a for-fee solution (see "Caveat Emptor: Is Free Right for Me?" in Chapter 5, Box 5.6). Be sure you also have the network capacity to support the number of users you grow into. Increasing course and user numbers is a great sign of success but will impact your budget.

EASE OF USE

The harder your selected technologies are to use, the higher your costs will be, because you're going to have to provide training and support for those who aren't familiar with them. Ironically, the most significant constant of technology is that it's always changing. That sounds a little sardonic, but try to describe what's easy technology for me or you to use when compared to someone just entering the field today. This is a warning that this column on the matrix is undoubtedly the first to be outdated. It is a snapshot in time, and as new technologies become mainstream or popular, they will enter your considerations.

It's hard to remember that not everyone uses technologies you may be familiar with, especially in school settings. In many schools, technologies like social networking, blogs and wikis, and cell phones aren't allowed, even for teacher use. Historically, new technologies go through a process of adoption that often begins with outright banning, including technologies like radio, television, and VCRs. The technology categories currently listed in the matrix came from a statewide needs assessment my former colleague Laurene Johnson and I conducted for one department of education. We asked target audience members to report their skill level and access to a long list of common technologies. They've been chunked together to fit the matrix, but the gist of what was available and most likely being used to support online professional development is there, at least for the end of the first decade of the new millennium.

Most of the participants surveyed felt comfortable with and had access to sending e-mail or surfing the Web (with online shopping or searching for a lesson plan given as examples). Attaching documents to e-mails or posting to a website, such as commenting on a blog entry or writing a product review at an online store, were more difficult for those surveyed. So using those kinds of technologies had increased costs in terms of training and technical support. Many of the participants felt comfortable creating a text document using word-processing software, less so incorporating graphics or other media; but sharing those documents with others in an online environment, such as through the use of a file server, drop box, or attaching them to a discussion list, was rated pretty low. Again, that meant higher costs for training and support if those technologies were used. Few had participated in online collaborative environments, videoconferencing, or webconferencing for any purpose. In retrospect, conducting this needs assessment and determining the appropriate technologies to use yielded a higher ROI, since the original technology considered would have either prevented people from participating or required the greatest expense in terms of training and support, and our client might not have achieved the outcome they desired.

RISK

I learned about the value of risk analysis from a presentation by Martin Ripley, then representing the Qualifications and Curriculum Authority in the United Kingdom, at a national summit held by the Partnership for 21st Century Skills in 2005, and then in more detail later that year when we invited him to work with the West Virginia Department of Education. Risk analysis is a consideration when developing large technology-based systems, which your online professional development system might just be. We intended to serve just a couple hundred users with ours, and to date have served more than 8,000, so that probably qualifies as a large system, although there are certainly larger ones. There's one critical factor about risk analysis I learned from Martin Ripley: The less tolerant you are of risk, the more your system will cost.

What are some of the risks you might consider? Deadlines are one. Are your deadlines firm? Does your system have to be online by a particular date? If that date is not flexible, are some of the milestones along the way? If your deadlines are firm and your project is falling behind, it will take more capital to get it back on track. What happens if you don't meet deadlines? Will you lose a contract or funding if you miss a deadline? That could be a cost you might not recover from.

Access, or uptime, can be a risk factor you might consider. Does the system have to be available 24/7? What if it's down for 1% of the time? Or 0.1% of the time? Are those acceptable levels of risk? If you're developing the system in-house, how will you accommodate your tolerance for these risks? Again, be sure to ask providers, including your Internet service provider or system's hosting service, to document their uptime to ensure it meets your accepted level of risk.

Having an acceptable minimum number of users can be a risk factor. You can have the most beautiful and thoughtful content on the Web, but if no one enrolls, your ROI will be dismal. The data security issues discussed earlier are risk factors, as are issues related to having dedicated and trained support personnel. Risk factors can fluctuate over time, too, where you might accept less risk as your ultimate project deadline approaches.

Consider what will or won't break your project and whether you have the funds to overcome delays. An information sharing outcome may be a relatively low-risk project, while a grant-funded project that requires evaluation data indicating changes in educator practice bears higher risk. And while it may seem like you have strong fortitude and high expectations by saying you're not willing to accept *any* risk, I suggest you reconsider that position. While admirable, there are very few projects, especially technology projects, in which some risk is not tolerated, and it's when you get down to the level of no tolerance that costs skyrocket.

Box 2.5 Caveat Emptor: Supporting Your Outcomes

The OPD Decision Matrix provides support for conversations you may have with online professional development providers. First, determine your desired outcomes and the type of measures you require, and then seek responses to questions for each of the factors that will impact your cost.

My desired outcome:	
Outcome measures:	

Outcomes and measures

- How well does the provider's solution meet your desired outcome? Ask for examples or endorsements from past clients.
- What kind of data can be provided to support your outcome measures? What kinds of supports or processes are provided? Ask for examples.

Technical support

- What is the extent of technical support that is provided? What support issues must you cover?
- Is it convenient? What are the days/times it's available?
- Is it easy to use? Does it include phone support?
- Do staff receive training? Are they friendly?

Content and program support

- What is the extent of content support? Are content issues resolved quickly and accurately?
- What is the extent of program support? What kind of support is offered over time as your program grows?

Data security

- What steps are taken and/or technologies used to keep data secure?
- What type of security is covered in standard program costs? What is the cost, if any, for additional security measures, such as secure transactions?

Technology

- What technologies are used? Are they readily available? Easy to use?
- Are proprietary technologies required? Do they require additional cost?
- What technology costs fluctuate with usage, such as data storage or data transfer?

In terms of **risk**, be prepared to tell providers what factors you have no tolerance for and which are more flexible. An experienced vendor should be able to provide data or examples that will help you determine whether they can meet your accepted level of risk or not.

ECONOMIES OF SCALE

At one time, the number of users was a decision point on the matrix. I once thought it was logical to assume that as the number of users increased the costs of the system would increase, but I no longer believe that to be true. Instead I believe that there are plateaus, or perhaps tipping points, in which a significant number of users are reached, that incur an additional jump in cost. For example, if your online professional development is a facilitated course that can only accommodate 20 people per class, once you exceed 20 registrations you incur the cost of an additional facilitator, which can actually be pretty significant. Or, while you can deliver a webcast or a teleconference to 10 people just as effectively as 100 people, depending on your service you may incur different levels of usage or data transfer charges for significantly large numbers. But each situation is unique, and you have to determine where your cost break points are depending on the format you're using and the costs (people, time, and technologies) that are associated with them. You'll find more about determining cost-effectiveness in Chapter 7 with a story of one study I was able to be a part of that indeed proved to be cost-effective and demonstrated an economy of scale.

CONCLUSION

While this chapter introduced ideas related to costs, perhaps more importantly it encouraged you to consider reasonable outcomes to meet your needs. Your outcomes influence your bottom line. Knowing the additional factors—direct and hidden—that can impact your outcomes can help you to determine what outcomes are feasible within the near and not-too-distant future. Those outcomes will help you make decisions about policies, practices, content, and actual technologies that you can then start budgeting for. No, there's no one magic formula, but hopefully you have a better idea of direct and hidden costs that will impact your bottom line. We'll return to cost in Chapter 6 after considering parameters relevant for developing an implementation plan, but all of those decisions will be shaped by your desired outcomes.

Review Box 2.6: "Take Action: Set Your Mission" and answer the questions related to determining your outcomes. These answers will give you information to craft your mission for online professional development. Your vision is the big-picture view of where you want to go; your mission is how you plan to get there. Along that trip, you'll need a map, or an implementation plan, which you'll develop over the next few chapters, and which will better help you determine your costs.

Box 2.6 Take Action: Set Your Mission

Review the outcomes for your online professional development system developed earlier in the chapter. Consider each of the input factors and determine how they might impact cost. This is the time to determine if you can justify your outcomes as feasible or whether you might want to modify either the outcomes or your timeframe for achieving them.

1. Determine how your outcomes should be **measured**. What data is necessary to help determine whether you've achieved your outcomes, and how will you get it?

2. Consider the type and amount of **technical support** you will need to meet your desired outcomes. What is the current load for support staff, and how will your project impact that load?

3. Don't forget to include the type and amount of **content and program support** you will need to meet your desired outcomes. How are these issues currently handled, and can you leverage those resources for your online professional development?

4. List the types of data you plan to collect and describe how that impacts the level of **security** required for your system. Consider data people will input as they register, participate in the training, and return to you for accreditation or recertification. Do you need secure transactions and storage? How long will you have to keep that data in your system?

5. Consider available **technologies** and the infrastructure you have to support them. You don't have to be too specific at this time because you'll explore those in more detail in Chapter 5. List technologies currently supported and any being considered. How different are proposed technologies from what is currently available and used?

6. Determine **how easy the proposed technology is to use**. You may want to survey prospective participants or inventory existing technologies commonly used. If you plan to introduce new technologies, consider the training and support costs necessary to ensure you reach your outcomes using those technologies.

7. List **risk factors** you are concerned about. Indicate whether you feel they are high, medium, or low risk. What risk factors are you absolutely unwilling to tolerate? For medium- or low-risk factors, what are some contingencies that might come into play if they are not met?

Did your outcomes change? That's okay. Go ahead and revise them, if necessary. It's best to have reasonable and feasible outcomes to yield the highest return on your investment.

3 How Do I Get Started?

In initial consultations, most people talk about online professional development as if it were simply a package you could go out and buy. Just head down to your local PD superstore, buy the "OPD Box" off the shelf, bring it home, plug it in, and off you'd go! Online professional development rarely stands alone. It's a component of a larger system that usually involves a school or district or larger region. Whether you're developing online professional development for a school system in which you currently work or you hope to provide services across a region, what you design and deliver will interact with the people and components in those systems—components that you have to consider up front or you'll have to backtrack later, jeopardizing your timeline and budget.

This chapter is intended to help you consider some of the components you're likely to have to deal with during the planning phase (see Figure 3.1) to develop a strong implementation plan. As you consider your needs, take inventory of what you already have, including policies, practices, material resources, and those people who control them. These are the gatekeepers—people who either have to be informed of what you're doing or who may actually make decisions about moving forward, at least as it relates to their realm. Having buy-in from these folks is critical. By the end of this chapter, consider who should do what by when. I use the term *gap analysis* for this process, and it's the first part of developing an implementation plan that will ultimately include timelines, budgets, and descriptions of the actual technologies you select.

TAKE INVENTORY

This chapter begins the development of an implementation plan for your system. You've already considered some of the big-picture needs for your project, hopefully codifying them as written vision and mission statements. Now it's time to get into some of the nitty-gritty. The following factors, which are not presented in any hierarchy or priority, are some factors you may or may not have considered when describing your needs.

> **Figure 3.1** Conducting a gap analysis involves taking inventory of what you have and projecting what you need.

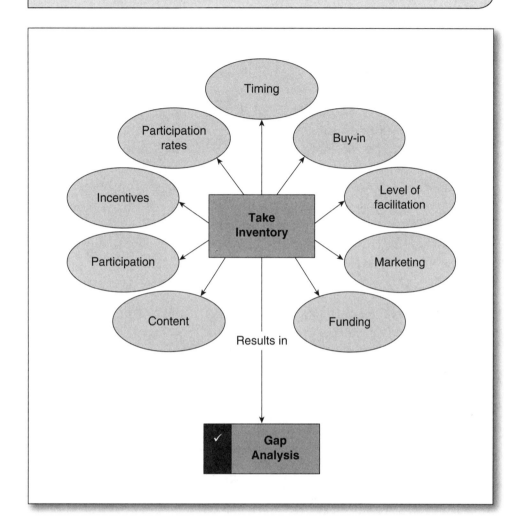

Determine Content to Deliver

This is usually the easiest component to figure out. In many cases, it's some new content, resource, or pedagogy that becomes popular that is the initial trigger that sparks the desire for online professional development. In every project I've worked on, the topic has already been determined. But before you make the final decision, it's important to consider what you already have and how successful it is. Much online content has been drawn from face-to-face offerings, and these can be a good source of content that you may want to deliver. Putting content online may make it available to a wider audience or may capitalize on the capacity for online technologies for improving the experience.

Also determine if there are gaps in your current offerings, or if they are not as successful as you prefer. You can also determine what content to develop by reviewing student performance trends, conducting surveys or focus groups, or other interactions with your prospective target audience. Staff in your curriculum and instruction and professional development offices are likely to be your gatekeepers. The type of content you select (e.g., basic information, skills, or attitudinal) will have influence over how it's designed and delivered. Those considerations will be addressed in Chapter 4, which focuses on instructional design.

Don't forget to keep a long-range view in mind. Your content will become outdated over time, and you will likely want to add new topics. What will be your replacement or refreshment cycle? What related topics might you consider? In my first large-scale project, we worked so hard to get one course up and running that we weren't prepared when the participants *requested* a second course the following year! So don't forget to think about your content needs across the years.

Know Your Audience

Knowing who your audience is, what they do or don't like, and what they expect to get out of the experience is crucial. Instructional designers often conduct an *audience analysis* by interviewing potential participants, creating audience profiles, or otherwise trying to get to know the audience members better so they can design content and activities that will be successful. I'll cover audience analysis in more detail in Chapter 4, but in terms of this planning stage, there are a few things to consider before you get too far down the development process. If it doesn't meet the needs of your audience, they're not going to take it. And if you force them to take something that doesn't meet their needs, it will have little impact. Even well-intentioned professional development on very relevant and important topics has met with disaster simply because it was not delivered in a way that met the audience's needs.

Determine your audience's technology skills.

Since you're going to deliver this online, before you can determine what technologies you're going to use, you have to know if your audience can use them. I really want to emphasize this point. You can't assume that everyone has even basic technology skills. Skill levels vary even in this day and age when it seems like Facebook, MP3 players, and smartphones are the norm. Just because technology is available, it doesn't mean it's used. This is especially true in schools, many of which struggle to provide adequate access to technology. At other times, your audience may surprise you. Consider the lessons learned by the World Health Organization in Box 3.1: "Be Open to Your Learner's Needs." It's best to determine the skill level of your specific target audience before you go too far, perhaps through a survey, interviews, or a focus group. You can help your audience develop new skills, but you can't start too far out of their comfort zone.

Box 3.1 Be Open to Your Learners' Needs: Using Twitter to Support Online Professional Development

For many years, there have been few opportunities to train and provide ongoing professional development for health care workers in Micronesia. Steve Baxendale, who serves as the Project Coordinator for the World Health Organization's Pacific Open Learning Health Net, was hired to address this great need. One effort included providing online professional development to college professors in the area so they could then turn around and offer online learning to health care workers across the 14 Pacific Island countries and territories his office serves.

There are many infrastructure issues in this area, and not just technology infrastructure issues. Based on a positive experience providing online professional development in the States, Steve set out to capitalize on the power of online learning in his new setting. He learned a few things along the way. He notes, "You have to be very open to your students. You're building a community of learners. You can't be a know-it-all."

Steve built a professional development program using some more traditional online technologies, but his students taught him the value of using Twitter and texting. Twitter, the popular micro-blogging service, only allows messages of 140 characters or less. That doesn't sound like a lot of room for deep content learning. But because bandwidth was such an issue at many of the sites, his participants found Twitter more reliable for communicating with each other—and with him! "Using Twitter worked well," he said, "but it's not something I'd have thought about originally." His students routinely use IM (instant messaging) and SMS (short message service, commonly referred to as texting), as well. The lesson here may not be that you need to adopt every latest and greatest technology but, instead, that you should pay attention to your students and use the solution that is right for them. For more information about this project, see Box 3.3: "Learning From Experience: Pedagogical Principles of Distance Learning."

Determine your audience's access to technology.

I was surprised to find out how many educators I've delivered online professional development to participate at school rather than home. While there may be exceptions, school technology is still used for online professional development by a lot of educators. With that being the case, you may find that you need to develop media that meets the limitations of school technology.

It's usually not the school computer that is the concern, but the network. School networks are notoriously tight—blocking streaming media, social networking, instant messaging, and all kinds of e-mails that you might normally get at home. If your audience can't see your streaming video of the greatest pedagogical practice ever, you need to consider alternative methods of delivery. If you have a learning management system (LMS) that sends out e-mails with URLs or that come from commercial domains, you may not be able to communicate with your audience.

Determine why your audience will participate.

Educators are motivated to take professional development for many reasons. For some, it's because they are told to. Their school may be adapting a learning community model, and all faculty will be required to participate. Others may take professional development because they need to keep their job by earning a required number of continuing education units for recertification, or maybe they're looking for some form of advancement or a change of jobs. Still others may participate for the aspect of collegiality and the enjoyment of learning something new. These are all different levels of motivation and will impact the content you select, its design, and the utility of the technology you select to deliver it.

One consistent finding from my interviews, and my experience, is that all too often people sign up for online professional development because they think it will be easy (see Box 3.2: "Top 10 Online Professional Development Myths"). They probably go online to shop or communicate with friends, and the flexibility of being able to participate in professional development at home in their pajamas sounds a whole lot better than sitting in a workshop all day. Unfortunately, many of these people find out that online professional development is often more rigorous than traditional face-to-face settings. That's because you can pull in a world of resources in one place, and you can embed that experience during actual practice, so teachers can go try new ideas in their classroom and report back. That takes a lot more effort than sitting in a workshop for a day, pajamas or not.

In terms of motivation, if your audience plans to take your online professional development because they think it will be easy, but it's not, and they have other options, they'll leave in droves. Determine the reasons why your target audience will take your professional development. Review the current types of professional development being offered. Determine if they are successful, or popular. It's hard to convince someone to take your professional development online, unless there's something in it for them that they are not currently getting.

Box 3.2 Top 10 Online Professional Development Myths

During my interviews, the topic of myths about online professional development came up several times. The following list of Top 10 Myths was originally inspired by Melinda George from PBS TeacherLine and Ross White from LEARN NC but is corroborated by many of the experts I spoke with.

1. **Online professional development is easy.** Just because you can shop online, it doesn't mean you're prepared for online learning. Remember, it's not the technology that matters, but how it's used. When it's used to provide high-quality content and rich learning experiences, you can be challenged, but in a good way.

2. **Online professional development lacks rigor.** Rigor is different from ease. The experts I spoke with described their understanding and use of learning theories, instructional design strategies, addressing the needs of adult

learners, effective online pedagogy, and access to education and subject-matter experts to inform the development of their products. Many participants find online professional development *more* rigorous than other settings.

3. **All online professional development is the same.** There are 1-hour synchronous webinars with chat and video, book studies, mini- and long-term courses, online learning communities that communicate in real and virtual environments, and on and on. If you haven't found enough examples in the book so far to understand that there are many different types of online professional development, just keep reading.

4. **Teaching online is like teaching face-to-face.** Successful online providers emphasize the need for rigorous training of online facilitators. You don't have the same visual and verbal cues in an online setting as you do face-to-face, and it takes time and effort to develop effective habits and strategies to meet the needs of your online students.

5. **Online professional development is just a textbook online.** White hopes that this notion has dissipated some, but because there's a lot of online content that is composed of text and images, it's hard for people to visualize the interaction that occurs in conjunction with that content. If someone doesn't see flashy animations and video—the bells and whistles—he or she can discount it as being similar to a textbook online.

6. **Online courses have learners glued to the computer.** As opposed to a chair in an all-day workshop? Many successful online professional development providers have less seat time per session and instead require participants to get away from the computer and go implement a new strategy or skill in their practice, and then come back and share their experience. How often does that kind of implementation occur in a face-to-face setting?

7. **Online professional development is isolating and lonely.** It won't be unless you design it that way! There can be a true sense of community in online learning as well as a sense of presence in some media, such as virtual environments, that enhances communication and collaboration and nurtures professional relationships.

8. **If you pay for it you should get your credit.** As George noted, "You can't expect to get credit from a college course if you never attend the class," but that hasn't stopped the e-mails she and her staff receive from people who have signed up for online professional development but never attended a single session.

9. **Graduate credits from online professional development are "throw-away credits."** To be sanctioned by a university, online professional development programs often undergo extensive review and must meet all standard requirements for face-to-face classes, some of which may include additional activities or projects and oversight by university faculty.

10. **Online is cheaper than face-to-face.** It depends on your outcomes. High-quality content development can cost just as much for either delivery format, but you can reach an economy of scale in delivery, and you can do some things online you can't do in more traditional settings. Focus on what's the most effective return on your investment.

Box 3.3 Learning From Experience: Pedagogical Principles of Distance Learning

Organization: World Health Organization

Contact: Steve Baxendale, Project Coordinator, Pacific Open Learning Health Net

URL: www.polhn.org

Date First Implemented: 2009

Audience: College professors learned how to modify an existing face-to-face course for online delivery.

Need: *What Was the Initial Trigger?*

Steve Baxendale was hired to develop continuing education opportunities for health workers for the 14 Pacific Island countries and territories covered by the World Health Organization's Representative Office in the South Pacific. Because of the shortage of health workers and the multiple duties they often performed, it was important to provide ongoing training for health workers where they did not have to leave their communities for long periods of time.

Intended Outcomes:

The project targeted college professors currently offering courses in a face-to-face setting. The intended outcome was that these professors would learn to design and deliver effective online versions of courses in their area of expertise.

Incentives:

Graduate credit

Instructional Design Considerations:

The preference is problem-based learning, sometimes incorporating case studies, often modeled after real events. The designers try to make the material relevant, including making sure people represented in graphics and animations look like the target audience, which in this case includes people from Micronesia.

Lessons Learned:

Doing a needs assessment and including all of the relevant stakeholders has been a successful means for getting buy-in. WHO contacts health-related governing boards and institutions, health facilities, content experts, and practitioners (members of their target audience) as much as possible to determine what professional development is necessary.

The administrative system (academic services) initially relied on was not set up for online courses, so WHO had to make an effort to provide student support specific to an online setting. The online students don't follow the same procedures as other students because—in many cases—they can't. They're often isolated, and their work obligations don't allow them to attend classes on a regular schedule.

> **Evaluation:**
>
> Course evaluations are conducted at the end of the professional development. Most questions are qualitative. Baxendale corroborates the notion from other providers that there is a tension between funders' wanting data to demonstrate impact but not providing sufficient funding to actually observe the participants in practice.

Identify Incentives for Participation

Motivation leads to considering what kind of incentives your participants are going to want. I'd like to think that all educators are dedicated lifelong learners who seek out the highest-quality professional growth opportunities to participate in throughout their career. There are people like that, but the reality is that life is busy, and that's no less true for educators. Teaching doesn't happen just inside the school walls during the school day, and many teachers take home grading and lesson planning, or provide afterschool help on and off campus through tutoring, homework hotlines, sponsoring clubs and activities, and even online support for students at night. That doesn't take into consideration educators' personal lives, filled with family obligations and keeping up with friends and personal interests. Because life is busy, even the most dedicated educators will need some sort of incentive to participate in your online professional development.

In the "if you build it, they will come" line of thinking often encountered, someone envisions a utopian online learning community in which busy educators will sacrifice nights and weekends because their professional growth is the incentive. There's a difference between growing a community based on interest rather than growing a community to promote professional growth on a topic someone else thinks is good for you. Yes, professional growth is an incentive for many people, but it's perhaps an insufficient incentive for most people—and not just educators. If that is your only incentive, please reconsider why you think online professional development is the answer. Or better yet, consider some of these other incentives, some of which cost very little to provide.

Most educators are required to obtain some number of professional development hours or continuing education units to be recertified. These types of incentives are well met by online professional development. Try to determine areas of need for teachers who must receive these kinds of recertification points. Depending on what level of education (bachelor's degree vs. master's or higher) or certification, teachers may have more or less flexibility about what types of units they receive. In one district I taught in, as a teacher with a master's degree I had many more options for recertification activities than those with a bachelor's, who were required to take graduate-level courses in their area of endorsement. A good strategy is to try to figure out if there are types of recertification points that are required but difficult to obtain that your online professional development might meet. As for me, there were no graduate programs in my area of endorsement within several hundred miles, so I couldn't have taken a graduate class on campus if I had wanted to. Online professional development would have been a good fit there.

Recertification points for professional development can often be offered at the local level, and you don't always have to be an accredited, degree-offering institution for your participants to receive credit for taking your professional development. It's a good idea, when you get to the marketing considerations for your program, to pull together a summary of information about your course, including an overview, table of contents, objectives, outcomes, and time required for completion. Share it with your prospective audience or their districts to try to determine appropriate recertification units up front. I've had several districts accept online professional development I've helped to develop elsewhere because it met their needs and requirements. In this situation, a little work up front can lead to incentives, and you don't even have to provide them—the district does!

Many educators do want graduate credit for the professional development opportunities in which they participate, and if you're not an accredited, degree-offering institution, you might be able to partner with an institution that is in order to provide this incentive. Some institutions of higher education require that a faculty member either deliver the content or oversee the delivery in some way, perhaps reviewing final products from participants. This person is often referred to as the teacher of record. You will also likely have to submit your content for review by a faculty member or may be required to include a capstone project, such as a research paper or presentation, depending on the policies of the institution you cooperate with. These institutions usually have additional fees that must be added to your participant cost, such as an application fee (if they are not already enrolled in a degree program at the institution) and a fee per credit hour granted. These can be steep, especially when added on top of fees you may charge, but students enrolled in a graduate program are already familiar with these fees and may be willing to pay them if your program meets their needs.

Beyond recertification and graduate credits, many educators may be encouraged to participate if your incentives include classroom materials, equipment, or other resources. Book study participants might get a free copy of the book. Participants in technology professional development might receive a laptop, whiteboard, or other technology to use in their classroom. Others may get a classroom set of curricular materials. This can be a win-win situation for a district that has invested significant money in new curricular materials, pedagogical interventions, or technology. These resources will have greater potential for positive impact once your teachers know how to use them appropriately.

Teachers may also be encouraged to participate if they receive release time, either a course release or even a release from a school duty, to participate in online professional development during the school day. And, of course, stipends are the incentive that will draw in many people. If you plan to offer stipends, they should be comparable to other offerings.

Identify incentives that have been successful in the past, because personal edification is not enough. If your professional development will compete with existing offerings, what incentives do they provide? Determine what kind of incentives you will offer to make your online professional development more inviting.

Calculate Participation Rates

As mentioned in Chapter 2, there are levels of participation that are tipping points into higher levels of service. My example was that if you deliver courses that are facilitated, and your class-size limit is 20, once you go over 20 people you need another facilitator. But increased numbers will also impact your need for additional content, technical and administrative support, and even data storage and transfer. Your concern here is whether you have minimum participation requirements to deem your project successful—and to keep the funding coming—and whether you can handle larger numbers should you be more successful than you planned.

Review past participation rates in other professional development offered in your area. Based on those rates, what are reasonable expectations? Project how many people you'll *need* to participate at start-up and then how many you'll need to sustain the program. Will they draw from other programs, or are you serving a new audience? Again, why should they participate in your program over others? Projecting use over several years is important for considering how to scale up your approach. Think ahead 3 to 5 years. It's also good data to use when talking to providers or vendors who want you to use their solutions. Do they have a minimum level of service? Some have a minimum fee, and you need to determine if you can provide enough participants to make that fee worthwhile. Others may have a cost-sharing arrangement. Can their solution support your projected growth? Find out the implications of increased numbers on cost and reliability of the service.

Determine When People Will Participate

Online professional development can be as rigorous, if not more so, than more traditional forms and delivery modes. Because of that, you can't expect to put something online and let people "work it into their schedules." Online professional development should be considered comparable to other delivery methods with similar obligations of time—at the very least. Provide adequate time for people to participate. You know educators are busy people. Combine that with the fact that many of them access online professional development using school equipment, and you should consider how those factors influence when they are likely to access your content.

Encourage schools and districts to build online professional development opportunities into the school day or the school calendar. If you already provide workshops on inservice or early-release days, you can allow educators time to access online professional development during these same days. I developed some online professional development for cohorts of teachers at the same schools. While the teachers at some schools completed the work on their own, others would meet together in a computer lab during inservice days to work through the content together. They all went through the content; what I did was provided them the flexibility to access it in a way that best met their needs.

It depends on the activities and the expected outcomes you plan to achieve. Some may be more suited to allocating time during the school day, while others may be more suitable for after hours in an area that is more comfortable and quiet. Consider the incentive of release time and allow participants to access online professional development during predetermined times during the week, such as an hour one day a week. This may not work in all situations based on contractual obligations, but don't rule out investigating these options.

Collaboration and reflection are additional important design elements to consider when developing content and activities. Consider ways these elements can be built into the culture of the schools participating in the online professional development. For example, many schools have learning communities that meet on a regular basis. Choose online professional development to support the topics being discussed in the face-to-face communities and reflect on how it can enhance that initiative. Consider time to allow participants to share what they have learned with others, either in person or online. Just as teachers often have to provide a workshop after attending a face-to-face workshop or conference, have those participating in online professional development share what they have learned. They could do a presentation in person at a faculty or staff meeting, or they could use technology to share information through a blog, school website, or online learning community. From the perspective of the developer, this is also helpful marketing of your product to other potential audience members.

Consider current expectations for time allocated to professional development. How will online professional development support those expectations? Will it make it easier for people to participate? Or will limited access during the school day be a barrier for your audience?

Get Buy-in

Locally, you need to get buy-in from different stakeholder groups that will be impacted by your online professional development, some more directly than others. The first, technical support personnel, may be obvious, because it's a technology-laden activity. As was mentioned earlier, make sure you involve them from the beginning! I've never met technical support personnel that have actually tried to block or undermine online initiatives, but they can be reluctant or hesitant to respond if you've added to their work without their input. You're going to need their buy-in—at some point—and earlier is better and *easier* than later. If you're developing a plan within a school or district, your technical support personnel may be best suited to help with your gap analysis to determine if you have adequate software, hardware, and network infrastructure to support your plan. Also consider additional support personnel that might be required for your plan based on the number of participants you plan to serve. They know the infrastructure best and can be a valuable resource as you move forward. And since it's a technology project, it's likely they'll be interested in it, and they may become strong advocates for your program.

If you work within a school district, you really need the buy-in of administrators from the beginning, especially building-level administrators whose teachers may be enrolled in the program you're planning. It's amazing how administrative support can really improve the success of a program, yet if they're not actual participants, they're often left out of the process. Principals are the designated instructional leaders, fiscal agents, and resource managers for their schools and are ultimately held accountable for the success of the school. Let them have a voice in terms of what content is provided, what resources are available, and the supports they can offer in their own building. Keep the lines of communication open throughout the process. Having this support can go a long way in terms of meeting your expected outcomes, especially if principals may be asked to provide evaluative information about the program once it's operational.

Of course, if your audience will include teachers, it's important to get their buy-in. Addressing the topics in this chapter, like determining appropriate content and providing relevant incentives, will go a long way towards getting their buy-in. They also shouldn't see it as a burden or an add-on to what they are already doing. You have to help your audience members, whether teachers or administrators, understand the relevance of your online professional development and how it will help solve the problems they face. When you truly do provide a solution to their problems, buy-in won't be an issue.

Determine Level of Facilitation

This is a biggie. Facilitators are a big-ticket item because they can only work with so many participants at a time, regardless of whether you're running courses that have actual classes or facilitating a learning community where interaction is more fluid. Facilitators also require pedagogical and technical training and ongoing support. They may be content experts but unfamiliar with online learning or with the specific technologies you're using. However, many people see online professional development as a means to provide self-paced learning and reap the benefits of automated instruction that does not incur the costs associated with facilitators.

I feel comfortable in saying, yes, in some cases you can create successful self-paced professional development that does not require facilitation. But it depends on the outcomes you're trying to achieve. Consider other instruction. What skills and or topics have successfully been automated for . . . third graders? Algebra students? English language learners? Education in general? There are some success stories where students can learn basic content, like verbal information (facts and figures), or simple processes or procedures by interacting with simulations or animations. Educational technology has made some gains in this arena.

Go back to your outcomes. What do they tell you about the type of learning that you want to occur? Using an animated game to practice basic math skills is different from teaching teachers how to monitor and analyze different levels of student numeracy development and to identify misunderstandings or incorrect strategies and plan appropriate interventions. But that's a pretty typical desired outcome for professional development. There are some skills that can be addressed without facilitation and some that are better addressed with facilitation. Atomic Learning, as mentioned in Chapter 2, is an example of a company that provides nonfacilitated tutorials, often screen captures of common technology tools, that have helped many teachers (and others) successfully develop technology skills. Presenting or sharing information or developing basic knowledge about a topic might be automated and successful without a facilitator. Developing complex skills or changing people's attitudes and behaviors, or the culture of a school, are pretty complex outcomes to achieve without facilitation.

So many people want to provide self-paced, nonfacilitated online professional development that instead of saying you can or can't do this, I encourage you instead to consider, "What content has to be facilitated?" Because you may have some that doesn't have to be. You decide what's best for you and whether your needs include facilitators (see Box 3.4: "Caveat Emptor: Facilitation Models"). For more detailed information about preparing facilitators, see Chapter 6.

Box 3.4 Caveat Emptor: Facilitation Models

Instead of looking at the cost of a facilitator as a burden, I encourage you to consider the return on investment for that facilitator. What kind of learning outcome is desired? Below are three different models that I've used in order to help meet the request for less expense for facilitation. Each case is a statewide implementation of online professional development using a course-based approach lasting 10 to 15 weeks. In all cases, changes in participant knowledge were measured. In terms of return on investment, a corresponding average completion rate is given for each case. What is the "learning return on investment" of a completion rate of 90% versus 50% or less? You have to determine what you're willing to accept.

1. **Compensated and trained facilitators.** Master teachers were trained to facilitate a 13-week online course for teachers in their schools. All received from 3 to 12 hours of facilitation training in person. The facilitators received additional support in the form of a printed manual with suggestions on how to organize group activities, run discussions, and other common topics. The completion rate for this model was more than 96% sustained through offerings over a span of 5 years.

2. **Volunteer and trained facilitators.** Based on the success of a previous offering, a state client requested a repeated offering of a 10-week course and would pay for participant registration but not for facilitators. We asked for and trained volunteer facilitators from the participants who registered for the course. Training was conducted online through a 1-hour live webinar that was also archived. These facilitators had access to an online manual with explicit directions for each activity. Facilitators were not responsible for monitoring whether participants actually participated or completed the course. The completion rate for this course, that was previously over 90% using the compensated and trained facilitator

model, was approximately 50% during the first year. Several volunteer facilitators did an excellent job and volunteered to facilitate a second course or sought other opportunities for paid facilitation with other providers.

3. **No facilitation.** I helped a state develop a 15-week course that was completely self-paced. Participants had to keep a checklist of their activities and submit it to a site coordinator upon completion of the course. Suggestions were provided in the online content for groups that had access to a facilitator, including alternate activities for groups, but no facilitators were trained. The course ran for 3 years, and the completion rate was approximately 13%.

Get the Word Out

I've met a lot of excited and motivated project managers and developers who have worked for months on an online professional development project without anyone in the target audience even aware it was being developed. I once walked into a presentation for 200 teachers who were going to be required to enroll in a course I had been developing for them for 3 months, but who were not told until that very day that they were *required* to take an online course. Talk about motivation problems!

Consider how you will market your online professional development from the very beginning. You need to get the word out to districts and schools, whether you're working from the outside or inside. How is this currently done? What methods have been most successful? Will you use both print and online means? Perhaps you can present, online or face-to-face, at conferences or meetings that members of your target audience normally participate in.

Your marketing material should demonstrate how your online professional development will meet the needs of your participants. It may also help them understand how it fits into their current system or philosophy of professional development. If you are augmenting or replacing traditional forms of professional development, people need to feel your solution will be the right choice for them. You may need to win over some people who believe that the *only* way to provide professional development is face-to-face.

You may also want to cultivate champions for your effort. These can be at any level, whether district and school administrators or classroom teachers. They may be individuals or groups, such as teacher unions or school boards. Stan Freeda from OPEN NH says his program has been trying to seed the districts he serves with people who have taken their courses. "Successful participants tend to encourage others to take their courses," he says, "and can also give face-to-face support for those who might need it." OPEN NH also budgets annually for a 2-hour face-to-face orientation in four sites across the state.

Determine who the recognized leaders are in the system where your online professional development will be delivered. Try to get them on board early. They may be able to corroborate needs but can also help you better navigate the culture of the school or district. No one knows what teachers will or won't accept like a fellow teacher. Once you're up and running, your marketing efforts may change their focus, but don't wait until your launch date to announce your online professional development. Start early and build momentum so people are anticipating your system.

Identify Funding Sources

It's too early to determine exactly how much money you'll need to develop and implement your online professional development, but you can identify sources of funding. The best advice I can offer you on this topic is that schools and districts have access to resources that they may not realize could be used to support online professional development. Most districts have existing professional development offerings. Some large districts may have extensive offerings for staff throughout the year, including summer workshops, that are coordinated by designated professional development staff at the district level. Can those existing people and funds be used to provide online professional development? Perhaps to augment existing programs? Or maybe you can automate some professional development, like new employee orientation or compliance training, that can free up resources to be used elsewhere. Regardless, determine how new online professional development offerings will operate within the current system and culture of professional development and what role it will play.

In schools that receive federal dollars through Title programs or others, online professional development may meet the needs of these different programs. Professional development is a common requirement for schools receiving these funds. In some cases, funds can be combined to support a program that serves multiple audiences. For example, online professional development that helps all teachers in a school develop literacy pedagogies for students of all academic backgrounds may be able to draw on funds from special education, educational technology, limited English proficiency, as well as other school improvement funds. The trick is getting people from these programs together to talk and determine the advantage of combining these funds to result in something bigger and better than what the isolated funds might provide.

Partnering for Success

It seems that with most of the people I've worked with, with similar experiences reported from many of the experts I've interviewed, when an organization decides to implement online professional development, they decide to develop everything from scratch. We educators tend to be pretty territorial and maybe just a bit reluctant to share. I encourage you to consider what online professional development solutions may already be available. There are many online professional development providers out there who have already developed some great content that you might be able to use—some for free! Find out what's already available before you embark on developing content from the ground up. Make sure you review the profiles of successful online professional development providers throughout the book and you'll find some online professional development content—some linked to classroom resources for students—that you can use for free. Teachers' Domain from WGBH in Boston (profiled later in this chapter) and the NSTA Learning Center from the National Science Teachers Association (in Chapter 7) both offer free and fee-based, high-quality classroom content and online professional development developed in collaboration with content, learning, and media experts. Additional organizations may already be providing content in your area.

There are some signs that the reluctance to share may be changing, however, especially with the push for Creative Commons licensing and open-source materials that are becoming popular on the Web. The Creative Commons licensing scheme will let you know how you can use content you find on the Web in your own work. You may have to use it as is with no modification, or you may have complete control to customize it to your needs. One caution is that you usually don't get any support for the content you find that are open source or follow a Creative Commons license, or you have to be very proactive about finding support through discussion forums or other sources. And the content you find may or may not interface with your selected technologies, so just be aware you may need to invest a little time to bring it fully into your online professional development. For more information, visit the OER Commons online (www.oercommons.org).

There are several successful online professional development programs that are available to help when you want to develop your own content, but do so with a knowledgeable and trusted guide. Many of these organizations are profiled in this book. They offer helpful models and templates; experienced instructional designers and facilitators; and other advice related to marketing, administration, and other concerns. Some allow you access to their expertise and resources by joining their program. Many teach you how to develop high-quality content that promotes interaction and engagement by actually enrolling you in a class where you create your own content for a course you can deliver. Some can even provide a platform for you to deliver your content if you join their program. They're out there, successful, and have done a lot of this legwork for you, so don't ignore these valuable resources. You don't have to start from scratch! For more information, check out Box 3.5: "Caveat Emptor: Partnering for Success."

Box 3.5 Caveat Emptor: Partnering for Success

We've reached a point where online professional development is no longer a novel idea. Dozens of providers across the country and beyond have learned lessons and developed successful procedures that you can benefit from. You don't have to do this alone. But is a partnership right for you?

Melinda George from PBS TeacherLine notes that "partnerships work well when your expertise complements each other." She suggests not taking on something out of your area of expertise. Knowing your strengths is a critical first step. She notes that TeacherLine and others have learned a lot about what makes good online learning, but because TeacherLine is not an organization

(Continued)

(Continued)

with subject-matter experts in all areas, she looks for strong partners in those areas. You can follow this example. Figure out what you're good at and what resources you have, and then find organizations that complement them, in order to develop a strong partnership. Programs like Virtual High School are actually cooperatives that districts can join and benefit from, and some programs deliver materials to educators in multiple states. Two of these are Teachers' Domain from WGBH, which serves educators nationwide through partnerships with Public Television stations; and e-Learning for Educators, sponsored by Educational Development Center and Alabama Public Television, which delivers materials to educators through state partners.

Al Byers, from the National Science Teachers Association (NSTA), notes that an effective partnership can have the greatest impact on how well their materials are received and the impact they have on professional growth. He notes that when their materials are deployed as part of a larger strategic professional development plan that incorporates incentives and milestones and has administrator support, success is greater than if their online portal is presented simply as a URL that is forwarded via e-mail to a large number of teachers.

Henry Pollock, former director of Florida School Leaders, echoes the sentiment that many players in the education space don't like to share. In his state, when the Department of Education would release a request for proposal (RFP) to develop a program, there were several regional entities that usually bid and won contracts. But what they ended up with, according to Pollock, was "five flavors of the same ice cream." In developing Florida School Leaders, Pollock implemented a partner-based model where no one entity was given more than 50% of their budget for development of a single component, and all had to serve as subawards to the others. The result was that all partners led a significant piece of the work, one that was a particular strength of their organization, while also contributing to the other parts of the whole, and all material was delivered statewide through a portal controlled by the Department. But this opened up each partner to entirely new audiences they were not used to working with or delivering to.

Do you really need to do this alone? Review the descriptions of these and other online professional development providers and consider whether there are suitable partners out there that will meet some or all of your needs.

Box 3.6 Learning From Experience: Teachers' Domain

Organization: WGBH

Contact: Howard Lurie, Associate Director, Educational Productions Department

URL: www.teachersdomain.org

Date First Implemented: 2002

Audience: K–12 science teachers

Need: *What Was the Initial Trigger?*

WGBH started by taking sections of high-quality video footage captured during the filming of the popular television series Nova and putting them online to support science teachers. Teachers' Domain offers more than 36 professional development courses in science content and pedagogy and additional offerings on teaching strategies that can be applied in different content areas.

Intended Outcomes:

Teachers' Doman addresses topics that are traditionally considered hard to understand, whether for students or teachers. Their goal for professional development was to look at areas in STEM, particularly in science, primarily in upper elementary and middle school, for teachers who needed additional credit for recertification. The focus is helping these teachers deepen their content knowledge and master effective pedagogy.

Incentives:

Credit for recertification is offered through PBS TeacherLine and some state programs. Graduate credit is also available from Adams State College and Indiana University for an additional fee.

Lessons Learned:

Teachers report that courses are rich in terms of media and content and can be very challenging. There is a gap between what superintendents and other administrators want teachers to do and what teachers want to do—what teachers feel like they need to do. Consultation with experienced classroom teachers has encouraged Teachers' Domain to streamline their professional development opportunities. Lurie emphasizes that Teachers' Domain tries to "meet teachers where they are." They run teacher focus groups, and teachers often ask for things they can use directly in their classroom.

Teachers' Domain does not provide or facilitate the courses themselves. They produce the content, embed that in a digital platform, and license the content and activities (not the media) to districts and schools. Teachers' Domain has a partnership with PBS TeacherLine that has the capacity to train facilitators or deliver courses developed by Teachers' Domain.

They are trying to find a balance between the 3-hour, graduate credit course that comes with a registration fee combined with hefty tuition costs versus a shorter, more self-paced activity that is faster to get through and less expensive. They have teachers who need to review a topic or just check their understanding on a topic rather than enrolling in a comprehensive course in which the topic they need is just one small portion.

Teacher's Domain has to deal with some complicated rights issues with the media they use. They have to be very clear with actors, producers, and others

(Continued)

(Continued)

who create the media as to how it might be used. Schools and districts can license the content, but Teachers' Domain streams the media. They provide the following different levels of access to media:

- Everything can be viewed online.
- Some can be viewed and downloaded.
- Some can be viewed, downloaded, and shared.
- Some can be viewed, downloaded, shared, and remixed.

When a teacher takes a course from Teachers' Domain, whether directly or through an approved organization that has licensed the content, they become familiar with the other materials on Teachers' Domain that they can use in their classroom. It builds loyalty to the brand and provides value added to those who participate in their professional development.

CONCLUSION

Too often I'm called in to work with people who have never considered these factors and have already spent significant time and money developing content. You need to consider all of these factors, regardless of whether you're buying an online professional development solution or growing it yourself. To help you organize your thoughts on those factors, review Box 3.7: "Take Action: Gap Analysis to Describe Your Needs." You can use it to support internal meetings with different stakeholder groups involved in the development process or when talking to any vendor or contractor who will be involved in your project so you know they can deliver what you need.

In terms of "What do we have?" include policies and practices, not just material resources. This column also might be thought of as "What is the status quo?" or "What is the current practice?" You've started identifying your needs, or perhaps your wants, in earlier chapters. Return to your vision and mission to make sure your needs remain consistent.

Remember, the gatekeeper is the person or persons that you need to involve as you move forward. You may need their approval or you may need them to participate in the development process. Ultimately, you need to determine who has the final say for developing your system. Who is the gatekeeper about what topics are covered? Can building leaders at each school make those determinations, or are they decided by district professional development coordinators? Who is the gatekeeper for what technologies are used? Is it the technology staff at the district, or is it the individual user? Who are the gatekeepers about incentives and embedding the online professional development into the school day or calendar? Will participants be able to access your system during school, or will they be doing their work at home? No, you're not going to be able to fit all that information you find in those little boxes; use it as a guide to gather that information to better determine what you need.

Box 3.7 Take Action:
Gap Analysis to Describe Your Needs

Factor to Consider	What Do We Have?	What Do We Need?	Who Is the Gatekeeper?
What content will we deliver?			
Who will participate?			
• What technology skills does my audience have?			
• What level of access does my audience have to technology?			
• What motivation does my audience have for participating?			
What are the incentives for participation?			
How many people will participate (1–5 years from now)?			
• At start-up?			
• 3 to 5 years from now?			
When will people participate?			
Who else should be involved?			
• Technology staff			
• Administrators			
• Target audience			

(Continued)

(Continued)

Factor to Consider	What Do We Have?	What Do We Need?	Who Is the Gatekeeper?
What role will facilitators play?			
• What content has to be facilitated?			
• What content does not have to be facilitated?			
How will we get the word out?			
What funding sources are available?			

What Does Good 4 Online Learning Look Like?

There is some counterpoint in the instructional design world as to whether instruction is designed differently for online learning than for face-to-face interaction. While I sometimes have to use different media online, I don't do things much differently for *designing* in either setting. To me, instructional design is finding the right fit to match the goal of the instruction with the needs of the audience and the setting in which they are learning. Sometimes, I use the same materials, media, and activities in both settings, and sometimes I don't. It depends on those three factors: (a) who your audience is, (b) what your content is, and (c) what media you have at your disposal. Often, you don't get leeway in one or more of those, so you have to customize your design within those parameters.

You may be thinking that since you're not going to develop your own content but purchase it, this chapter isn't for you. It's important, however, that you be an informed consumer about what is and isn't effective instruction. If you don't keep the quality of the design of the instruction in mind as you're reviewing material for purchase, you may be blinded by the technology. While there are entire books written about and degree programs in instructional design, there are some things you can still learn in a short period of time to better determine if your content is well suited to your needs. This chapter will give you suggestions for improving the quality of your online professional development, whether you're developing or purchasing your content.

You may want to use some of the suggestions in this chapter to develop your own content, or maybe you will use them to describe the kind of content you want—your content specifications (see Figure 4.1). These specifications can be included in your implementation plan. This chapter comes before technology selection (Chapter 5), because the learning comes first. You have to know what kind of learning you want to occur to select the best technologies to support it.

Figure 4.1 Understanding instructional design can help you develop content specifications or your actual content.

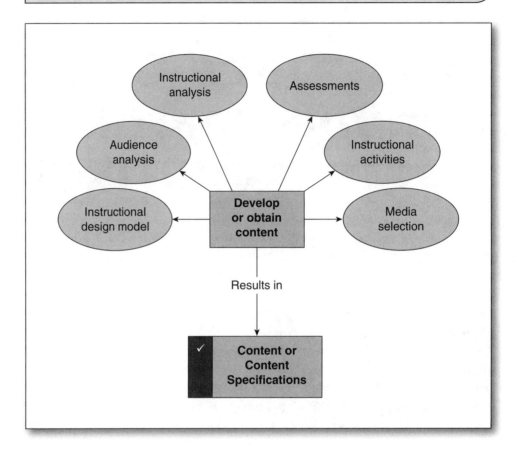

WHY INSTRUCTIONAL DESIGN?

Instructional design is one of the most critical aspects of your online professional development as well-designed content promotes successful learning. Most project managers will demand interactive and engaging online professional development, but they often confuse that with the technology "bells and whistles." Yes, online learning should be engaging to the senses, and there is media that can be very interactive and entertaining, but the biggest bang for your buck will result if your *content* is interactive and engaging. Even the most powerful and most expensive technology isn't going to do you any good if you don't have high-quality content that is engaging and presented in a way that meets the needs of your learners. Steve Baxendale from the World Health Organization strongly believes "there is a direct correlation between the quality of the course, the quality of the instruction, and whether a student completes it." In his experience, he's observed that students will drop out of a badly designed course in the first 3 weeks. Even if you have beautiful graphics, animations, and HD video, if it's not interesting, relevant, or useful, your users will just turn it off. Content comes first. Well-designed content is interactive and engaging.

The term *design* implies some systematic process, and that process is usually codified in an instructional design model. There are several popular instructional design models that can be used to guide your design process. Select one that meets your own philosophy, style, and needs. The ADDIE model developed for the military and still used today includes a series of steps under each of the five phases that give it its name: Analysis, Design, Development, Implementation, and Evaluation. Many teachers around the country are familiar with a popular model called "Understanding by Design" developed by Grant Wiggins and Jay McTighe (2005) that begins with the end in mind. Kathy Cennamo and Debbie Kalk (2004) developed a spiral model that capitalizes on the ability of digital technologies to support rapid prototyping. I use a model that is fairly linear and is commonly referred to by the name of its original developers, Walter Dick and Lou Carey, or the Dick & Carey Model (see Dick, Carey, & Carey, 2008). This model has some steps similar to ADDIE, like analyzing the learners and the content, developing instructional strategies and materials, and an iterative evaluation feedback loop. I find the audience analysis and the instructional analysis especially helpful. As with most models, the developers don't prescribe methods for doing the steps. Instead they give suggestions and options. The models are resources designers use to make better decisions during the design process (Ertmer, York, & Gedik, 2009). Following are some helpful steps for designing instruction.

The Design Team

An instructional designer is often asked to work with a subject-matter expert (SME), sometimes called a content expert, to identify the content to be included in online professional development. Christie Terry from eMINTS says it's important to keep your SME focused on the content (see Box 4.2: "Learning From Experience: e-Learning for Educators: Missouri"). They educate content developers about online education and what's possible, but she doesn't want them to get caught up in the technology, what she calls "the shiny pieces." She often finds herself telling outside entities, "We're working on the content now. We can worry about the shiny pieces later." She says it's important to clearly establish roles, and the role of SMEs is developing good content. "Once you've established those roles," she says, "it goes much more smoothly."

Through negotiation, and sometimes trial and error, an instructional designer helps the SME determine what content is essential, what the learning outcomes might be from the instruction, and established ways this content is often presented. That includes eliminating information that is not necessary, which can sometimes be a sensitive negotiation. The instructional designer can also help the SME determine the skill level the content should begin at by helping him or her describe necessary prerequisite skills. It's rare to design a single learning experience that can meet the needs of experts and novices alike, so you have to draw the line somewhere, and the SME can determine that. It's also helpful to get the SME to describe or demonstrate what success looks like. What should the learner know or be able to do at the end of the instruction? What does it look like?

Besides interacting with the SME, the instructional designer is charged with actually determining the scope and sequence of the content, developing the instructional activities and assessments, and selecting or suggesting the media and how it will be used to promote learning. The instructional designer does all this with the audience in mind. One of my mentors, Kathy Cennamo, mentioned above, emphasizes that the instructional designer (or the design team) has to become an advocate for the audience. An instructional designer identifies the needs and learning preferences of the learners; aligns the outcomes, activities, and assessments so the learners can be successful; and verifies or evaluates the product to make sure it does what it's supposed to—which is help the learners acquire the desired skills and knowledge. If you're thinking about hiring an instructional designer for your project, you may want to see how the designers you hire address these roles. There are many excellent instructional design programs across the country, so if you are looking for a designer, ask for training or education credentials and work samples. And in this day and age, if they don't have a digital portfolio, preferably online, you may want to look for someone else.

How the content is presented depends significantly on the technology solution you select and the skills of the last member of the design team, the media developer. With the increased use of online video, smartphones and their apps, virtual environments, and gaming to support professional learning, it's difficult to find a single person who will have all the media development skills you need. Sometimes it just comes down to whom you have available or whether you have enough money to bring in the talent you need for the media you want. Even if you can't afford HD video or an immersive gaming environment, you can still design high-quality instruction using less costly media. The instructional designer and media developer negotiate what is possible to get the desired learning results.

Working with a media developer can also take some negotiation. These are talented and creative people. Good media developers have tremendous passion about what they do and keep up on the latest trends and the standards in their industry, but their industries extend beyond education. I've been fortunate to work with some excellent media developers, but it seems like most of my videographers want to be George Lucas or Ken Burns when I just want a 3-minute shot of a teacher delivering instructional objectives. Sometimes, they can lose track of the main purpose of the media—to promote learning. The instructional designer helps to keep that focus in mind and encourages the media designer to use the best processes and outcomes to support the learner.

Box 4.1 The Sponsor: An Additional Voice in the Design Process

LEARN NC was established in 1997 at the University of North Carolina at Chapel Hill in response to a state-based report that highlighted the disconnected nature of the teaching practices in many of the state's classrooms. The report noted teachers routinely taught in isolation and had little opportunity to share their professional knowledge. According to Ross White, Associate Director, LEARN NC has codified a process for content development since that time that not only includes a subject matter expert (SME) and an instructional designer, but a sponsor representative, as well. The sponsor initiates the project. The sponsor is often the funder or someone who has critical oversight of course development, and he or she makes sure the resulting project is not only good instruction but also meets the initial needs of the intended audience. Sometimes, when left alone, an SME and instructional designer can develop good instruction that doesn't necessarily match the expectations or needs of the sponsoring organization, so the sponsor provides that reality check to keep the project on target, which also helps support meeting deadlines and budget requirements. The sponsor can also be the "tiebreaker" on decisions that may be split 50-50 by the SME and instructional designer. White notes it's best when the sponsor is available to review the project periodically, but often if LEARN NC has to compromise on one aspect, it's that review, because the sponsor may not always be available. See Box 4.3: "Learning From Experience: LEARN NC" for more information about this program.

Box 4.2 Learning From Experience: e-Learning for Educators: Missouri

Organization: eMINTS (enhancing Missouri's Instructional Networked Teaching Strategies) National Center

Contact: Christie Terry, e-Learning for Educators, Missouri Program Director

URL: www.elearningmo.org/support.html

Date First Implemented: 2003

Audience: K–12 teachers

Need: *What Was the Initial Trigger?*

In 2005, the eMINTS National Center was offered an opportunity to participate in a Ready to Teach grant to help develop online professional development to support its mission of helping K–12 teachers use technology to transform learning in their classrooms.

Intended Outcomes:

The Ready to Teach grant outcomes closely mirrored goals that eMINTS already had established: to build a cadre of educators who could both develop and facilitate online professional development and to create a presence in the state for its potential benefits. One of the driving philosophies of e-Learning for Educators is that the program is not going to succeed in isolation. Says Terry, "We definitely believe that, as a program, we want to be sustainable. Partnerships are the key to that. We need to work with as many programs as

(Continued)

(Continued)

possible and the territorialism that can crop up as an artifact of funding is counterproductive."

Incentives:

Professional development contact hours that can be used to meet professional classification requirements for state certification and optional graduate credit through local universities

Instructional Design Considerations:

e-Learning for Educators used the Ready to Teach grant resources, including course development processes offered by the Education Development Center (EDC). Over the past 5 years, Terry and her team have modified that process, especially using the Backwards Design (Wiggins & McTighe, 2005) and the 5 Es (Trowbridge & Bybee, 1990) instructional design models. They are the models eMINTS and e-Learning staff want teachers in their programs to use.

The team takes steps to educate their content development teams about online education and teach them what's possible, how to support collaboration, how to write good questions, and more, but they do not actually build the course online. If the content development teams think, "We really need this video . . . or interaction . . . or a discussion board," the team members themselves don't have the technical capacity to add those elements to the course. Those suggestions don't necessarily spark action without consideration either. They are taken care of by project staff with expertise in the technologies; however, just adding "techie" pieces to a course for the sake of having them is not encouraged.

Lessons Learned:

Individuals who apply to become course facilitators for the e-Learning for Educators program take a 10-week course on online facilitation. Facilitators also have requirements they have to meet as they teach to maintain active status, and their contracts have to be renewed each year. Some may include taking professional development courses offered by e-Learning, posting support materials that are shared with other facilitators, contributing to the e-Learning blog, or writing a short article.

eMINTS provides technical staff who handle all technical and administrative tasks, including setting up courses, loading content, preparing gradebooks, enrolling students, and following up with students with participation issues. They also report grades and are the interface with the universities that offer credit. This allows facilitators to focus on teaching and learning.

eMINTS provides districts with the capacity to deliver high-quality professional development, either using content provided by eMINTS or developed by the district itself. According to Terry, "This is about collaboration, not competition. It's okay if we empower a district to not need our services any more. There's another district coming on down the road." Districts are taught how to write their own courses and then encouraged to share with others. As Terry says, "It changes the relationship. We don't have the capacity to write all of the content we need to write." The districts are considered valuable collaborators.

Both eMINTS and e-Learning opted to use Moodle as their learning management system (LMS) because it's a tool that many schools have access to. They also incorporate freely available Web 2.0 tools and use Google Docs often. Terry says that you "want to model things that teachers can use in their classrooms. You've got to look at it from the perspective of your users. YouTube is blocked in most of our districts. Some tools have advertisements and won't be allowed by most of our districts. You have to go beyond 'how cool is it?'"

Evaluation:

In addition to project evaluations for the e-Learning for Educators grant program, eMINTS has their own evaluation survey that has undergone approval through the University of Missouri Institutional Review Board. Program staff try to be careful about not overdoing it, not "surveying people to death." The current model is pre/post with a follow-up 6 months later. Common questions include, "Did you apply it in your classroom? Did you find it useful? Would you take another course?"

See the book's companion website for more information about the profiled programs. **www.corwin.com/rossonlinepd**

Box 4.3 Learning From Experience: LEARN NC

Organization: University of North Carolina at Chapel Hill School of Education

Contact: Ross White, Associate Director

URL: www.learnnc.org

Date First Implemented: 1997; first online courses launched in 2000

Audience: K–12 educators in North Carolina

Need: *What Was the Initial Trigger?*

Based on the success of initial work with six pilot districts, LEARN NC collaborated with the NC Department of Public Instruction, institutions of higher education, and other entities to develop online professional development that is then made freely available to school districts in the state.

Intended Outcomes:

LEARN NC originally intended to provide access to vetted teaching resources as well as support for online learning to all K–12 teachers in the state. Rather than being an online learning provider, LEARN NC set out to license or purchase an

(Continued)

(Continued)

LMS that every district in the state could use. LEARN NC initiates and oversees the development of online content by partner organizations.

Incentives:

Continuing education units and certificates for completion

Instructional Design Considerations:

The backwards design process is central to the instructional design philosophy at LEARN NC. White acknowledges that any time you work with a content expert with deep knowledge and passion for their content, you can struggle with instructional design in terms of determining reasonable objectives for the learners and chunking that content appropriately. LEARN NC develops objectives first, and then develops assessments to guide content development. Backwards design also gives instructional designers the opportunity at every step to ask for research or evidence to support proposed content, and many content experts are surprised to have to consider those questions. LEARN NC has codified a process for content development that includes a team of people including an SME, an instructional designer, and a sponsor.

Lessons Learned:

There are more than 80 school districts in North Carolina classified as rural, and much of the early use of LEARN NC came from those districts. White has noted some change in the past year where larger districts that develop content in the online program are now more likely to offer it for statewide use.

LEARN NC first provided discussion forums to teachers in order to promote professional dialog, but they were turned off in 2001. LEARN NC discovered that the open format of the discussion forums wasn't focused enough, so educators didn't find enough purpose for participating. Based on that experience, LEARN NC is now much more purposeful about the use of technologies to support learning communities. Their use of discussion forums is now much more focused, usually limited to a cohort of individuals and moderated by a content expert. Most are also limited in duration, which may not be a traditional learning community approach, but it has been a much more successful model especially in terms of value added to their participants.

LEARN NC's model of sharing content with local districts has been a hallmark of success of the program. They have to operate courses on a cost-recovery basis. It took time to convince funders that giving the content away was an effective model of using state tax dollars, whereas trying to create a revenue-driven model would have limited the program's reach, resulting in a less effective use of that money. According to White, "Revenue-generating models aren't bad, they're certainly necessary, but we just knew that we could move the needle further if we could offer systems a free option." White is also proud of the fact that the model allows them to provide that content to local school systems that can then customize its use to meet their particular needs. He would like to see other states use their content for noncommercial purposes as well as share their content. He recommends noncommercial providers look at Creative Commons licensing as a way to share content and maintain intellectual property rights.

LEARN NC tries to develop content for a 5-year cycle, but White believes 3 years is a more realistic timeframe. Hidden costs for the program include updates or revisions to the content. Incorporating new and emerging technologies are also a cost consideration over the life of a course.

Evaluation:

All participants must complete an end-of-course survey in order to receive their certificates. A 6-month follow-up asks similar questions to the end-of-course survey as well as whether the participant has implemented skills or knowledge from the course into practice. Based on their involvement with the e-Learning for Educators program, LEARN NC has newly implemented a precourse survey that asks the same questions about content and pedagogy as the end-of-course survey. It is not a survey focused on skills and abilities but dispositions, allowing the survey to be used across courses regardless of the content. While desired, White notes that "few funders are willing to invest in the time and effort it takes to create a rigorous objective-based test" to measure changes in participant knowledge.

See the book's companion website for more information about the profiled programs. **www.corwin.com/rossonlinepd**

Know Your Audience

As mentioned previously, instructional designers are charged with being advocates for the learners—your target audience. You *want* them to be successful, which means they need to develop the skills and knowledge you have deemed valuable enough to focus on. To do that, try to understand who they are and why they'll enroll. As mentioned in Chapter 3, this task is often referred to as an *audience analysis*, and it's just as important whether you're buying content or developing it on your own. It's crucial to know your audience.

You can gather data about your audience in different ways. Optimally, you'd like to interview or meet with potential members of your audience, whether through individual or focus group interviews. You can observe your audience in action, such as teachers in a classroom setting or building leaders at a strategy meeting, possibly recording these visits for further analysis. Some designers will create profiles or scenarios that represent members of their audience—trying to come up with the most critical attributes. You can give them names and histories and post them. I like to find representative pictures of the people I'm working with, so I can picture them better in my mind.

Try to determine why audience members are taking your online professional development. Is it a choice? Are they required to? What are their expectations for participation? Do they just need to complete it? Or are they looking for dynamic interaction with other like-minded individuals so they can build a lifelong network of colleagues and mentors? Their goals, values, and motivation can impact how you design your content significantly, as you can include elements to increase motivation, but you've got to know what will be motivational to your specific learners.

Determine the knowledge and skills the audience members bring to the setting. You'll want to design or find instruction that is cognizant of their prior knowledge and experience but then builds on it. You don't want to cover information they already know. You also don't want it to be so far ahead of what they've done in the past that they get lost or disengage. At the very least, you can determine the education levels of your audience members. Keep in mind that educators have successfully completed college. Some have multiple degrees. And they've gone through some sort of mentoring or training program to get there. Be respectful of the knowledge and skills your audience brings and match your content to their education background, reading level, and vocabulary.

Determine other factors about your group that may influence their participation. Will your audience members be very similar, or will they come from a range of backgrounds? The latter, obviously, can be more of a challenge, but if you can find out ahead of time that they'll be a heterogeneous group, your content should provide options. Steve Baxendale from the World Health Organization notes that because he works in Micronesia, the scenarios he uses are set in Micronesia. He even takes steps to ensure the media he incorporates includes people who look like they are from the area. He notes that if you're working with teachers who may be resource-poor or who work with older equipment and facilities and your videos are all shot in a pristine lab with all the necessary supplies, they'll turn off completely. In that case, he says, "shoot in resource-poor labs" and your audience is more likely to believe you.

I like to consider three participant levels: those who need extra support and possibly remediation; those who will do fine with the general content; and those who require enrichment and so need additional sources of information, possibly provided by linking to outside material. The learners may not realize that's how the information is presented. All of it's there, but I know some will not follow the links to enrichment material, just like some people will not read box features, text blocks, or supplementary information. I put it all in, though, making the essential information prominent, and leave it up to the learners to decide if they want to view it.

Design Good instruction

Online professional development *is* instruction, and we know a lot about designing good instruction. We have learning theories, design models, and research on "what works" in a variety of instructional settings. We know "how people learn," and every content area has defined or described critical knowledge and skills, sometimes expressed through standards. It doesn't matter whether you're buying or developing the content—use what you know about good instruction, and be sure it is evident in your online content. It's not special or different just because it's online or whether you're in a classroom, a chat room, or on an island in Second Life.

An *instructional analysis* helps to define the scope and sequence of instruction. It's an examination of all of the essential skills and knowledge in your content laid out in some sort of hierarchy. The hierarchy can progress all the way down to the prerequisite skills your audience members require. You probably wouldn't go to this level of detail if you're going to purchase instruction, but you do have to determine up front what skills and knowledge you want your purchased content to cover. You can create an instructional analysis in a narrative, outline, or flowchart, but I prefer to use a concept map. The framework in this book was derived from a concept map. I used software for that one, but you can just use sticky notes on a posterboard or wall. Use what feels comfortable for you.

Begin by getting the SME to articulate the ultimate outcomes for the learning—describing what the audience members should know and be able to do as a result of the professional development. If your personal learning theory has a behavioral bent, consider the conditions under which the learners might have to use their new knowledge and skills and the criteria for what makes a successful learner. It can take a little time and effort to come up with the best wording, but what you're doing is developing a guiding statement that informs all of your subsequent content needs.

From that end goal, the next step is to determine what the learner needs to know or should be able to do to reach that goal, working backwards from the big picture by repeatedly asking, "What do they need to know to do that?" You end up with a more finite list or progression of skills and knowledge that, when combined, meet your goal. Identify all crucial skills and knowledge. You get to the point where you think, "Well, they should already know how to do that," and you can stop. You might have to rearrange things a little, and sometimes you come across some overlap in the content. Some items may be collapsed during the actual professional development, especially in order to save time. The instructional analysis is a great tool to share with your SME or other SMEs to be sure you've gotten all of the essential information and not included unnecessary information.

In the following Figure 4.2, a diagram and corresponding outline show a simplified version of the very top levels of an instructional analysis for professional development on the use of assessments. The analysis continues downward, in some cases through many more levels, into content for school leaders (who deal most with accountability measures and informing stakeholders) and content for teachers (who focus on teaching and learning). Note that III.C.1. is a prerequisite skill. This training was not about writing lesson plans, but using assessment data, generating better assessments, and incorporating them into lesson plans.

Figure 4.2   Instructional analysis example

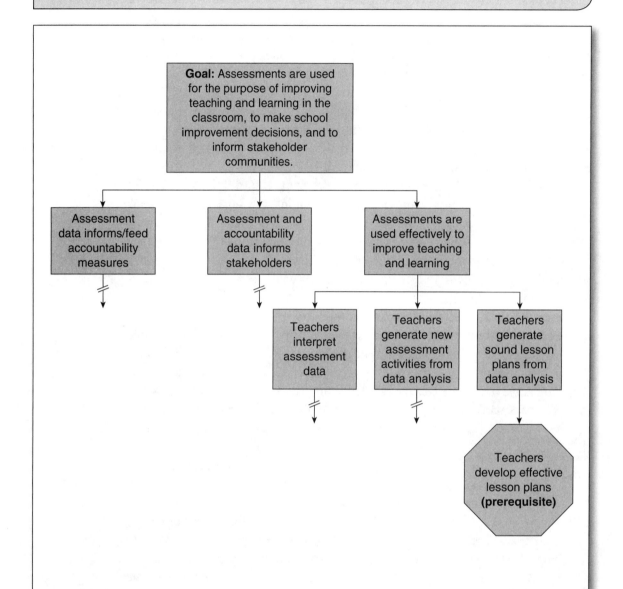

Goal: Assessments are used for the purpose of improving teaching and learning in the classroom, to make school improvement decisions, and to inform stakeholder communities.

    I. Assessment data informs/feeds accountability measures.

    II. Assessment and accountability data informs stakeholders.

    III. Assessments are used effectively to improve teaching and learning.

        A. Teachers interpret assessment data.

        B. Teachers generate new assessment activities from data analysis.

        C. Teachers generate sound lesson plans from data analysis.

            1. Teachers develop effective lesson plans (prerequisite).

The instructional analysis is a powerful document that covers many other critical elements of good instruction. You can use it to determine objectives. Most people like to know why they're taking a training course and what's expected of them, and objectives are a good way to tell them. State your objectives in language that is friendly to the learner. Objectives make a good framework for a review, too, so often you'll see them again at the end of instruction I design. An instructional analysis also helps you know what *not* to include. Generally, you're going to have to work within a restricted time format, like an hour-long webinar or a 4-week class, so you have to draw the line somewhere. This can be a good reference to SMEs who, like me, tend to want to try to include everything they know about a topic. If the learner doesn't need the material to complete the module, don't include it, but save it. That can be your *next* course!

The instructional analysis also lays out potential sequences for the instruction, which don't have to be linear. You can allow for branching or some individualized learning paths, but your content will now be grouped or chunked together. It's important to keep critical information together so that the learners build skills and knowledge as they progress rather than leaving it to chance and missing critical foundational information necessary for meeting the higher level outcomes. Your instructional analysis can also help you determine what some appropriate assessments might be, which is the next topic.

Design Your Assessments First

As I've mentioned before, there are popular instructional design models that focus on the end result and then work backwards. If you've completed an instructional analysis, you've already identified the expected outcomes—what the learner should know and be able to do—and you know the context in which those outcomes are usually exhibited. Now you just need to figure out the best way for the learner to demonstrate her or his new knowledge and skills, and then work backward to make sure you include all the information and practice so the learner can complete the assessments successfully. There should be no secrets. Nothing on the assessments should be a surprise. You *want* them to succeed. Good design helps learners succeed.

Assessments also make good learning opportunities, so allow your participants to practice them during the instruction in the format they'll appear in later. Activities can also serve as assessments embedded in the course if the participants create a product that is reviewed. No matter what format is used to collect assessment data, you have to determine the best way to do this online. Your media developer can be helpful here, but remember that the learning comes first. Don't let the media obscure the assessment. If you can, find out how other people incorporate online assessments by enrolling in their online courses or participating in social networks or online learning organizations. Many offer free resources and examples.

Determine how the assessment data will be collected and scored or graded and how you will provide this feedback to the learners. Forced-choice assessment formats can provide immediate feedback, and not just outcome feedback—which is whether a response is correct or incorrect. Feedback can include a link back into the content for those responses that were incorrect, so the learner can review. If you're purchasing content, be sure the assessment methods match the objectives (including *your* objectives), are covered adequately in the content with sufficient practice, and are a suitable method for demonstrating skill and knowledge for the content you've selected *and* the technology. There's more specific information about assessing learning in Chapter 7.

Increase Motivation and Engagement

I mentioned that most people like to know why they are learning something. That's true of most people, but the need to know why may be especially true for adults. This is one of the main assumptions of *andragogy*, which refers to designing learning for adults, and is a term usually attributed to the work of Malcolm Knowles (1990). Generally, adults want some say in what they are learning and want something they can use right away. They're more interested in developing skills relevant to helping them solve immediate problems rather than just learning factual content. Theory and research are important, but place them within the context of application. How will learners use this material when they get back to their school or classroom? What the principles of andragogy do in terms of designing online professional development is improve the possibility that the content will include engaging experiences that increase motivation.

Andragogy also suggests that adults come to learning opportunities with a variety of experiences, some that support the learning and others that do not. If there are common misunderstandings in a content area, your content can address them—but provide reasonable and plausible reasons as to why they might be incorrect. Some of your audience members may be wedded to a particular teaching strategy or resource that has shown little or no impact on learning. You can't just tell them they're wrong. Help them understand that while their chosen practices are popular, we now have information that demonstrates that new ways covered in the training can be more effective. Using examples closely related to the everyday experiences of the learner, including stories from other teachers or schools like theirs, may have more sway than stating "research says. . . ." In fact, stating "research says" turns some people off.

Andragogy is an overarching idea that helps keep the learner in mind. Another useful concept for motivating learners is Keller's (1987) ARCS Model of Motivational Design. The ARCS acronym stands for Attention, Relevance, Confidence, and Satisfaction. For examples of strategies for increasing online learner motivation, refer to Box 4.4: "Supporting the ARCS Model."

Good instructional design guides the learner through new information and experiences much in the way that a good coach motivates a winning team. The *A* in the ARCS model suggests that, from the beginning, the content has to gain the Attention of the learner, but then continually direct her or his attention to critical information throughout the experience. If your content explicitly demonstrates how it will solve someone's problem, you've demonstrated its Relevance. Like attention, relevance needs to be made apparent throughout the instruction. Incorporating role models or experts may also impress the relevance of the content upon your audience, but be sure that you choose people that your audience can relate to and that their actions and behaviors exemplify outcomes that learners can feasibly attain.

Your learners should be Confident that they can do what you're asking them to do, and your content should have the supports necessary to build that confidence. Choosing appropriate language is important. I tend to prefer conversational language; however, different settings may call for different language; your audience analysis can really be beneficial here. Ultimately, if your learners believe your content is relevant and they leave your online professional development with skills and knowledge they can use right away, you've gone a long way towards having Satisfied learners. At the end, your learners should be fully prepared to complete an assessment that focuses on promoting growth in a way that honors the learner and the content.

The principles in andragogy and Keller's ARCS Model of Motivational Design suggest some key factors to keep in mind for content designed for adults, who are, after all, the audience for your online professional development. You can dig deeper into both concepts, and I don't want to imply this brief overview is a thorough treatment of either concept. I've given you some examples to consider, and you're likely to come up with more. My best advice is remember who your audience is and treat them with respect for their background, knowledge, and expertise. Just like you, they are educated professionals who want to know why something is important and how they'll use it. You can use these principles and the strategies I've described whether you're designing your own online professional development or reviewing content for purchase. I know you can!

Box 4.4 Supporting the ARCS Model

Attention

- Use graphics or video
- Incorporate concrete, realistic examples the audience can relate to
- Organize the learning using a problem statement or problem-based context
- Use humor, but sparingly

Relevance

- Demonstrate correlation to standards or criteria
- Include opportunities for self- and group reflection
- Design activities and assessments that are practical and result in products of consequence
- Incorporate role models or experts through testimonials, scenarios, or case studies

(Continued)

(Continued)

Confidence

- Provide adequate support for differentiated learning
- Respect the audience and what they bring to the experience
- Use appropriate language for the situation
- Include stories or experiences from people "just like them"
- Start with an activity all of your audience will be successful with and gradually increase difficulty

Satisfaction

- Include authentic situations through case studies, role-playing, or simulations
- Include positive reinforcement and feedback throughout the learning
- Don't include any surprises on the assessments

Box 4.5 Take Action:
Instructional Design Considerations

No technology can make up for bad design. Make sure you have appropriate resources—people, materials, and policies—to ensure high-quality design. Consider the following questions and concerns before you begin any content development.

- What instructional design process will you use to develop your content?
- Do you have or need the following personnel:
  o Instructional designer
  o Subject-matter expert(s)
  o Media developers (graphics, video, web programming, other)
  o Project manager or sponsor
- Determine methods to describe your audience. What are their
  o Background skills and knowledge related to the content
  o Technology skills
  o Access to technology
  o Motivation for participation, including goals and expectations
  o Education background
  o Heterogeneity or homogeneity
- How will you determine appropriate skills and knowledge to be covered in your online professional development? What must be included? Is nice to include? Should not be included?
- What assessments will help your participants demonstrate they have mastered your content? How will they be presented online?
- Consider guidelines or principles that support adult learners and encourage motivation and engagement. You may want to use national standards or develop your own instructional design guidelines.

GETTING YOUR HANDS DIRTY

Following are some common processes you might consider using if you plan to develop content. Some, like creating a storyboard and script, are probably best suited to developing longer courses. There are also some suggestions for how common instructional activities can be designed or structured for online presentation, a common request I receive.

Create a Storyboard

In a big project, a storyboard is a common step for pulling together the necessary information and media for your content. You might associate storyboarding with creating movies, but it has also found a home in instructional design. Different people complete the storyboard to a different degree. Some designers put *everything* on their storyboards, including all the text for display or narration, graphics or mockups of graphics, and sample media. Mine aren't usually that detailed, since I prefer to use word-processing software for large amounts of text, but it just depends on what you're comfortable with. In a shorter event, like a 1-hour webinar, storyboarding can be combined with the actual content development, because presentation software works for both. In that case, the storyboard becomes the presentation.

A storyboard will help finalize the scope and sequence of the content, activities, and assessments. It's also an opportunity to reflect on considerations like how to apply elements from the ARCS Model of Motivational Design or other design elements you prefer. Another critical use of the storyboard is to describe the requirements for necessary graphic and media elements, although their final form could change. At the very least you want to rough out some ideas for your media elements, but you can do it by a text description, for example: "need to demonstrate *X* practice in a real classroom here, would prefer a video." Depending on available resources, that classroom video could become a narrated slideshow or even a scenario in text with graphics. Yes, now it's time to start thinking about the technology, but know that the learning should prevail over technology features.

Presentation software can be used to create a storyboard, because it supports text, graphics, and other media, like videos. Slides are easy to rearrange, as you can usually view the presentation slides in a "slide sorter" or "lightbox" mode and quickly change their order. I use a different color for the background or as a border for slides in different sections so I can spot them easily in the slide sorter mode when the slides are reduced in size. I also try to put the key concept, title, or most important information in a very large font prominently displayed on the slide, again so I can find it when it's reduced, but I may use a very small font to add detailed information. If you don't want to use presentation software, storyboards can be created using concept mapping software, word-processing software (although this isn't as easy to rearrange), or even sticky notes or index cards. You have to admit, cards and notes are pretty portable and easy to rearrange, but they're also easy to get out of order, damage, or lose. Use what you're comfortable with.

Figure 4.3 is a simple example of a storyboard screen created from a template made in PowerPoint (and used as the basis for the script example in Figure 4.4). It contains content from an SME with notes and suggestions for her review. Note that a final decision about the media is not determined at this point, as it can change based on budget, availability, or other factors. Purple was the color selected for this module, and purple shading is behind the module name in all the slides in Section 1 for this course. You can put other necessary elements on your template instead of what is shown, perhaps including information related to navigation, narration, or actually adding graphics. While notes appear on-screen in the example, they could instead appear in the notes section in PowerPoint.

Figure 4.3 Storyboard example based on a template created in PowerPoint

Title: Looking at Reading	**File:** 007	**Module: 1:** Introduction
Objective: Describe a comprehensive literacy program		
Main idea: • Reading is the process in which information from text and the knowledge possessed by the reader act together to produce meaning. Good readers skillfully integrate information in the text with what they know (Anderson et al., 1985). • Despite perceptions to the contrary, reading is not easy for most children. Reading experts have come to realize from over thirty years of research that learning to read is a very complex linguistic achievement, rather than a natural and easy accomplishment. In a paper prepared for the American Federation of Teachers titled *Teaching Reading is Rocket Science,*(2000), leading reading expert and researcher, Louisa Moats notes that "teaching reading is a job for an expert . . . moreover, teaching reading requires considerable knowledge and skill acquired over several years of focused study and supervised practice." • Need to convince the participants they can do this, that research is valuable. Need to move from "research says" to being practical. Need to convince them this is important.		**Media:** Example: Lessons from a master teacher (illustrating why I can be a master teacher). Possibly a video, testimony, or story from a real teacher. **Notes:** Do a search for articles on Louisa Moats and determine why you think she is considered a recognized authority on teaching reading.

Edvantia (2004). Development of the content for the online assessment course, "Assessment and Intervention in a Comprehensive Literacy Classroom" was initiated by Edvantia, Inc. through a cooperative agreement with the U.S. Department of Education (No. S283A950018-05) and developed by Edvantia into an online course under contract with the Tennessee Department of Education.

Write a Script

For large projects, a script is an essential document. It is a detailed account of *all* information necessary to develop the final learning material, and it can be a fleshed out version of a storyboard. For a typical course, my script will contain items like the page name, the name of the file or associated files, all of the required text that will be displayed on-screen or used in narration or animations, and related information, as well as a description of all media elements including their file type and name. I also leave room for notes, because I'm often working with others, and this is our place to communicate about the actual content, ask questions, and seek clarity. It's important to keep all that information in one place. If you're creating learning objects (see Chapter 5), you may include the metadata information that you require.

Using word-processing software makes it easy for all of your learning material to go through the editing and quality assurance processes you may have. All specific style questions, for example, using "Web site" versus "website" or determining how references or external resources will be cited, should be taken care of in the script before it goes to the developers. In final form, it becomes the master document from which all information shows up online. The ultimate goal of the script is to ensure that none of the content has to return to the SME or instructional designer once it's given to the developers. Returning to ask for additional information or clarification wastes time and money and introduces the opportunity for error, especially in the presentation of text-based information. The storyboard and the script can also help prevent the all-too-typical curse of "project creep," which refers to trying to keep adding content or elements to the point that timelines and budgets are blown out of proportion.

Figure 4.4 is an example of a page from an actual script. It's the page that resulted from the storyboard example shown in Figure 4.3. Again, script templates are very helpful, especially if you have a team of people working on them. You may include additional or different items on your script, especially if you're creating true learning objects. This is just an example of a format that works for me.

The script example illustrates several of the design components mentioned so far and some coming in the next section. For example, the screen focuses on only one concept, and the most important information is placed prominently on the screen. No one would have to scroll to see the text above the video. Supplemental information, including an external link, is placed in a separate text block to demonstrate that it's not critical information that is assessed. It's actually a feature for this training, and the features have consistent icons, noted in the media elements table, to draw the learner's attention and let him or her know what it is. Consistent elements can increase learner satisfaction. The language is written for an adult, but it's not as complex as a research journal might be, even though information from research is presented in the content. The choice of second person makes the language more conversational and user-friendly, and there are obvious attempts to instill confidence in the learner (i.e., "You can be such an expert"). Since this online professional development was designed for teachers, the video of the master teacher talking about her practice not only grabs the learner's attention, but also addresses the relevance of a topic that may not be of high interest to all of the target audience—research. Using a peer in the video also hopefully increases motivation and engagement

Figure 4.4 Script example based on the storyboard slide in Figure 4.3. Note the greater detail and the final decision on media.

File name:	sec1007.htm
Screen title:	Focusing on Reading

Display on Screen:

Reading is the process by which information from text and the knowledge possessed by the reader act together to produce meaning. Good readers skillfully integrate information in the text with what they know (Anderson, et al., 1985).

Despite perceptions to the contrary, reading is not easy for most children. Reading experts have come to realize, from more than 30 years of research, that learning to read is a very complex linguistic achievement. It's not a natural and easy accomplishment. In a paper prepared for the American Federation of Teachers titled *Teaching Reading IS Rocket Science* (2000), leading reading expert and researcher Louisa Moats notes that "teaching reading is a job for an expert . . . moreover, teaching reading requires considerable knowledge and skill acquired over several years of focused study and supervised practice."

You can be such an expert. The years of research were conducted with teachers of reading just like you in classrooms just like yours. This training will help you master some of the skills necessary for assessing your own students and designing effective reading instruction to help all your students become successful readers.

One teacher's voice	Insert video here
"Your learning has not stopped here, your learning has just begun." This is the insight offered by this master teacher, who continues to monitor new research and how those findings impact her teaching and help more of her students succeed.	

Meet the Expert

Louisa Moats is a nationally recognized authority on reading and the author of numerous articles and books on reading, writing, and learning disabilities. Her publication, *Teaching Reading IS Rocket Science,* prepared for the American Federation of Teachers, helps teachers recognize the need to apply reading research in classroom reading instruction.

Also by Louisa Moats:

Whole Language Lives On http://www.edexcellence.net/detail/news.cfm?news_id=45

Media elements:

File name: expert.gif **Type:** GIF	**Description:** Meet the Expert icon
File name: sec1002.mov **Type:** MOV	**Description or script:** Lessons from a master teacher illustrating why I can be a master teacher. Reflections over time.

Notes:

The following interview questions will be used for this and subsequent videos throughout the training.

- Compare your feelings as a new reading teacher with the way you approach your position today.
- How do you select appropriate reading materials?
- How do you prepare for a reading lesson? How do you select assessments?

© Edvantia (2004). Development of the content for the online assessment course, "Assessment and Intervention in a Comprehensive Literacy Classroom" was initiated by Edvantia, Inc. through a cooperative agreement with the U.S. Department of Education (No. S283A950018-05) and developed by Edvantia into an online course under contract with the Tennessee Department of Education.

as the video was shot of the teacher in her classroom (someone "just like you") with all of her teaching materials around her. The video also helps to address why the learners are taking this course, in part, and how material from the course might be applicable to their own setting.

Instructional Activities and Media

How do you create an effective online activity? It depends on the learning objectives, the purpose of the activity, and the available technologies. There are so many different but valid answers depending on your resources. For example, if you want to use the popular think-pair-share activity in an online course, you could conduct it by having your learners think about information presented in a document, graphic, or video; then pair up through a wiki, discussion board, phone call, or shared document online; and share their results through another document, graphic, video . . . or a concept map, blog, e-mail message . . . there are so many possibilities. The best way to determine how to do that is to really figure out what you want the learner to know or be able to do after completing the activity and match it to how technology can support different kinds of learning in Chapter 5.

I've provided a few more examples, however, in Box 4.6: "Instructional Strategies in an Online Setting ala Marzano." This is based on a handout I use during instructional design workshops to get people thinking about the many ways technology can support common instructional activities. The examples relate to the nine instructional strategies identified by Bob Marzano and his colleagues at McREL (Marzano, Pickering, & Pollock, 2001) in their popular *Classroom Instruction That Works* series. It is one of the most popular resources for identifying instructional strategies, and many educators are familiar with it. If you're familiar with these nine principles, the examples should be helpful. Remember, it's not the technology but *how you use it* that is important.

Box 4.6 Instructional Strategies in an Online Setting a la Marzano

1. Identifying similarities and differences
   a. Use analogies through case studies and scenarios presented in text with or without graphics, including downloadable documents for offline review, or include animated presentations or movies
   b. Use metaphors through stories presented by video or video-like animations
   c. Incorporate graphic organizers (e.g., Venn diagrams)
   d. Present data in easy-to-read graphs and tables, with salient points highlighted

(Continued)

(Continued)

2. Summarizing and note taking

   a. Include online journaling through blogs and wikis

   b. Suggest writing prompts for digital stories and multimedia scripts

   c. Share with colleagues via e-mail or an online forum

3. Reinforcing effort and providing recognition

   a. Clearly define and relate incentives for completion

   b. Define successful completion of activities, using rubrics, checklists, or exemplars

4. Homework and practice

   a. Embed new skills and knowledge in real activities in schools and classrooms

   b. Indicate completion levels visually in course navigation

   c. Use exemplars in various media formats

   d. Link to relevant information for practice or enrichment in various media formats

5. Nonlinguistic presentation

   a. Use graphics to reinforce text content, especially graphs, tables, and diagrams

   b. Use video, slide shows, gaming, animations, and simulations to demonstrate processes or action

   c. Interact in a virtual environment or social networking application

   d. Use graphic organizers

6. Cooperative learning

   a. Set norms for group participation

   b. Provide individual and group variations for activities

   c. Provide guidelines for leaders or facilitators

   d. Grow from an active to a dynamic learning community

7. Setting objectives and providing feedback

   a. State objectives in user-friendly language

   b. Allow the learner or community to set their own goals

   c. Use KWL charts (organizers that help students identify what they **K**now, what they **W**ant to learn, and what they **L**earned about a topic)

   d. Develop self- and group-reflective activities

   e. Compare one's own experiences to others through case studies, exemplars, and real-world stories

   f. Include formal assessments, such as quizzes, surveys, open-ended responses, projects, portfolios, and other means

8. Generating and testing hypotheses

   a. Make predications about outcomes to scenarios or simulations

   b. Incorporate relevant, real-world problems

   c. Have learners develop materials of consequence they can use immediately in their practice

9. Cues, questions, and advance organizers

   a. Provide opportunities for self-reflection to activate prior knowledge

   b. Include advance organizers that show the framework of the content or activities, length of setting, and options for learner control and navigation

   c. Use KWL charts

   d. Ensure navigation is obvious and redundant

   e. Guide the learning through visual clues including highlighting, arrows or pointers, text formatting, and other means

   f. Provide guidelines, timelines, job aids, and activity templates

One common approach to developing online professional development is repurposing training from a different format. Some people decry this method as not taking advantage of the power of the technology, but it depends on your outcomes. And if you have good content, you can use it as the basis for a new and powerful experience that does employ some of the power of the technology. It may take some work, though, to take advantage of the online environment. Al Byers from the National Science Teachers Association suggests modeling what you want your learners to be able to do. He's found that the common model of once-a-week, instructor-driven interactions through a discussion forum isn't a good fit for science education that often involves manipulatives or learning objects and hands-on application. Design activities that are appropriate to the skills and knowledge required by the content.

One of the biggest mistakes I've seen occur time and again by someone who wants to develop online professional development for the first time is not budgeting enough time to create high-quality content. Without considering all the steps in the process, the result is often lackluster content, usually basic factual information that serves as poor instruction and takes little advantage of the technologies being used. It may be posted online just to meet a deadline—one that may be many days later and many dollars more than budgeted. For a sample timeline, review Box 4.7: "Take Action: Content Development Timeline." You may have your own internal process you need to follow that is similar or even adds a step or two; however, review these suggested steps to see if you've included everything. This is probably the fewest number of steps you'll have to follow when developing your content. Luckily, some of them, like the audience and instructional analyses, might be completed only once to support several different courses or projects.

Don't forget all of the supporting materials that are routinely associated with learning, whether online or not. They are an important piece of your content delivery. Students have expectations for information to support their learning, such as glossaries, search engines, manuals or tutorials for using the system, and a way to get help. Many learning management systems (LMS) allow you to include background information about a course, the developers, or the facilitators. Another commonly requested feature is a sample course. I developed an introduction to online learning and tutorial for using the LMS that then served as a sample course. It actually made that sample course have greater relevance to the experience. If you're launching from scratch, you have to consider all of these pieces, not just the content you're going to deliver, and have it all developed, reviewed, and posted when you get ready to launch. You don't want any "Under Construction" signs, and you really don't want to go back and have to edit your interface. Revisions at that time are likely to be expensive. Luckily, many providers offer templates or forms to complete most information supported in their LMS.

Box 4.7 Take Action:
Content Development Timeline

Count back from your expected launch date. Depending on the scope of your content, these steps can take from 1 week to many weeks each. For each step, also consider who is responsible. Generally, make sure each step is completed before moving on to the next, because any changes will just waste time and set you back. Once your script is in final form, however, text and media development can likely occur simultaneously.

Design Step	Person(s) Responsible	Timeframe
Conduct audience analysis		
Conduct instructional analysis		
Create storyboard or outline from instructional analysis		
Develop script and identify all supporting materials (handouts, activities, media, etc.)		
Review script for content (revise)		

Design Step	Person(s) Responsible	Timeframe
Review script for grammar and style (revise)		
Create or obtain media elements		
Review media elements (revise)		
Format or integrate all elements for web delivery		
Evaluate system (revise)		
Launch		

USING MEDIA TO HELP (OR HINDER) LEARNING

How do you choose the right media? Again, most clients come to me thinking "interactive and engaging" and immediately suggest video. Video *is* interactive and engaging, but it's not the only medium that is. Instructional designers study research on how best to design and display text, graphics, and other forms of media. Following are a few basic tips to help make the most of your media whether you're designing new material or reviewing material for purchase. There's one critical point in terms of deciding which media to use: Just because you *can* doesn't mean you *should*. All decisions for media selection depend on *how it supports learning*.

Text

Text is really useful! Whether presented onscreen or in a downloadable document for offline reading, there's a permanence to text that can help make information clear, as opposed to images, music, or videos that are often open to interpretation. It's easily distributed and can reduce the cognitive load for your learners, unlike images and video. It is useful in asynchronous and synchronous settings, and your audience—educated professionals—will be comfortable with the conventions of text. There are some limitations to text, as it's not as expressive as speech and can be misunderstood. Humor can also be difficult to get across in text.

Most people read onscreen differently than they do a printed document. We usually read slower onscreen, because monitors have lower resolutions than the printed page, and many people skim. Onscreen, people look for critical features, like titles and hyperlinks, and often skip a bulk of the information. They're looking for the information they need, and they have full control to skip what is of little interest. Most people will read more information online in an educational setting if it's relevant to them because the credit offered at the end is an incentive to keep going, but there are a few things to keep in mind when you present text onscreen.

First, follow Standard English conventions. English is read left to right, from top to bottom. That sounds rudimentary, but it's too easy to place text in all manner of places on the screen or in a graphic, and some people do so to the detriment of their content. Left-justify your blocks of text following conventional text layouts (imagine a book, magazine, or newspaper) and use sentence-case capitalization (like these sentences—avoid the use of all uppercase *or* lowercase letters). A dark font (e.g., black) on a light background (e.g., white) works best; and pick one font. You can vary that to some degree, but too many colors or fonts is distracting. The text has to be readable, and black text on a white background is perhaps the easiest to read for most people with normal vision. Red and yellow, as text or a background, can be difficult to read for people with limited visual capacity. And for colorblind people, it's going to look black and white (or shades of gray) anyway. Also, white text on a black background is usually a no-no, especially for many visually impaired people.

Chunk your information for screen display. Focus on one concept per screen (see the script example Figure 4.4), put the important stuff at the top, and segregate or isolate the enrichment or supplemental information. If you have to scroll, it's probably too long. People may be more willing to scroll in a learning situation, but try to avoid it when possible. If there is a lot of text to present, such as case studies, research briefs, and other supplemental reading, it can be put in a form that can be downloaded and printed; otherwise, consider providing print-based copies, like a companion book or course pack of materials. Some people will print out the screens, whether they are designed to be printed or not, so be cognizant of how much text is on each screen and how it is organized.

Graphics and Images

Pictures may be worth a thousand words, but they may not be the words you want your learners to remember. Images can be helpful, because they can convey many things at once, including emotion and mood, which can be difficult to put into words. A picture conveys information literally—it's what you're looking at—but there can be a lot of things to look at, and you may need to guide your learner to the most critical attributes or important information to draw from the picture. Tables and charts can go a long way toward simplifying complex information, especially a large amount of data, and are some of the best types of graphics to use to improve learning.

To support learning, the graphics and images should be highly redundant with the primary content medium, such as text or a narration. They should illustrate or expand upon the primary information. New information should never appear *only* in a graphic, because many people skip over graphics or don't spend as much time with them as they would text. Purely decorative pictures should be used sparingly, because they can detract the learner from critical information. But we do like to look at pretty things, so there's a balance you can strike between decoration and function.

A consistent look and feel to graphics, images, and colors is helpful as it can guide attention appropriately and even bolster confidence as your learners will become comfortable with the features they represent. Give your navigation, icons, and other consistent graphic features the same look and feel. I avoid combining clip art, stick figures, or cartoons with images of real people in the same project. Real people are more engaging than cartoon people visually, especially if they really *are* real people similar to the target audience and they're demonstrating a skill you want your participants to master. However, a good graphic designer or even clip art sets of engaging characters can be used effectively. Just try to avoid combining styles. If you do combine images of real people with graphics, try to tie them together visually through the use of similar font, border, or other media elements.

Audiovisual Information

Be cautious of including audiovisual information, like narration, animations, and simulations, just because you can. Speech is a very powerful form of communication. It can be more expressive than writing or images, as it can convey the feelings and emotions of the speaker more clearly. But speech, when inserted into online content as audio, forces the learner to work harder to interpret what is being said and to make meaning. Try not to use audio alone, unless it's especially significant, like a famous speech or a compelling speaker. Even then, you can combine the audio with one or more images of the speaker or the subject to make it more engaging and provide context.

Narrations are tricky, because not all learners want to listen to information. Heed the adage, "Teach don't tell." At the very least, narrations should not simply be the text onscreen read out loud, unless used as a learning accommodation. Many people can read faster than most narration, so most of your learners can get through text-based information faster and with greater understanding. If you feel compelled to use narration, it should complement the information onscreen, perhaps being used in conjunction with a slideshow or video, but you have to acknowledge that your learner always has the option to turn it off, even if it's just muting the sound.

The most important advice I can offer if you're going to include audio, either as podcasts, screencasts, animations, or even in video, is to use a good microphone. Audio is a deal-breaker. People seem more accepting of poor quality video than audio, especially with the rise of YouTube and other video-sharing sites. And since you're likely to edit your audio and will save it in a format that can be transmitted on the Web, you're going to lose some quality. Get the best quality possible at the beginning. You don't need to break the bank for a good microphone, but go beyond the basic computer microphones and get a good unidirectional microphone and a stand. Digital recorders have become very affordable and are more portable than a laptop.

Record in a quiet room, and be aware that many common items emit sound that can interfere with your recording, like air-conditioning, lights, and even your computer. To improve the quality of your audio, you may want to use a screen to cover your microphone to prevent the popping sounds some people make when they speak, or a desktop sound booth to reduce ambient noise. You can make both easily and inexpensively. There are many free audio editors or enhancers available, such as Audacity by SoundForge, Myna from Aviary, and The Levelator from The Conversations Network, that allow you to improve your audio after it's recorded. These sites also include helpful tutorials and user forums to get you started on improving the quality of your audio.

Video

While video is the media request I get most often, it is perhaps the most difficult, time-consuming, and expensive type of media to develop if you're going for quality. Yet video can be compelling, and it's especially helpful for demonstrating a process or sequence, such as a teaching strategy. The number one rule of video in education is: *Use video to show action!* Don't videotape your narrator. It's a waste of time, money, and bandwidth with little return on your learning investment. If you want to include a video of an interview with someone, include action footage to *show* what the person is talking about. I've been fortunate to work with some excellent videographers, one of whom has provided the information in Box 4.8: "Getting the Most From Your Video." I've picked up tips and tricks from them, and even do some minor editing of my own, but the greatest asset I've found for creating high-quality video is an expert.

You can get better self-recorded video if you keep a few things in mind. Staged video can often be pretty awful, as your viewers will think, "That's not how it is in *my* classroom!" I've met some developers who actually script out video and stage the whole thing on a set, but that doesn't work well for me, and it is a lot of extra effort for a product that is usually not much better, or all that great. In terms of videotaping in schools, I try to be as unobtrusive as possible and respect that the learning in the classroom is the most important priority. If you bring in a couple of people with videocameras, you're going to draw some attention. In order to get the most out of the situation, I try to prepare the teachers I'm visiting before I visit but let their classes play out. Shoot it all; you'll edit it out later. I tell them some examples of what we want to see, developing a shoot list before I visit and explaining what each shot might look like. If you can't describe what it looks like, video may not be a good choice. Don't go in hoping you'll figure it out.

In the classroom it's my job to tell the crew where to focus. I've got my shoot list in hand and am listening to the teacher and the other interactions in the classroom to get as many good examples as possible. For me, the best-case scenario is two cameras—one on a tripod that stays focused on the teacher at all times, and one handheld camera for other interactions and supporting footage. But even with one camera, try to work with the video crew to let them know when to focus on the teacher and when they can get other shots. Videographers are used to changing their shots often to increase visual interest, but that's not as necessary in an educational video. Very often you need to stick with the teacher so your learners can understand the whole process you're trying to address. Most lessons have an introduction (e.g., "This is what we're going to do today, boys and girls"), a demonstration by the teacher, and a wrap-up. During those parts of the lesson, I make certain to keep a camera focused on the teacher.

Cameras make some people nervous, which can lead to mistakes. If they're critical, like when a teacher misspelled the title of the book the class was reading, I stop the action and do it again. That misspelled title could have been on the board through every shot in the video, which would have made the video unusable or extremely embarrassing if used. I've gotten into some friendly disagreement about that practice, because I'm impacting the classroom. You have to use your best judgment. The kids knew the title was wrong and told their teacher. It often takes just few seconds to back up and get everyone back on track. Some mistakes become opportunities for learning, like the time another teacher was having difficulty connecting her laptop to a projector and called on a student for help. It was a great example of the culture of respect she had obviously nurtured in her classroom. You can't fake that or script it out. No teacher deserves to be embarrassed simply because she or he was nervous. Keeping errors in can cause you to lose a lot of credibility with your learners, as most would focus on the incorrect information and dismiss much of the other great stuff going on in the classroom.

There are some factors you do have great control over. Remember, audio is a deal-breaker. Use the best-quality microphone you can afford here, too. I prefer a wireless microphone so the teacher has flexibility to move around. Lighting is also important. Classrooms often have poor lighting for video. A good videographer will know how to compensate for poor lighting in an action setting and is an artist in an interview setting. I only tell people to wear makeup if they usually wear makeup. It's especially helpful for interviews. And encourage people to wear something they have worn before and feel comfortable in. No new haircut; no new dress. I have a list of dress tips that I send out before visiting, but the most important one is to wear solid colors— no stripes, checks, or other strong patterns—in "jewel" tones and to avoid red, black, and white. If that's confusing, I can make it even easier. Wear blue. Blue looks great on camera.

Careful preparation increases the likelihood you'll get better video. Once you've recorded it, it needs to be edited, stored, and delivered, and you'll need lots of time to get to that final product. Editing is the most time-consuming part of the process, because you do it in less than real time. It can be painstaking to find exactly the right spot to edit a clip or to insert information, and so editors often spend time going back and forth over a few seconds of video until they get it just right. This is where much of the expense comes in. I've heard lots of estimates, but I figure it takes at least 1 to 3 hours of editing for every minute of final video. It depends on the quality you're willing to accept.

Box 4.8 Getting the Most From Your Video: Hints From a Professional

I've been fortunate to work with several excellent video professionals who have taught me a lot about developing high-quality video. One of them is Stew Harris, an award-winning producer who for years generated stories for ABC's *PrimeTime* and *20/20*. He now shares his expertise with nonprofits and educational institutions through New Media Mill, his company in Washington, D.C. These tips are from him.

If you're going to spend the time to create video, it's important to find a good videographer. Finding a good one will make the difference between a dull product and one that will rivet viewers.

- **A producer calls the shots.** If it's one of your first video endeavors, strongly consider hiring a producer early in the process and keep them involved through fruition. A producer is the person who will put your vision into an action plan and translate it into "television speak" for the technical people who capture video and sound and the post-production experts who finish the project. A few of the things a producer will want to know are how long the video(s) will be, how many locations will be used, and if there are interviews.
- **Shoot the best quality you can afford.** It's hard to get into classrooms, so take advantage while you can. While you have plans for your current project, you may want to reuse or repurpose your video for different segments or formats. Shoot the best you can afford in case you need to go back to it later.
- **Good video requires a great camera.** Consumer cameras deliver videos that appear flat and lifeless, because they often have poor color saturation and don't permit selective focus. If your videographer can assure you that you will be shooting with "a three-chip camera of 1/2-inch or more," you're more likely to be working with someone who is more aware of what comes out of their camera. Also, don't be fooled if they tell you it's high definition. High definition can look worse than standard definition if the camera doesn't render rich color or selectively blur out backgrounds.
- **Get the best audio quality possible.** Your video crew should bring external microphones. They shouldn't rely on microphones built into the camera, even on a good camera. Wireless microphones are handy in classrooms where teachers move around a good bit, but they can pick up interference from devices that transmit radio frequency, like sirens and even some cell phones. For best performance, I like to use an XLR (three-pin balanced) microphone but the minimum I'd recommend is a 1/8-inch mini stereo input (which is not an RCA-style input). An audio engineer is a great addition, if you can afford one. Since the audio is so important, the audio engineer can let you know if you really need to stop the shooting in case cords come unplugged, batteries die, or for other reasons that sabotage your audio. Without good audio, you're sunk.
- **You can do better with the lighting.** Generally, the video crew won't be able to augment classroom lighting in an action setting, but they can perform a manual "white balance" to calibrate their camera. If your

videographer doesn't know what that means or they tell you their camera does it automatically, keep looking. Interviews often use a technique called "three-point lighting," and an experienced videographer will likely use this phrase or talk about the different kinds of lights they routinely use for "key, fill, and backlighting" for interviews.

- **It's all about the tripod.** Any videographer worth his stuff will bring a tripod, and hopefully a monitor, which will show you what your video will look like right then and there. Your videographer should not rely on handheld shots, unless you're looking for a motion sickness effect. Whether you're using one or two cameras, set the main camera on the tripod, frame the shot where the action will be, take your hands off the camera, and let the action occur in the shot. If you need close-ups or action shots, do it at the end of class. Don't try to capture everything going on, you're trying to get the best representation of the classroom instruction.

- **Interviews make training videos more interesting.** Interviews where people give background, have insights, and share stories can be quite riveting. You not only have the action footage from the classroom, but you have their interview as a narrative track. Combine the two so your viewers have the full picture. Repetition is as important in video as in education. Don't be afraid to repeat that classroom footage in your interview sequences.

I want to reiterate that video, while the request I get most often in terms of media, is also one of the most difficult and expensive to develop well—so that it promotes learning. Use video specifically for showing action. Avoid talking heads, unless you're a fan of David Byrne. Consider whether you can create video-like elements, such as animated presentations or podcasts that are a sequence of still images with narration, that get your point across. Your decision will be based on what you want your learner to know and be able to do, and if video is the best or only way to do that, then use video.

CONCLUSION

Your outcomes will vary at the end of this step depending on whether you plan to develop or purchase content. If you're going to develop your content, be sure you have access to the appropriate personnel, including an instructional designer, SMEs, and media developers. If you have never used an instructional design model, considering finding an instructional designer who has, and determine her or his familiarity and success with that model. Review Box 4.5: "Take Action: Instructional Design Considerations" to be sure you're prepared to take on content development. You need people, materials, and processes in places to be successful. Use Box 4.7: "Take Action: Content Development Timeline" to ensure you have enough time and the right people to get the job done. You have to get the design right. Remember, no technology can make up for bad design.

If you're going to purchase content, consider using the checklist in Box 4.9: "Caveat Emptor: Evaluating Media in Online Content." This may also be a helpful checklist for evaluating your own content. If you're not that far along in the development process, return to this step later.

Box 4.9 Caveat Emptor: Evaluating Media in Online Content

You can use the following checklist to guide your review of the use of media in online professional development, whether you are buying it or reviewing media your team has created.

	Yes	No
Text • Is the amount of text onscreen appropriate? • Are large blocks of text presented in optional printable formats? • Does the text follow standard language conventions? • Is the text easy to read on the background(s)?		
Graphics and images • Do graphics illustrate and expand upon the content? Are they necessary? • Are graphics used to make complex concepts easier to understand? • Is there a good balance between decoration and function? • Is there a consistent look and feel to graphics, images, and colors?		
Audiovisual information • Are audiovisual elements essential? • Is the audio quality acceptable? • Do audio elements, like narrative, complement information on the screen? • Can users toggle sound on and off?		
Video • Is video used appropriately to show action or demonstrate a process? Is it necessary? • Is the video believable? • Is the audio quality of the video acceptable? • Is the overall quality of the video acceptable? • Is the video in a format you can view?		
Learning outcomes • Does the media support the purported learning outcomes of the content? • Does the media support our project outcomes?		

What Technologies 5 Are Right for Me?

After a thorough analysis of your content, you're prepared to determine technologies that will be the right fit for you. The technologies are the fun part, but I didn't want you to be blinded by the technology by presenting it too early. If you've done your background work, you're better prepared to be more objective in your technology selection. This chapter explores the wide range of technologies available to support online professional development. Certainly, you will be familiar with some, and maybe there will be some new ones in the bunch. Unfortunately, simply by putting a description of technology down in print, it's doomed to be obsolete, or at least my description will likely be out of date in short order. Technology changes pretty rapidly, and any description of technology is going to become dated. If you wait for the ultimate technology, however, you may never get it, so consider the best option and plan for growth.

Before we dive in, I want to emphasize the often-repeated mantra that it's not that you use technology but *how* you use it that matters. Focusing on your outcomes will help you determine how you will use technology. You don't want to buy an expensive online system that supports animations and videos and interactive webconferencing if all you need is something that allows teachers to share lessons and have discussions about them online. Instead of just listing technologies and features, I group them by learning activities common to professional development—*how* you might use them. As you review your technology options, keep in mind any technology standards you may need to address when deploying them (see Figure 5.1).

Figure 5.1   By considering how you plan to use technology, you'll better be able to define your technology specifications.

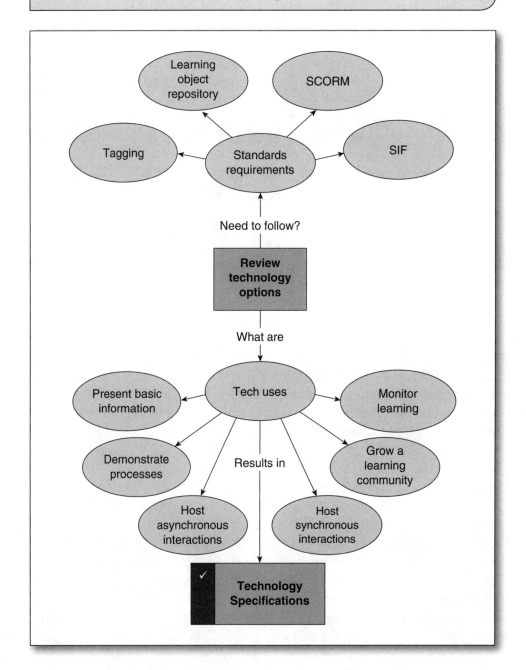

And one final note: Any time I mention an application or developer, I'm not endorsing any one product or brand. There isn't enough room to cover every application here, so instead I'll focus on the learning activities they can support in your online professional development and include at least two of the most popular applications of each type in my description, when necessary. I recommend a quick web search based on these examples to find additional options. The book's companion website will be a place where these and additional applications can be found—I encourage you to go there and recommend others.

A WORD ABOUT LEARNING OBJECTS

If you've taught or designed professional development, you've created, used, and reused all kinds of learning objects. In online learning there is a specific meaning to the use of the term *learning object*. A learning object has all the information and content necessary to complete a learning task. Part of a learning object may be an image, an animation, a movie, text, or a combination of media, combined with the instructional objective and context for that resource and a way for learners to know if they've mastered the objective. You can also add information to describe the object in the form of tags (usually referred to as metadata), so that the one object can be cataloged, found, and used over and over in different settings. Common metadata tags include the title, creator, keywords, and a description.

For example, if I create an animation that demonstrates how to use hand-held personal response systems (what many teachers refer to as "clickers") for a test review, it could be a pretty handy activity for many courses. If I have teachers in a language arts pedagogy course and others in a social studies pedagogy course, I may want to include that animation in both courses. I can copy it and paste it into both courses, but what if I have to make a change to the animation? I'd have to replace it every place I used it, which takes time, and I might miss one. That's sloppy data management. If I created that animation and added the extra information to it to make it a true learning object, I could store it in one central location, an online database. Then, both of those courses, and every other course that uses it, would link to and use the one and only version of my learning object; and any time I made a change to it, every course would use the most current version. Generally, learning objects are stored in an online database called a *learning object repository* (LOR). Some learning management systems (LMS), which are described at the end of this chapter, include or can link to an LOR.

That all sounds really great—only one version but used many times—but it can be time-consuming to create learning objects. If you create true learning objects, you have to decide on a standard to use, and everyone who creates and edits learning objects in your system has to know how to add the data accurately. Based on which standard you use, there are dozens of metadata tags that you can add to a learning object. Some LMS can help you add the metadata to your learning objects as they are initially put into the repository, but adding metadata to existing content that you created previously or that you purchase or borrow from someone else can be cumbersome and time-consuming.

There is also the question of what exactly defines a learning object. Is it a page? A lesson? A unit? A course? And media elements, too, can be learning objects on their own, or they can be combined with other media into a larger learning object. The general answer is that a learning object should have everything you need to address a specific skill or piece of knowledge. It should be able to stand on its own, but it should also be reusable, which is the whole benefit of learning objects. Determining what should or shouldn't be learning objects in your system takes some expertise, and if you want to go down this road, you may want to bring someone in who has helped design a learning object repository before. It's also better to start with a tagging or metadata scheme than trying to retrofit existing content to meet the standards you adopt. For more information about building learning objects or an LOR, refer to Box 5.1 featuring Liz Glowa, who is a nationally recognized expert on this topic.

Box 5.1 Building a Digital Repository: Advice From Liz Glowa

Liz Glowa is a national leader in the promotion of digital objects and providing guidance to educators on how to implement a reusable learning object strategy. She has worked directly with staff at several state departments of education and provided national leadership through her work with the SREB SCORE initiative, which is the Sharable Content Object Repositories for Education (SCORE) initiative developed by the Southern Regional Educational Board (SREB) (see the book's companion website for links to these and other resources). Glowa provides some comments as to why you might want to consider developing a digital repository and suggestions for how you might get started along this path.

1. **Help your learners find the best content.** Searching the Web for content can be overwhelming, and there's usually little guarantee of the quality. Because learning objects are tagged and can be linked to organizational schemes like state or national standards, your users are more likely to find exactly what they are looking for when they search your LOR. The digital content objects in your LOR can also be vetted, so those people who find them in a search are able to make better decisions about whether the material is going to be useful. A formal vetting process can be an expensive undertaking, but an LOR also supports ratings and comments from users that many educators may find more relevant since it permits them to see how others like them have used the content.

2. **Separate your content from your delivery system.** As those who have done it will tell you, transferring existing content to a new LMS can be a painful procedure, often requiring lots of time and money. But as products change, merge, or become obsolete, the decision to keep your current LMS may change. Glowa notes that when digital content resides in an LOR, that transfer is much easier—if you move to a new product that integrates with your LOR. The content is independent of the LMS, and the metadata tags help you map the content attributes to a new product much more quickly and efficiently.

3. **Provide a familiar interface to other learning repositories.** Several reputable organizations, such as the National Science Digital Library from the National Science Foundation, have developed LORs according to international technical standards and populated them with high-quality content. If your LOR is developed according to these same standards and uses a similar tagging scheme, you can link your LOR

with others and actually search external LORs through yours, thereby expanding your reach. Once your users become familiar with your LOR's interface, they will appreciate having "one-stop shopping" through your LOR.

4. **Don't start from scratch.** Implementing an LOR requires commitment and allocation of resources. The goal for this initial investment is to improve the quality of experience for your users, eliminate duplication, and more effectively manage your digital assets so you'll see savings in cost over time paired with higher quality learning experiences. There are existing metadata schemes you can use, and Glowa suggests you build upon the guidelines others have created. She served on a team of national online learning experts that helped to develop SREB's SCORE metadata scheme, which is drawn from international standards. Many of the national LORs use Dublin Core.

5. **Work together.** You may want the benefits of an LOR but your organization or district may lack sufficient size or resources to tackle implementing one. In this case, Glowa suggests working with others to implement an LOR at the consortium level. This is how The Orange Grove, Florida's Digital Repository, came into being and now provides digital content for educators across that state. LORs have the ability to support subrepositories, so multiple districts could come together to develop the infrastructure for an LOR and add customized digital content to their own subrepository that benefits from the larger system's architecture. She suggests you may have to spend more time up front in terms of business rules and operations, but the end results include the benefits offered by more efficient content management.

6. **Think ahead.** When asked where LORs are headed down the road, Glowa notes that we need to think beyond the concept of a learning object to the broader idea of a digital content object. There are all kinds of documents and objects that are created in schools that are now in a digital format and must be managed. These may be related to curriculum, policy, certification, and of course, professional development. Many of these materials are sitting in proprietary databases that don't talk to each other. Glowa suggests that all of these digital objects can be tagged and managed by a digital repository, and this central method of managing all of this digital information not only provides benefits in terms of efficiency, but makes it much easier to provide connections and linkages. For example, digital content about student performance can be linked to professional growth plans that can be linked to digital content intended to address student needs. That's the holy grail of professional development—tying professional growth directly to student needs and outcomes—and Glowa's vision includes a way to get there.

For online learning, perhaps the most common standard you will run into is the Sharable Content Object Reference Model (SCORM), which originated from one of the largest e-learning providers, the U.S. Department of Defense. In a nutshell, SCORM is a specification for LMS and content so that content can easily be shared between different LMS. It's really where the idea of learning objects came about, or at least got some real traction. Learning objects can be developed to these specifications so they can be considered "SCORM-compliant." If you create SCORM-compliant learning objects, you can quickly and easily deliver them to any SCORM-compliant LMS. If you're not going to have a lot of content and a lot of users, you may not have the personnel with the time or resources to become fully skilled in creating SCORM-compliant learning objectives. However, if you do purchase a SCORM-compliant LMS, you can upload SCORM-compliant learning objects quickly. It's something to consider, especially for larger course-based projects.

For any content you create, you will want to tag it with some standardized tagging schema. You may not want to use the extensive Standard for Learning Object Metadata developed by the Institute of Electrical and Electronics Engineers (IEEE LOM) or Dublin Core, but you may want to use social tagging. This consists of title, description, and keywords. You may be familiar with the concept of tags from social networking applications. Basically, if you create a piece of content and post it, whether a discussion response, a lesson plan, an image, or a video, you add some keywords—tags—so other people can find it quickly. Tagging is a much simplified version of creating content that is searchable, but it's obviously not as reliable or powerful. Users often create the tags, and sometimes they are misspelled, or different people may have different conceptions of the meaning of tags. Often, though, they can pick from common tags to improve accuracy.

PRESENTING BASIC INFORMATION VIA TEXT AND IMAGES

A lot of online learning gets panned as simply being a "textbook online," but there are still many reasons to present basic information via text and images. As covered in Chapter 4, there are benefits for using text and images, and professional development offerings often include background information, white papers, research reviews, descriptions of practice, policy examples, case studies, data sets, and many other types of information that are well suited for text presentation. Generally, if you have a lot of detailed information and you want people to be able to view and review it at their own pace, text and images can be appropriate. If the content is important and relevant to those using it, they'll appreciate this tried-and-true format for sharing information.

Of course, you can post text and images to any webpage, whether you plan to hard code it yourself using HTML (Hypertext Mark-up Language)—the standard programming language for the Web—or intend to use methods that don't require your knowing web-programming languages, like a blog, wiki, or some form of LMS. Some come with editors that look similar to word-processing applications, so you can type or paste your information into the editor and format it. But if you've got a lot of text on a single concept, you may just want to post a document created on your favorite word-processing software.

Common word-processing applications have become sophisticated enough to support images, graphics, hyperlinks, and more, so they're actually much more than a static page. You can also format them in Adobe's Portable Document Format (PDF) to retain critical formatting and to prevent people from editing them. Many providers use documents to supplement their online activities. It's not the most interactive use of the Web, but it does work in some settings, because you're providing consistent access to high-quality information.

Presentation software, like Apple's Keynote and Microsoft's PowerPoint, are also handy tools to use to present text and images. They have further functionality that makes them useful for mini-lectures and even some advanced information presentation. Presentation software can be used to create timed and animated presentations that can include audio and navigation buttons or links that can provide branching options. These can be saved and shared online in their original format or as slide shows that users can't edit. There are several applications that extend the functionality of PowerPoint beyond simple text and image presentation, which are covered in the next learning activity type: demonstrating a process, sequence, or procedure.

DEMONSTRATING A PROCESS, SEQUENCE, OR PROCEDURE

Once you move into the realm of skill building, you might want to demonstrate some kind of action. This may be a pedagogical process, an assessment procedure, or a sequence of steps any educator may have to follow, from the routine to the highly complex. Action implies motion and that's where web-based technologies can really shine, even using common technologies found on most computers.

Presentation software is not only a jumping-off point for other applications, but it can be used to show animations as well. You can create these through a progressive series of slides that build upon each other as a sequence of images in a series, or a set of slides that appear to be animated. But if you have access to some additional authoring tools, you can actually create more powerful multimedia animations. The benefit is that many people, including many teachers and others who could serve as content experts, know how to create basic presentations and could send that content to someone whose role is to convert it to something more interactive.

One option is to export a PowerPoint presentation into Flash, which is perhaps the most common animation software used on the Web and is supported by most web browsers. You can do this through free software, such as OpenOffice or some online converters, or by creating versions of your slides that can be imported into Flash. This would take some additional expertise, however, as they'll probably need to be tweaked, and Flash programming is a more advanced skill. The benefit, however, is that Flash files are designed to be easily displayed over the Internet, so you can get an animation online that is suited to lower bandwidth delivery. In order to go this route, you'll probably need access to at least one person who can program in Flash; plus you'd benefit from having some guidelines for your content experts, perhaps giving them templates and either prohibiting the use of certain types of graphics or giving them a bank of images to use in their presentations.

A more powerful approach to extending PowerPoint into a truly robust e-learning environment is through tools like Articulate's Presenter, which allows you to create online lessons or full courses right from PowerPoint, or Adobe's Captivate software, which can import PowerPoint presentations you've created. You can add narrations or animations, embed video, and incorporate many other functions, all in a Flash-based course shell with a table of contents, navigation, and other common lesson features. There are other products available from these and other vendors that support additional learning tasks, like quizzes and online hosting of content. They do come at a price to match their powerful functionality, but if you're going to create a lot of learning objects of this type, the help these tools provide can offset the investment. Of course, you can also do all this directly in Flash if you have that expertise.

If you want to demonstrate a process on your computer, but put it online for a wider audience, create a screencast. Screencasting software records actions on your screen as an animation or video that you can post online. This is especially helpful for creating "how-to" demonstrations of software or websites, perhaps even helping people become familiar with the technologies you use in your online environment. You can add narrations or other audio, images, hyperlinks, and some have other features like highlighting critical information; and different editing tools will be included to clean up your demonstration. Adobe Captivate supports screencasting, as does the popular Camtasia application from TechSmith. There are even free screencasting tools, like CamStudio and Wink for the Windows operating system, and some web-based services you can use to create and host screencasts, like Jing and Pixetell. Costs vary, sometimes based on the functionality you choose, and some free or low-cost products may include watermarking on the files you create.

You can also create audio and video files using common applications, some free, and post them online in different formats. An audio file alone can be embedded in a webpage or can be turned into a podcast for web display or uploaded to a digital player or even a smartphone through a service like iTunes. Several states have created iTunesU sites to host professional development offerings. As mentioned in Chapter 4, audio alone has limited application, but you can quickly increase the effectiveness of your audio by combining images, even a sequence of still images, using presentation or podcasting software. Audacity is one of the most popular editing tools for audio, and GarageBand for the Macintosh operating system is popular not only for audio podcasts, but also for incorporating images or video, at which point it's often referred to as a vodcast. Audio and image files on the Windows operating system can be imported into PhotoStory or MovieMaker, with the latter also supporting video.

Of course, video is a great format for demonstrating a process, especially new pedagogical processes in classrooms. Tips for creating better videos are presented in Chapter 4, but consider whether you really need to have video in your online professional development. Yes, high-quality video can be an exceptional teaching resource, but it can also be expensive and time-consuming to create when, for some skills, a series of animated slides with narration may suffice.

HOSTING ASYNCHRONOUS INTERACTIONS

Asynchronous simply means people don't participate in something at the same time. E-mail is asynchronous, as is posting to social networking sites like Facebook. Phone calls, chat, and webconferencing are *synchronous*. Asynchronous interactions provide flexibility for your participants. Facilitators can post an assignment at the beginning of the week and participants can reply by the end of the week. Or participants may want to post questions of interest in a learning community that others can respond to when they have time, whether during a planning period or from their home at night. Asynchronous options also decrease the pressure to respond immediately, so participants can take more time to craft thorough and thoughtful responses.

Threaded discussion software was one of the earliest types of asynchronous technologies and is still very common in online interactions. The thread simply refers to the thread of messages that participants post, like those found on sites like MySpace or Facebook. Because they are topical, threaded discussions work well for many types of groups, and you shouldn't discount them because they may seem to be "old" technology. Often, a moderator or facilitator posts a topic or key question and the participants reply. Sometimes they reply to the facilitator, or they may reply to each other. It can take some practice to develop good questions for discussion, as it can for participants to create substantial replies. At their best, threaded discussions help people learn new information, assess and reflect on their own knowledge and experiences, and build strong professional connections with colleagues in the same building or across the country. Many social networking sites and LMS include some type of discussion software.

E-mail and mailing lists are also valuable technologies for supporting asynchronous interactions. They can be cumbersome, however, unless the end user has some form of organizational scheme for e-mails or if the mailing list messages can be archived in a central place online so they can be searched and reviewed. What is convenient about them, though, is that many people are very used to using e-mail, and if you can get messages to them in their preferred e-mail inbox, you don't have to rely on their logging in to your system just to keep up. While you may not want to use e-mail or mailing lists for your primary content delivery, you will likely want your online environment to generate e-mails for important announcements, like new course offerings, results of assessments, messages from facilitators, and other system-generated messages. Make sure your service actually sends copies of the full messages from your lists, not just a notice that a new message is waiting. The last thing I want to do is to have to log on to an LMS just to read a short one-line e-mail about the system being down for an hour when I won't even be awake.

There are reasons to use both blogs and wikis in online professional development, again, based on what you want to accomplish. Being very much like an online journal, blogs make great resources for journaling activities or portfolios of individual learning. Participants who attend professional development, either online or face-to-face, can use their blog over time to demonstrate how they've put their new knowledge and skills into action. Talk about accountability! They can upload documents, like lesson plans or school policies, include pictures or videos of new pedagogies in action, and include reflections about personal growth. Blogs can support reflective practice, with the asynchronous communication comprised of me communicating with myself over time about my thoughts, goals, and achievements. Of course, blogs support commenting, and other members of a learning community can subscribe to an individual blog and offer support asynchronously, as well.

Wikis not only support group projects but can support an entire online learning environment. You can often create separate pages or complete sections in your wiki, and most allow different levels of permission or access. For example, you may use a wiki for a learning community where only some pages are editable by the group and others are maintained by an administrator. Sometimes it's hard to tell when you visit a site whether it's a wiki, a blog, or some other tool. And while some districts block social networking applications, it's less common to block a blog or wiki. There are many free or low-cost blogging and wiki applications, especially for educators. You may have to put up with advertisements on free applications, though. Thankfully, there are now simple and easy ways to convey information online that don't require complex web programming skills.

HOSTING SYNCHRONOUS INTERACTIONS

There are times when you may want people to work together at the same time. It can be difficult to reach consensus on a threaded discussion tool or e-mail due to the time delay. Sometimes, you just need to find out something fast and can't wait. There are text-based options for synchronous interactions, like chat, which can be included on websites, social networking applications, webconferencing, and LMS. Chat is helpful when delivering live professional development sessions over the Web because participants can ask questions to the presenters in the chat feature and they're recorded. Sometimes you just can't get to all the questions, but if they're recorded in the chat feature, you can save the chat transcript and send out follow-up information with responses to all questions asked or post them for future reference.

Chat can also be used for some logistical purposes. Participants can use chat to introduce themselves, tell us where they're located, and tell us how many people are in the room with them. Trying to introduce a large number of people over the phone is complex, and people often don't know when to speak or end up speaking on top of each other, wasting time. Chat makes that process more efficient as the presenters can begin with the audio portion while people are introducing themselves in the chat window. You can always stop

10 minutes into the presentation and do a summary of the participants for them. And if you need to keep track of participants, asking them how many are in the room gathered around the computer or phone is well suited to chat. Sometimes you don't realize five or 10 people are sitting around a conference phone but logged in under one name.

As helpful as chat can be, sometimes I just get tired of typing. Luckily, there are several options for voice communication. Don't forget the phone! I know this is *online* professional development, but online audio is still not foolproof, and I find very few people who have microphones or external speakers for their computers. Without them, the internal microphones and speakers can actually cause interference, as the microphone can pick up sound from the speakers and send it back into the ether and your audio becomes a series of echoes, squeals, and squawks. There are two simple solutions. If you're going to use audio through the computer, insist everyone use a headset with a microphone or use the phone.

A good audioconferencing service is also a strong consideration if you plan to do a lot of group sessions. It allows multiple people to call in to a single number. These services offer special features, like "lecture mode," as one service calls it, where your presenters all call in on one number and all the participants call in on another. You can mute or unmute all the participants at one time or as individuals. Some allow participants to get into a question queue and have their phone line unmuted to talk directly to the presenter. I also recommend you use a service that provides toll-free numbers for your meetings. You have to bear the cost, but many people are disgruntled by long-distance charges, and many schools will not allow people to call long distance internally. By using a service, you're likely to get lower rates than an individual can, and you can pass those costs along in the form of course fees, if you need to.

You may also want to incorporate videoconferencing in your online events, although you have to consider bandwidth. There are still schools and homes with dial-up Internet connections, and many school districts block streaming media, so you have to be sure your participants can actually use the service. Videoconferencing is becoming more common, though, and a home DSL connection can usually support video over webcams. Be judicious, however, about when and how you use videoconferencing. It does take some practice, and it has some limitations, especially in group settings. Without practice with the webcam, presenters may look down at their desk to read their notes so you get a view of the top of their head for much of the time. When groups try to use a single webcam in a room, you usually just see tiny stick figures off in the distance. There are free options for videoconferencing, such as iChat on the Macintosh operating system, and Skype and ooVoo are cross-platform, free applications (for now). Some smartphones also support videoconferencing, and it will be interesting to see how these and tablet computing devices influence the use of videoconferencing.

Give special consideration to your outcomes and the type of information you need to share, however, before incorporating any video. A talking head is not very engaging, and if the critical information can be spoken and the speaker doesn't have to do anything physically to convey the information, consider audio plus a picture of the speaker. Better yet, pair audio with a presentation of relevant text, graphics, and images. If you want to watch a classroom in action, consider taping it ahead of time and display a short clip. If you have folks who can't access streaming video, put it on a website ahead of time and have participants watch it before the session. In some cases, you may still need to send out videos on CD or DVD.

Webconferencing software, a single multifunction application that supports multiple forms of media, has become affordable, with some scaled-down applications available for free. It has been a real boon to synchronous professional development, as webconferencing applications have all the tools you need to create and deliver high-quality professional development that meets the two magical criteria of being interactive and engaging. Webconferencing is a contact sport.

There are several common features in most webconferencing services, with more being added all the time. Chat is a common one, along with audio over the Internet, phone, or both. There are also usually interactive whiteboard applications built in, and supporting presentation software, like PowerPoint, is probably the most often used feature. Sharing documents can be helpful, especially long documents, but make sure there is a way for users to download documents for their own review before, during, or after the webconference. Actually cocreating documents is an especially useful feature that can be used by groups of learners completing activities for a course or for reviewing work with a facilitator or presenter.

Another common feature is polling or survey software, which can be used effectively to keep people engaged and to gather data about the presentation. But polling takes some planning and can easily be used poorly, such as when questions are nonsensical or really only have one correct answer—negating the reason for using the poll. Instead, use polling and surveys to inform your presentation as formative assessment. Include a poll at the beginning to better understand your audience. Use polling to introduce critical topics by gathering the participants' experiences and using that information to determine which information is presented or emphasized. Use polling software to check for understanding of critical concepts and ask if the participants need more time or an additional session. Polling can be used for needs sensing by asking participants for critical topics to cover in the future. Polling and survey software can be used for evaluation during the event, or you can post a link to an online survey and send participants to it after the fact. One hour is about the maximum anyone should be asked to sit and interact online, and you may want to use that time on content presentation and interaction. You can't guarantee, however, that people will complete an online survey after the fact, unless it's a requirement for credit.

Webconferencing software is a powerhouse tool. It's been interesting to see how these products have evolved, and I'm curious to see what comes next. Best of all, the prices have dropped significantly in just a few years. There are also free or low-cost services available online that provide some of the functionality of the full webconferencing suite of tools. You can collaborate online through chat and an interactive whiteboard on Scribblar.com, and iChat (on your Macintosh computer) now supports presentations and screen sharing. There are many more collaborative technologies online, so adding a webconferencing component to your online professional development, no matter what your outcome, could become a reality and one you should really consider for increasing interaction and engagement.

GROWING A LEARNING COMMUNITY

It was probably MySpace or Facebook that introduced most of us to the world of social networking. Social networking technologies combine many of the features already discussed, such as discussions, chatting, discussion forums, blogs, and tagging, along with photo sharing, links to videos, and many unique applications built just for them. They combine these features with user management, so once you've created a profile, you can create or join groups and pull in the features you want most. A district or school could use social networking software to create a learning community portal, then create groups for different roles, like all of the principals, all second-grade teachers, and all language arts teachers, or allow participants to join multiple groups. They are appropriate supports for a learning community or other school-based teams. You can also create short-term groups, like a curriculum group that meets for a few weeks or months. You can also use them to focus on long-term efforts in which the group members change over time, like a group to monitor and discuss the implementation of early literacy interventions or dropout prevention.

If you want to grow an education-oriented learning community online, my first recommendation is to go join one. Too many people who plan to begin a learning community have never participated in one—on- or offline. They're not only unaware of what the technology can do but *how* it can be used. You'll find lots of interesting features you can add to your online learning community, like blogs, videos, and photos, but pay close attention to how the features are used and *if* they are used. There's a lot of dead content out there that people have posted just because they can. Instead, see which features seem to have the most traction by getting the most participants. It might be a chat-based interview with an education leader or a space for sharing lesson ideas. Photos and videos can be fun, but determine how other sites use them to support outcomes similar to those you want to achieve.

At the heart of most successful learning communities is a passionate person or core group of people who generate momentum and sustain the community (see Box 5.2 featuring Sandy Fivecoat, CEO of WeAreTeachers). These people dedicate a significant amount of time to making the community successful. Let me emphasize that—*significant* time. They may organize events, lead discussions, find guest presenters, or nurture other members to champion community activities. This champion (or group of champions) is perhaps the most critical element for the success of a learning community. The technology will not build community for you. *You* have to do that. A learning community can take a lot of time, especially in the beginning, and you need to dedicate personnel—including technical, content, and program support personnel—to reach a successful outcome.

Box 5.2 Growing a Dynamic Learning Community: WeAreTeachers

WeAreTeachers is arguably one of the largest social networks for teachers, reaching more than 140,000 participants. CEO Sandy Fivecoat and her team launched it in 2008, and have since built a successful business model to sustain participation, including giving away more than $75,000 in grants to teachers who participate. She shared the following suggestions for those wanting to capitalize on social networking in their online professional development efforts.

1. **Determine the scope of your network.** Establishing a limited teacher-to-teacher network within a district has some obvious benefits in terms of meeting goals and supporting initiatives, but Fivecoat feels the greatest benefit for using social networking is connecting and sharing with others globally. You may find a restricted community appropriate to your needs at first, but consider if and when you might want to expand to a larger audience.

2. **Teachers need a reason to use your network.** Fivecoat notes that there are many different networks for teachers to join, but if you don't offer sufficient high-quality content, teachers may join but not come back. Content is the best differentiator, and for teachers, the most valued content includes experiences from other teachers that describe how to address specific student needs. In her experience, research and basic how-to demos don't speak as well to teachers, unless those demos are by teachers showing how to use a product successfully with real students. Teachers won't come just because you build it. The lesson here is ensuring that the content on your network is relevant to your audience; let them tell you what they need.

3. **Give back to your members.** WeAreTeachers provides incentives, in the form of mini-grants, to its members to provide content. These may be vendor-sponsored grants, but it's a two-way communication. Product developers can ask questions of teachers in the network (e.g., How do you ensure your use of play supports learning?), and teachers have direct communication back to product developers. Teachers create videos to respond, and community members vote for their favorites. You may not need to give away grants, but do consider the incentives your members will receive through participation. With all the competition out there, professional growth alone is not sufficient.

4. **Use a comprehensive approach.** WeAreTeachers is focused on providing value to its members and uses a thematic, program-based model to do so. Programs have a beginning, middle, and end. After members identify a critical topic, Fivecoat looks for a sponsor to provide mini-grants to teachers to explore that topic. Teachers report their experiences, sometimes providing lesson plans or ideas relevant to the topic, and the winners of the grants may also create short videos or podcasts of their grant-funded

projects that are posted back into the community. For some programs, Fivecoat uses a commercial distribution company to target large groups of teachers through mass e-mails that often bring new members to the site. Some may stay active just for the length of the program, but others will continue participating in other programs. In your own network, consider a comprehensive approach that uses a single initiator as a focus for multiple opportunities for participation, thereby providing a high return on your original investment.

5. **Leverage other social media.** One of the unique aspects of WeAreTeachers is that they push content from their site to other social media sites, such as YouTube, Ning communities, and Twitter. Says Fivecoat, "We blog and cross-blog with all key thought leaders in the education community." She believes the portal concept doesn't have much future. Instead, she encourages a "thoughtful distribution" process so teachers can find your content—well-branded, of course—in the places they prefer to visit. They've even made it easier for teachers to join by using Facebook Connect so that participants don't need to create a unique account just for WeAreTeachers. Instead of trying to isolate your content and your users, consider how you can push your materials to wider audiences through the growing number of social media applications.

There are many free social networking applications you can use—a web search turns up dozens. The trick is finding the one you like the most that has the features you need. Some sites are hosted for you, while others allow you to host them on your own server. The popular blogging software WordPress has a social networking application called BuddyPress, and there are open-source applications like Elgg. BigTent includes advertisements as many free applications do. I'm still waiting for the one application that will become the market leader that has as much functionality and ease of operation as the formerly free Ning. Many web developers have created different applications, like "apps" on a smartphone, that could be added to Ning to increase its functionality. Time will show whether these same apps will become popular on other sites or whether the cost of Ning or some other social networking application will be justifiable to enough users to make it the leading application. For more on this topic, review Box 5.6: "Caveat Emptor: Is Free Right for Me?"

Of course, there are additional applications that educators are experimenting with. Twitter is popular for growing personal learning networks, and some people are beginning to use it to support professional development efforts. And the use of mobile devices, like smartphones, is gaining ground. A for-fee service that has caught my interest is one especially developed to support coaching and mentoring of educators online called TeacherStudio. Developed by former teachers specifically for the education space, it includes synchronous and asynchronous communications, grouping, and file sharing, but it organizes these around common educational practices, like instructional strategies, lesson plans, and full-fledged professional development activities. You can also indicate in your profile whether you are or aren't looking for a mentor in any education-related topic or practice. Everybody's an expert in something, so you could be a mentor in the use of digital portfolios but want to work with a mentor in response-to-intervention strategies at the high school level. A key feature of the site is the use of video and video-like documents (like slide shows, animations, and narrated presentations, as described earlier), but unlike YouTube or TeacherTube, the videos are grouped with other supporting materials, so you will have additional information and all necessary materials linked to the video and organized all in one place. New bundled services like this will likely continue to enter the market, and what they do is make it easier for you to include a range of technologies quickly and easily.

Virtual environments (VEs) are another technology being used to support learning communities. You participate in a VE through a computerized alter ego, called an *avatar*, which may or may not look anything like you. You navigate through this environment in different ways, sometimes walking, sometimes flying, or even teleporting. But the main purpose, at least in terms of education, is to connect and interact with others for professional growth. VEs can support a range of text- and audio-based communications, and educators are using them to replace onsite meetings as well as to conduct short- and long-term professional development opportunities. You may be able to interact with your favorite author or education leader or attend a conference entirely in a VE or in conjunction with a face-to-face event.

Perhaps the leading VE in education is Second Life, although there are others available, like ReactionGrid. They require a free application you install on your computer that allows you to enter and navigate the environment and communicate with others. If you actually want to own a piece of Second Life, referred to as an "island," you have to use some real-world money, and you start from scratch. There's a pretty steep learning curve for creating objects, not to mention entire buildings and communities, but you can visit existing education spaces with just a little bit of practice. If you're interested to see how educators are using this engaging technology, I suggest you join Second Life and visit some of the existing education islands. ISTE's island is a great starting point, as there are lots of tips for getting started and learning how to navigate and perform common actions (from sitting down to flying), but there are other education spaces, and most education organizations are very willing to let you join them in Second Life. For the story of how one district has been using Second Life to grow its learning community, see Box 5.3: "Getting My Second Life Together With SLEEC."

Box 5.3 Getting My Second Life Together With SLEEC

I'm sitting on the couch in SLEEC Island's main building comfortably dressed in blue jeans and a Henley, but I can't get my spiky blonde hair to cooperate. It's better than the brown hair I had last week, though, and I was glad to swap it out. Actually, it's my avatar, JR Quander, who's having the bad hair day; and he's sitting with two instructional technology teachers from Escambia County School District in Florida in the reception area on the county's island in Second Life (see Figure 5.2). SLEEC stands for Second Life Educators of Escambia County, and Lauren Thurman (whose Second Life name is Laural McCallen) and Lori Weedo (Second Life name Lori Galli) are talking with me about their experiences. They're in Florida, I'm in Virginia, but our avatars are having a comfortable chat on SLEEC Island.

Escambia County has been using Second Life as one of several means of providing professional learning opportunities for its teachers since 2008. Initially, the intent was to allow the 60 technology learning group facilitators from across the geographically large county to meet during the day without having to travel. That has expanded to meetings during and after school as well as providing additional opportunities for professional learning and growing professional learning networks.

Thurman and Weedo purposely started small and built consensus and motivation with the intent of branching out and including other teachers in Escambia County. SLEEC membership now includes educators from across the globe, but its primary focus is still Escambia County. Building community was their first priority, and offering more formal opportunities for professional development, such as mini-courses or workshops, came later. As the community has grown, ideas for these opportunities have been generated by the community members themselves—an example of a truly dynamic learning community.

While SLEEC offers some formal professional development opportunities, including a day-long conference held in October 2010 that featured nationally recognized presenters from across the nation, Weedo and Thurman note that there are many additional opportunities available from education organizations in Second Life that are available for free. You can connect with practitioners, researchers, industry leaders, or other experts so that teachers can interact with them, where they might not get that opportunity elsewhere.

Thurman and Weedo acknowledge VEs are not for everyone, but neither were many technologies, such as the early use of the World Wide Web by educators. VEs do have a learning curve to be able to navigate and use their features, but they are evolving, and they provide one opportunity in an arsenal of opportunities to support professional learning. Weedo hopes that their teachers keep an open mind because "teaching is a profession that includes a lot of aspects of growth. You don't stop learning because you've taken your college courses. You still need to grow as a teacher." She believes that they owe it to their students to investigate new and engaging ways to grow and learn. And she comments that one of the things she thinks about when she considers VEs is that "learning can be fun. This is just the tip of the iceberg for teaching and learning in virtual environments." Weedo agrees: "Our students are our teachers. Students will be excited when their teacher brings in something new and engaging, even if it's outside of the box a little bit. We can cover, cover, cover material. It doesn't mean they've learned it if they're not engaged." She says that Second Life is a great place to keep learning by connecting with other educators.

You can learn more about SLEEC in Box 5.4: "Learning From Experience: Second Life Educators of Escambia County" or by reviewing the educational VEs and resources listed in the references.

Figure 5.2   From left to right: Lori Galli (Lori Weedo), JR Quander (John Ross), and Laural McCallen (Lauren Thurman) on SLEEC Island in Second Life during our interview for this book

Box 5.4 Learning From Experience: Second Life Educators of Escambia County (SLEEC)

Organization: Escambia County School District, Florida

Contact: Lauren Thurman (Second Life name: Laural McCallen), Instructional Technology Teacher; and Lori Weedo (Second Life name: Lori Galli), Instructional Technology Teacher

URL: http://sleec.edublogs.org/

Date First Implemented: 2008

Audience: Original participants included the 60 Technology Learning Group facilitators from the county as a means to support their professional learning community model. The intent is to eventually include more of the 3,000 teachers in the district to participate in professional growth opportunities. Membership is open, though, and SLEEC has members from across the globe.

Need: *What Was the Initial Trigger?*

SLEEC Island started as a means of investigating Web 2.0 tools with teachers in Escambia County. Their Technology Leadership Group was interested in investigating avenues to support problem-based learning through Title IId funding.

Because of limited funding, travel was limited, and meeting during the day within the county was difficult. After attending a presentation by noted education expert Kathy Shrock about how her district was using Second Life, Thurman and Weedo were encouraged to investigate the virtual environment.

Intended Outcomes:

A driving force was to find a vehicle that would allow members of the technology learning groups to meet virtually, and they have. Thurman and Weedo worked at building a community that will eventually take on more formal activities, rather than providing structured activities at the onset. They have the expectation that content and program specialists, especially those who are geographically distant, will use the island as a virtual campus for professional development. By providing this opportunity for Escambia County's teachers, they envision that their teachers will also visit other educational areas in Second Life and attend professional development opportunities there.

SLEEC supports a growing virtual gallery of student and teacher work, called the Technology Integration Matrix, where teachers can share materials from projects they have worked on. One of the first topics of study was how to support project-based learning, both in and out of Second Life, and move those practices to the classroom.

Incentives:

Educators will have an opportunity to receive in-service points through the district's ERO (Electronic Registrar Online), which will then count toward their certification points. The opportunity to interact with one's professional learning network, especially for geographically separated colleagues, is also an incentive.

Instructional Design Considerations:

SLEEC's design was originally focused more on a community-based design than an instructional design. They have focused on building a strong initial community, because it is hoped that those efforts will result in the request for more formal or structured professional development opportunities generated from within the group, thus becoming a more dynamic learning community.

Lessons Learned:

Skills training has not been as successful in Second Life as have opportunities that include interaction and communication with others, such as building and nurturing a professional learning network. There are also unique 3D objects that have been created that take advantage of the dynamic nature of the environment to provide engaging opportunities for presenting learning.

There is a learning curve to be able to navigate and use some of the features in Second Life. But once you do, you can find many different professional learning opportunities in different educational environments—many available free for educators. You don't have to own your own island to benefit from professional learning opportunities in Second Life. Thurman recommends that anyone interested in this environment should first plug in to some of the

(Continued)

(Continued)

existing organizations that have virtual environments. "You can sit quietly and observe for a little bit, but then get engaged," she encourages. "Have conversations with people and keep networking with other educators."

Often, those people who are reluctant to ask a question in a live setting are willing to pose their question in sessions held in Second Life, sometimes by posting it into a chat window while a speaker is presenting. Responses can come from other people in the audience as often as from someone who might be designated as the speaker.

Evaluation:

Teachers take participant surveys. More formal evaluation is likely as more courses and mini-courses are supported in SLEEC. Second Life offers unique tools to support data collection and evaluation, such as linking to free Google Docs. SLOODLE tools let you use tools in Second Life to send data to the LMS Moodle. Teachers are able to post follow-up reflections while they are attending sessions "in-world" that will go directly to a Moodle course they are enrolled in. The SLOODLE will also enroll the avatar, log chat sessions, provide quiz chairs (a virtual waiting list), link to presentations that can be uploaded through Moodle to Second Life via a presentation board, provide an editable glossary, incorporate a blogging tool for the avatar to wear, and other features.

See the book's companion website for more information about the profiled programs.   www.corwin.com/rossonlinepd

MONITOR LEARNING

No matter what your outcome is, at some point you'll want to determine what people are learning. Evaluating online professional development is presented in more detail in Chapter 7, but there are several different types of technologies you can use to monitor what your participants are learning. The easiest to incorporate are those that support forced-choice formats, such as multiple-choice or true-false questions. These offer convenience because they automate data collection and reporting, perhaps also linking participants back within the content in case they need to review information and retake an assessment. Many also include options for open-ended responses, but a real person is going to have to review them. These assessments give you some quantifiable measure that can be reported for accountability purposes, like offering recertification credit or continuing education units. There are several online forced-choice assessment generators and survey tools, and LMS can include them.

When you move into facilitated professional development, you may want to be sure that participants can upload different materials to demonstrate their learning, such as documents generated as a response to a reflective activity, lesson plans, presentations, videos, and others. Tools like blogs and wikis are also helpful for creating online portfolios and journals, which can be monitored and evaluated or used for self-monitoring of one's own learning. Security of data becomes an issue as you begin to collect artifacts that correspond to scores, grades, or data related to recertification. And you will likely need to collect and report scores or grades, which you can do through an online gradebook, another common component of LMS.

Having mentioned LMS throughout the book, it's time to turn to those systems and how you might use them to support your online professional development efforts. But first, if you aren't already locked into one specific technology, reflect on *how* you plan to use technology and create a list of different technologies you might consider evaluating for use in your own solution. Review the questions in Box 5.5: "Take Action: Exploring Technology Specifications" to see if you can be specific about the technologies you plan to use. It may turn out that, based on your content and audience, you will find an answer to all of your needs in a single LMS as described at the end of this chapter.

Box 5.5 Take Action: Exploring Technology Specifications

Review the examples in this chapter or visit the book's companion website for additional examples that address *how* you will use technology to support online professional development. Thinking through this will give you a general description of your technology specifications and could even be used to outline a more detailed functional specifications document, which could become part of your implementation plan.

How will your content and activities require you or your learners to . . .	What technologies will you consider?
Present information via text and images?	
Demonstrate a process, sequence, or procedure?	
Host asynchronous interactions?	
Host synchronous interactions?	
Grow a learning community?	
Monitor learning?	

INFRASTRUCTURE FOR ONLINE PROFESSIONAL DEVELOPMENT

Because of the growth of online learning, there are comprehensive sets of tools you can download, purchase, or lease to support a range of different learning activities and needs. It's gotten difficult to come up with a single term that describes these systems, as they are constantly evolving and adding new functionality. Some common names are learning management system (LMS), course or content management system (CMS), and others. Because the types of functionality they provide can overlap, and there is no standard term, I refer to them throughout this book as LMS, since ultimately the system supports professional *learning*. These systems are powerful tools that can handle all of the data for your courses, learners, and the common activities described in this chapter.

In terms of content, an LMS can usually support most media types that you would find on the Web and can be accessed by common web browsers. You may want the flexibility to code pages using HTML, Javascripting, or other web-programming protocols, or you may want to stick to posting documents developed on common word-processing or presentation applications. They often support different types of media, such as streaming video, audio, animations, and simulations in common formats, such as QuickTime or Windows Media Video files, Flash, or Java applets. Just make sure your LMS supports the media you want to use.

Whether you purchase or develop your own content, an LMS organizes it so your learners can access it in a way that becomes familiar. It's like using your favorite search engine, travel website, or other web-based resource. They become familiar with the navigation and organization of the LMS and will be able to find all of the information they need to successfully complete a course or activity. An LMS also usually combines functionality within one suite of tools, often including a method for creating assessments, a gradebook, and survey tools, and allows you to chunk your information into lessons, units, and courses of any duration you desire. They may support or incorporate e-mail, discussions, chat, webconferencing, or the creation of shared documents with others. They also usually track where participants are in a course, so they can leave and reenter the system quickly and get back to work.

In terms of management, an LMS should provide different levels of access to the course elements. Participants should only be able to enter the system and access the content, not modify it. Developers, on the other hand, may be given access to create course elements or entire courses directly in the LMS. If you hire external developers, you will want to give a more restricted level of access to them, so consider whether your LMS should provide this level of access.

On the learner side, your LMS should handle all of the data and information about your participants. It will likely track all of their account information, such as usernames and passwords, contact, and payment information. It may store information related to *all* professional development opportunities— whether on- or offline. Most can track which events people have registered for or completed, and they may be able to give up-to-date information about recertification points obtained. This may include scores on assessments or even course grades, if given. Some contain or link to user portfolios that store this type of completion data or may even contain course artifacts created by users.

On the management side, participants may be able to use the LMS to review and revise their own personal data as well as create personal reports, such as printing out certificates of completion or reporting recertification points to a governing body. These are especially helpful features, and your users may appreciate the ability to take care of these tasks on their own. Administrators are usually able to run reports and find out statistics related to registration and participation, like course enrollments, course completion rates, waiting list status, and any payment information. They should be able to manage all aspects of individual records, especially determining if user information is accurate and up-to-date, and may be able to import large data sets, like entire class rosters or even all participants in a district, through mass import features.

Many districts have been using an LMS or LMS-like application for years to schedule face-to-face professional development and track participation. If you sign up for summer workshops or inservice professional development online through a secure portal, it's likely you're using an LMS to do so. An LMS can actually be used by human resource (HR) departments that never use them for professional development, or they might be linked to HR data systems that track all relevant information about employees. Linking systems and sharing data brings up another technical standard you may need to consider—the School's Interoperability Framework (SIF). The SIF Association is a nonprofit membership organization composed of educators and companies that support them that has created specifications for the transfer of data between different hardware and software that schools rely on. If you're planning to connect to other data systems in a school district, find out if your LMS has to be "SIF-compliant."

So, when do you need one of these systems? The answer will depend on the outcomes you've selected, the type of data you collect, and the scale of the professional development efforts you undertake. If you're presenting or sharing information and are not tracking user data beyond page views or hits, you may not need one. If you collect basic user information, like allowing users to create their own username and password, you still may not need an LMS. Social networking technologies can be used to support different online professional development activities, from lesson or book studies on up to dynamic learning communities. If you want to assess user knowledge, you might benefit from an LMS that links assessments to content, but only if you need to track that assessment data for a critical reason, like recertification. Once you get to the point of having to track user data through the system, knowing specifically who those users are for critical reasons, what content they have accessed, and what content they have mastered, consider moving to an LMS. And, of course, if you have a large number of users, like an entire district or many users across multiple districts, an LMS might make tracking all of that data easier.

If you get into the job of creating courses, even just a few, you may benefit from the ease with which an LMS provides a consistent interface and experience to the users in your system—administrators, developers, learners, and facilitators. An LMS can provide structure for content developers and help organize courses and course elements into consistent components. Of course, an LMS will be beneficial if you're committed to using a standard, like SCORM, as it may actually provide templates or forms for you to enter this information as it's created.

Some of the experts I interviewed have had to go through what I'd consider "the unthinkable"—changing their LMS. Some have done it more than once. Ross White from LEARN NC says you need to consider standards and portability. What will your content look like if you export it out of your current LMS? What options do you have? He notes, "The more you tie yourself to any system with no portability, you'll end up hemorrhaging money." Henry Pollock from Florida School Leaders concurs and notes that because technology changes so quickly, "don't get too hung up on one type of technology. Try to be as platform neutral as possible." (Read more about this program in Box 5.7: "Learning From Experience: Florida School Leaders.") Christie Terry from eMINTS further recommends that you NOT tie your system's URL (web address) to a specific LMS product, like www.MyOPD.serviceprovider.com. She knows firsthand that your LMS can change, and you don't want your identity tied to an application you no longer use.

Should the unthinkable occur and you do have to change your LMS, Liz Pape from Virtual High School says they now rely on templates rather than discrete bits of content. That way, her programmers can write scripts that can convert the template elements from one system to the other, and no one has to touch the content. She also recommends that if you come up across this challenge, you notify your users early and often. Prepare them so they'll know how to do what they're used to doing, but also let them know what great new things they'll be able to do in the new system—which is one of the reasons for using a different product, after all. And as Liz Glowa mentioned at the beginning of this chapter, using an LOR can make that transition less painful and more efficient as the content is independent of the LMS.

Box 5.6 Caveat Emptor: Is Free Right for Me?

There's a significant and growing population of users that rely on Moodle, a free, open-source LMS. There are other free solutions—some whose free version may have limited functionality or support, like BrainHoney by Agilix or Canvas by Instructure—but Moodle most likely has the largest following and largest set of features. Free always catches my attention—at first; but remember that only the software is free. All of the other components of your system, like hosting, technical support, content, and facilitation, are not. If you decide to go with a free LMS, you have to consider how you'll provide the other components. If you have the hardware and networking resources to host a free LMS, plus someone with the technical expertise, you may see a high return on investment. If you have to pay for those things every year, or hire someone to support your free software with an annual cost for salary and benefits, compare those costs to for-fee applications that may include hosting and technical support in their fees. Depending on the scope of your project, you may end up paying less for a for-fee LMS.

Similarly, in the education space, Ning was once the most popular social networking application, perhaps because it offered a range of different functions for free. But free is not usually a sustainable business model, and Ning's services are now available for fee. But, just like considering your LMS, paying for a valued service can be justified. Sometimes you have to pay very little to get a lot in return, and if a technology can help you meet your outcomes for a small fee, you need to weigh your inputs versus outputs. A small investment could yield a high return on investment, while free applications may actually end up costing you money in hidden costs related to time, effort, and personnel.

Free applications work for some projects, but not for others. Know those options are available, but carefully consider all of the resources necessary to support your solution, free or not. Remember all the known and hidden costs will determine your total cost of ownership.

Box 5.7 Learning From Experience: Florida School Leaders

Organization: Florida Department of Education (FLDE)

Contact: Henry Pollock, former Director of Education Retention Programs

URL: www.floridaschoolleaders.org

Date First Implemented: 2005

Audience: Current and preservice K–12 educational leaders in the state of Florida

Need: *What Was the Initial Trigger?*

Florida School Leaders built upon the success of a previous program, FloridaLeaders.net, funded by the Bill & Melinda Gates foundation, that helped to establish a statewide network of coaches and mentors drawn primarily from retired high-performing school leaders.

Intended Outcomes:

State standards for principal certification became obsolete in 2000, and so the FLDE convened a group of participants from different stakeholder groups who spent about 3 years developing a new set of state standards for what a high-performing school principal is expected to do. To implement these standards, the state had to retrain all existing principals as well as work with all institutions of higher education that prepare the bulk of aspiring school leaders in the state. Florida School Leaders was developed to meet those needs. It was a hybrid model, with both face-to-face and online components.

(Continued)

(Continued)

Incentives:

Participants in university educational leadership programs received appropriate graduate credit and district school principal preparation programs received professional development hours for participation in approved William Cecil Golden School Leadership Development online modules and workshops.

Instructional Design Considerations:

To improve the collaboration between developers and provide a more consistent user experience, the FLDE developed its own website and required each of the partner organizations in the program to import their content into the state website. The state partnered with one entity that set up a consistent navigation and interface design to improve the user experience. This also resulted in a single-user sign-on to all content for participants.

Lessons Learned:

In Florida, when money is available, the state usually posts a request for proposal (RFP), and different regional entities submit proposals to develop programs to meet the requirements for that RFP. "What you often end up with," according to Pollock, "is five flavors of the same ice cream." Each region wants to develop and use its own training materials, but not that from other regions. Florida School Leaders forced regional entities to collaborate. Fifty percent of the award had to include subawards to other partners, so no individual entity could win the entire pot of money. The state had to provide some oversight and facilitated the relationships between organizations that were not used to collaborating. Each regional organization had areas of expertise, so the state allowed each to leverage its expertise but pull in the complementary expertise of others.

Pollock notes that sometimes, "there can be a disconnect between higher education and K–12 practitioners" in terms of what each feels is important for educators to know and be able to do. Higher education faculty tend to want to create materials based on a faculty member's area of expertise (e.g., law, finance, etc.), because that is often the reason they are hired. A school or district wants to have holistic materials in which different areas of expertise are embedded in a larger framework (e.g., legal requirements in special education, financial requirements across school programs, etc.) because that's how their job duties are structured. Florida School Leaders took the input from university faculty but organized it in a holistic framework to meet the needs of the district target audience members.

The state tries to provide a lot of just-in-time training opportunities as well as longer course-based materials. The site also has a community model in which participants could post information from their school or district to highlight promising practices.

See the book's companion website for more information about the profiled programs. **www.corwin.com/rossonlinepd**

CONCLUSION

I want to emphasize again that while there are many fun and interesting technologies out there, it's how you use them, or intend to use them, that's important. If you can upload thousands of pictures and hours of video, but no one is going to view them, you don't need those features. And even if you do find a technology that supports your outcomes, like a powerful webconferencing application, you may not need to use all of the features all of the time. Find those that match the type of outcomes you've identified as important and the learning objectives for your content. You can use Box 5.5: "Take Action: Exploring Technology Specifications" to consider what kind of technologies might best meet your desired outcomes and content specifications, or, if you're thinking about an LMS, use Box 5.8: "Caveat Emptor: Evaluating a Management System" to evaluate a system and talk with vendors. Links to additional examples of the types of technologies described in this chapter, including LMS, webconferencing, social networks, and others can be found on the book's companion website, as well as additional information and resources about SCORM, learning objects, and virtual environments. I encourage you to submit additional resources through the website, as well, so we can all keep learning.

Box 5.8 Caveat Emptor: Evaluating a Management System

If you decide you need a CMS, LMS, or a system that does it all regardless of what you call it, review several different options to find the right one for you. There are solutions at different price points, including some that are free, but determine if the functionality you're after matches what the system can provide. Following are some questions you can use to evaluate a system you're interested in. I recommend you get a full, synchronous, web-based tour of the product by an expert. Also ask for references from current users. You may also be able to obtain a free trial copy or sign up for an account on a demo site for a limited amount of time. No matter what you pay up front, you're going to expend significant resources—time, people, and money—over the life of your program, and changing platforms can be tedious and expensive, so make sure you test it out before you commit.

How will you manage data about course content?

- What operating systems and browsers does it support?
- How do you plan to use the system? For each, consider what technologies or media are supported and how easy they are to use.
  o Present text and images
  o Demonstrate processes and sequences through multimedia
  o Host asynchronous communications

(Continued)

(Continued)

- o Host synchronous communications
- o Monitor student learning
- How easy is it to add, edit, or delete content?
- How does the system track user progress through the content?

How will you manage user information?

- Can you assign different roles (e.g., participant, facilitator, developer, administrator)?
- How many participants can be supported?
- How is user participation tracked and reported? To administrators? Facilitators? Participants?
- How easy is it to import and export data? What reports are included? Can reports be customized?
- How easy is it to modify data? For administrators? Participants?
- What security measures are employed to safeguard data?

Standards

- Does it meet technical specifications like SCORM or SIF? Find out what version it is, and have the vendor demonstrate exactly how it meets these specifications. Even though a system may support SCORM-compliant content, you may not be able to create SCORM-compliant content with the system.
- Does it need to interface with other existing data systems?
- Does it need to support reusable learning objects?

Pricing

- What is the pricing structure? How many users does it support?
- How much data storage is included?
- How much data transfer is included?
- What kind of technical support and training is included?

Putting It All Together 6

The previous chapters have posed a lot of questions to consider in order to increase the likelihood of success of your online professional development. Now it's time to make some decisions and head to the finish line. There may be a few more questions to ask, but it's time to make some concrete plans to get your system ready to launch. This chapter will help you with that process by using information from the gap analysis, content specifications, and technology specifications to result in an implementation plan that will take you to your launch (see Figure 6.1). Included is a simple model I've used to create timelines

Figure 6.1 Your development timeline, including a budget, can be completed after determining some human resource issues.

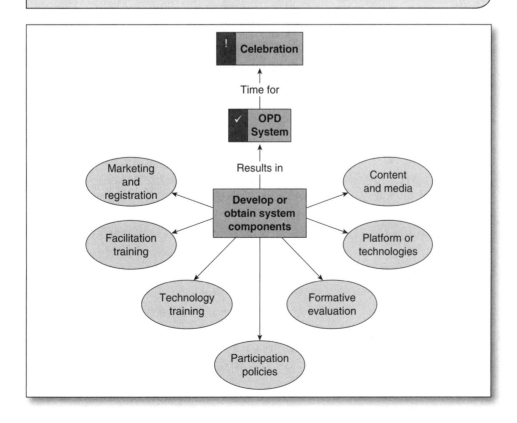

and calculate budgets that takes into consideration what you need to do to launch your system successfully as well as who is responsible each step along the way.

GATHERING ALL THE PIECES

The previous chapters focused on determining need, setting goals for desired outcomes, and crafting a plan to develop or purchase your online professional development system. It doesn't matter whether you're developing a course-based model or are looking for more of a learning community approach that has a more generative basis for programs or activities, the steps described are similar for either setting. Take a moment for a quick review before you consider the final steps necessary for launching your online professional development, which are focused more on the people that will be involved in your system.

State Your Vision

After determining your needs in Chapter 1, draft a vision statement for your online professional development based on those needs so that everyone on your team is clear about where you're headed. You may think that everyone is on the same page, but until you see it in writing, it can mean different things to different people. Seeing it in writing also gives you and other stakeholders opportunities to discuss and define terminology so you're clearer about the results you want. Describe where you want to be 1, 3, or possibly 5 years from now. Try to avoid jargon and too many adjectives. Be concrete. What will your program look like? What will it actually do? How will it address your needs? If you haven't already done so, write your vision statement now.

Use Your Desired Outcomes to Set Your Mission

If necessary, review the OPD Decision Matrix in Chapter 2 and revisit your desired outcomes. Consider your initial outcomes as well as those you may want to achieve down the road. If you're starting from scratch, you may want to start with a more foundational outcome so that you can build infrastructure and prepare your audience for other forms of online professional development. Be realistic about the outcomes you can achieve within a year after your launch. If your audience has never participated in a learning community of any type and has limited access to social networking technologies, jumping in at the level of a dynamic learning community may not be a reasonable expectation. But if your audience has been engaged successfully in a face-to-face learning community model that has already laid the groundwork, they may be ready to take it—or part of it—online to support ongoing professional growth.

If you haven't already, determine which of the following pieces are outcomes you expect to achieve a year from now, then 3 to 5 years from now:

- Present or share information
- Changes in teacher's or leader's knowledge
- Changes in teaching or leadership practices

- Active learning community
- Dynamic learning community

From there, consider the factors that impact your desired outcomes, like how they'll be measured, necessary support and resources, security needs, and others, as described in Chapter 2.

Describe Your Needs

Chapter 3 introduces parameters for a gap analysis so you can better describe what you have and what you need. This is the first component of an implementation plan. In addition to determining existing as well as new resources, identify the gatekeeper at each step of the way. For example, if all professional development in a district has to be approved by someone in curriculum and instruction at the district office, that person is the gatekeeper. If incentives for participation are tied to contracts or teacher pay scales, gatekeepers may include principals, staff from human resources, the superintendent's office, or even unions. The pieces to consider are listed below. Address these questions before you go into your actual development phase. The answers to these questions, in fact, will determine what you do develop; and by "develop," I mean create from scratch or purchase components, if not an entire solution.

- What content will we deliver?
- Who will participate?
- What are the incentives for participation?
- How many people will participate (1–5 years from now)?
- When will people participate?
- Who else should be involved?
- What role will facilitators play?
- How will we get the word out?
- What funding sources are available?

Develop or Obtain Content

Developing high-quality instructional content requires finding a match between your audience, content, and the media at your disposal. You need to know the demands of your content before you can select the right technology solution. If you're developing your own content, hopefully Chapter 4 introduced strategies you will consider for creating interactive and engaging activities appropriate to adults and the learning objectives. If you're purchasing or using free content, you still want to be sure these characteristics are present.

If you're hiring an external instructional designer or contracting with an organization to develop your content, Box 4.7: "Take Action: Content Development Timeline," in Chapter 4, should be helpful to set expectations and develop milestones for your project that a designer or developer can work towards. This timeline will help all the players see their obligations and determine whether the timeline is reasonable. It tells what each team member is responsible for, so it provides a level of accountability.

If you're purchasing or using free content, use the checklist at the end of Chapter 4, Box 4.9: "Caveat Emptor: Evaluating Media in Online Content," to be sure the content was developed to some degree of quality and that the media enhances learning. Request a guest account or other access to the content you are reviewing. Ask for any supporting information that may give you insight into how effective the content has been in the past and with which audiences. Be sure you can integrate any content into your existing or proposed system, making sure all media can be seen or heard on the technology your audience actually uses. If you're using a standard like SCORM or a tagging scheme, know who will add or edit that data and ensure it's accurate. If you're using free content, you'll need a backup plan in case it's no longer free, or just no longer available. If any compatibility or access issues have to be resolved, know who has to resolve them.

Determine Technology Specifications

Investigating all the different technologies and how they can be used can be a lot of fun. *How* technology supports learning is the most important thing to consider. There's no single solution. If, like me, you can get sucked into a new technology for several hours just playing with it and seeing what it can do, keeping your needs in mind might help you stay focused. In those cases where it's hard to stay focused or you become overwhelmed, walk away and consider what you've seen. And get a second opinion. Distance gives perspective, and getting input from someone else can help you make better decisions. Go back to *how* the technology supports your learning needs. If it's just fun, but doesn't promote learning, pass.

The quality of your content will be a determining factor in the success of your technology selection, even in less structured social interactions. If you already have some successful content, use it as a basis for moving forward. Once you know what technologies your audience has access to and feels comfortable with, you'll be better able to select a more appropriate solution to get your message across. If it's not used, it doesn't matter how interesting or engaging the technology appeared to be. In my experience, you can push most people one step away from what they are used to or are comfortable with, but the sink-or-swim approach rarely pans out. If your audience uses YouTube regularly in class, it may not be too much of a leap to look for a solution that supports video—even videos that your audience creates. Creating classroom video might be that one next step. On the other hand, if your audience has never participated in a social network and rarely uses e-mail, step back a bit in terms of your initial technology selection.

TAKING CARE OF BUSINESS

At this stage, you've laid much of the groundwork for success. Technologies can be identified and tested, and content can be under development or assessed by test users. It can be exciting to see all the pieces coming together. Once content and technology decisions have been made, there are a few additional human resource issues to consider before you share all your great information and make it public. You've spent a lot of time getting ready, and now you need to make sure people find and can use your new online professional development. Some of these considerations were mentioned earlier, but they are explored in more depth here since they're a little different from working with content and technologies.

Policies to Govern Participation

You'll have people who interact with your system directly, such as the learners who enroll and the facilitators who guide them, as well as those who will be impacted indirectly by your system, such as building administrators whose faculty members enroll in your online professional development and technology support personnel who may be called upon to help those using school technologies. It is helpful to have clear and explicit requirements for your participants and suggestions for those indirectly impacted by your system. This can be especially important if people external to your system may have a say in how successful your project is.

Facilitating an online course or an activity in a social network is time-consuming, and you need to be clear about the type of compensation your facilitators will receive. If you use them, paying for facilitators can be a big expense. By now, you've already determined what outcomes you hope to achieve and have considered what kind of facilitation model will be necessary to reach those outcomes, even if the answer is none. If you will have facilitators and you're working within a school district, your district may already have guidelines for facilitators in other settings, including how much they should be paid, if they are to be paid. Calculate how much total time is expected of your facilitators to determine appropriate compensation. Fees for facilitators vary but are usually based on the duration of the event, number of participants, experience of the facilitator, and enrollment fees. Other things to consider are whether your facilitators have to be practicing teachers, whether there are any degree or certification requirements, or if they should have any experience or training in online facilitation. Besides money, some facilitators may be willing to facilitate for different types of compensation. Perhaps the facilitator can receive professional development hours or continuing education units, or maybe participants in a learning community will agree to a rotation schedule for facilitation. Release time and access to technology are other popular compensation options. Regardless of the formality of your facilitation, have expectations spelled out clearly before you begin.

Some providers also use participation agreements for the learners who enroll in their online professional development. These may be loose expectations for what successful participation looks like, with little or no consequence for not following them, or they may be stricter guidelines for the quality and frequency of participation. In discussion-based settings, it's common to have expectations for participant responses that go beyond agreeing or saying they like something someone else has contributed. Emphasis is placed on going to deeper levels of analysis or reflection that draw on the content being explored. Participants expecting to receive graduate credit may have stricter participation requirements and products or other tangible outcomes that are required to successfully satisfy the degree program. Programs that offer continuing education or professional development credits, too, may have similar requirements, so align yours with the requirements or expectations for other forms of professional development your audience members may participate in.

I learned a valuable lesson from two former colleagues, Jackie Walsh and Beth Sattes, who are master facilitators in a face-to-face setting. Jackie and Beth like to start face-to-face workshops by setting norms for participation. In essence, this is a less formal set of participation expectations, but when developed by the group, perceptions of value are often greater. Remember, adults like to have a say in their learning, and asking them help develop expectations for participation is one way to honor this need. You can do the same thing online. It can be helpful for a "class" of participants who are going to go through a multiweek course as well as for groups that are participating in an online learning community, even if just for a short time. For an hour-long webinar, you may just let people know what participation expectations are to save time, but for long-term interactions, you should have the group contribute. Common norms include, "Ask questions," "Be respectful of the beliefs and experiences of others," and "Have fun!" I make sure that last one gets on the list every time.

The importance of buy-in from administrators and technology support personnel was discussed in Chapter 3. In terms of policies for participation, it's helpful to have guidelines and suggested advice for administrators and technology support personnel who may be indirectly impacted by your program. One common way to address pertinent issues is through a series of Frequently Asked Questions (FAQs). It's also important to have all ancillary material fully developed and published on your site before you flip the switch. You can add to it later, but remember, no "Under Construction" sign on any page! It's unprofessional, and you'll lose creditability. It's also helpful to include this type of guidance in marketing or promotional material, or include it in any packet of information you provide to participants when they enroll. A facilitators' manual, whether in print or electronic, providing handouts or information they could share with school administrators or technology support personnel, is another helpful resource to provide.

Technology Training

It's likely that at some point some of your participants and facilitators may need some technology training to be successful. At the very least, they may need to know how to do the things they already know how to do—like searching, communicating, and navigating webpages—on *your* system. The best-case scenario is that your interface design is so obvious that users adapt to it quickly—but don't launch an environment for the lowest common denominator of technology skills. You'll bore some of your more proficient users, and they might not come back. You also don't want your system to go too far outside the proficiency and comfort level of too many of your users. That "one step" rule is important to consider here. As technology specialists the world over will tell you, if it doesn't work, or it doesn't work as expected, people will turn off. It really may not be the fault of the technology, but still, they'll disengage.

Many learning management systems (LMS) have gotten pretty easy to navigate, but there are still a few things that can happen that your participants may be unaware of. For example, one LMS I used opened up the content in a new browser window. Users who had pop-up windows blocked never saw the content. Or sometimes the content would be open, but end up behind another window. The end result in both cases is confusion and frustration. In this case, a short User's Guide that contained screenshots and helpful hints was sent to participants when they registered. Web designers also commonly make information and functionality redundant (e.g., having menu items, shortcut keys, and other means to complete common functions) to cover all levels of users. You don't know how or when people will need help or where they'll go to find it, so putting it in multiple places is helpful. Common technical issues can also be reported in FAQs and provide your technical support staff with a list of common issues to check first and their resolutions. In some cases, you may want to consider creating a screencast of typical troubleshooting strategies.

It probably takes very little practice for most people to get used to the LMS options available today. You do still have to be careful which versions of browsers participants use. Some districts don't allow teachers to update *any* software on school computers, and many district tech support staff like to stay a version—if not two—behind the most current versions of browsers. This can cause some problems for your participants, mostly in terms of limited functionality. Make sure you notify participants of technical requirements for your LMS. And while not really a training issue, the number one most common technical support issue I face, hands down, is forgotten passwords. Several other providers corroborated this same experience. In the technical support and training you offer, make sure your participants know how to receive or reset their passwords. One LMS I used had three separate ways users could do this onscreen before they had to contact me, but contact me they did.

You may want to capitalize on the growing number of social networking applications that are becoming popular on the Web, which several online professional development providers report doing. Of issue is keeping track of participation once someone has left your site if you can't support the functions on your own. Will you require participants to upload a video of their classroom on YouTube or TeacherTube or create a digital story on VoiceThread? If you do, how will you track that information? The advantage of an LMS is that it provides a single place to store and report data. Moving to external applications means losing control of some of that data. Also be careful about how many different kinds of applications you connect to. Some people get tired of all the different usernames and passwords they have to keep up with, and whenever you can use a single sign-on for multiple applications, you're going to improve the experience for your participants. Several popular social networking applications, like Facebook, allow you to let your users sign in to others sites using accounts they've set up elsewhere, in this case using the Facebook Connect feature.

Very often, online professional development will use a variety of technologies, not just your LMS or network website. Your participants and facilitators are also likely to use word-processing, spreadsheet, and presentation software. Being able to collaboratively create documents through tracking changes and commenting can be very helpful in an asynchronous environment, but not everyone will know how to use these features. While there are some cross-platform applications, you're still likely to run into participants who have older versions of these applications on their school computers. Make sure facilitators and participants know how to save documents in different formats, including saving or exporting to Adobe's Portable Document Format (PDF). You may want to consider online versions of these applications, like Google Docs, but that can require an additional login and actually creating a Google account, which you may have to show some people how to do.

If they're uploading images or videos, your participants have to know a little bit about appropriate file types and appropriate methods for reducing file sizes for online display. It has become much easier to capture digital video, with smartphones and other popular videocameras being able to record video with the click of a single button. As I've mentioned, applications like GarageBand, iMovie, MovieMaker, and PhotoStory can also make video-like files out of still images and narration. The advantage to these is that they are much smaller than full video, but they can still convey information effectively. Videos and video-like files are helpful for capturing actual classroom practice as well as supporting reflection. If you want to see what's going on in classrooms or promote deeper levels of reflection, you may want to consider having your participants take videos and edit them with these applications, which also happen to be free, but you'll have to be sure everyone knows how to use them correctly or the technology will get in the way of your learning goals. Requiring their use can scare some people off.

Your participants will undoubtedly use some form of online communications, including e-mail, discussion forums, mailing lists, blogs, chat, and web- and videoconferencing applications. Luckily, most educators use e-mail now. Still, some may need some help with more advanced options, like attaching documents. Discussion lists can be confusing if you've never used them before. Not all discussion software uses the same format, and some people find the threading of messages—replies within posts or replies to replies—to be a little confusing. Generally, most people have experience using online communications, even newer ones, but I find it helpful to always provide a brief overview of topics related to Netiquette (Internet etiquette) and how to get the most out of online forums. You may not have to spend as much time on these topics anymore, but I still find people who like to USE ALL CAPS in e-mails, without realizing many people consider it shouting, or who want to "LOL" or use other popular shortcuts in every message, so you may need to lay the groundwork for a little more professional communication.

Webconferencing is still a novel occurrence in many schools, and if you work with educators, you're likely to find that few of them have used it before. When using webconferencing software, my former colleague Laurene Johnson made a screenshot of the application on which she then labeled important features, using statements like, "Your name should appear in the roster here";

"This is where you participate in the chat"; "This is where you raise your hand." It sounds a little rudimentary, but it was tremendously helpful. She would alternate that screen with one with important contact information—like our technology support hotline—as well as a reminder that all participants were muted until we got started. When you enter a conference room and you can't hear anything and no one can hear you, you might think something's wrong, and onscreen information can alleviate a lot of fears.

Webconferencing software can also be a helpful tool for orienting your participants or actually training them on the applications you may use, such as a social networking website or an LMS. A kickoff event using webconferencing software allows you to demonstrate your technologies in real time, and maybe even get people to interact while you're online so you can do a little troubleshooting and confidence building. If it's too confusing to go back and forth between your webconferencing screen and your LMS or social networking website, give your participants homework from the session, such as posting a response to a welcome message, downloading a syllabus or other course document, or finding and watching a welcome video.

For longer courses, an online orientation is a great way to practice the technology before graded activities come into play. Essentially, the first week of "class" is an orientation in which the participants learn how to use the technology. They log in, send messages through the system, post their first discussion responses, download a document, watch a video, or whatever else you need them to do in the actual course. If you have the luxury of a face-to-face training with facilitators, model the online orientation activities for them, and then they can go back and replicate it with their participants—but I've used the online orientation even if I don't meet my facilitators in person. Stan Freeda, project coordinator for OPEN NH, gave me some great advice based on the orientation his program offers. OPEN NH makes its online orientation more relevant by using material related to online learning as a focus of the orientation. For example, users may download an article or white paper about online learning and then post a discussion response based on what they've learned from that article. In that way, they're learning a little bit about online learning and what to expect from the experience while practicing the technology. It's a great idea to consider. For more information from this program, review Box 6.1: "Learning From Experience: OPEN NH."

And because technologies are constantly changing, it's likely your facilitators will need some kind of ongoing or periodic skills training. Even though you'll likely provide technical support, facilitators are often going to be the ones that are seen as the first line of technical support to your learners. Your facilitators should be comfortable enough to address common problems and basic troubleshooting while knowing when to direct someone to your technical support staff. Also, as I've mentioned before, many online providers investigate new and emerging technologies as they become available. If you do adopt new technologies, it's likely your facilitators will appreciate some help to learn how to use them. Your facilitators may actually be able to serve as a testing ground for those you're considering. They'll have a good idea of the technical skills of your target audience and will likely be able to give you valuable advice as to what technologies might best be incorporated.

Box 6.1 Learning From Experience: OPEN NH

Organization: New Hampshire e-Learning for Educators

Contact: Stan Freeda, Project Coordinator

URL: www.opennh.org

Date First Implemented: 2005

Audience: K–12 teachers in New Hampshire, especially those in schools with high-poverty, low-achieving populations

Need: *What Was the Initial Trigger?*

OPEN NH came about through participation in the e-Learning for Educators project funded by the federal Ready to Teach Program and organized by EDC and Alabama Public Television. Main partners are the New Hampshire Department of Education and New Hampshire Public Television.

Intended Outcomes:

New Hampshire has a large rural population and many smaller schools. There can still be a lot of travel involved in participating in local professional development, so OPEN NH is designed to help districts provide high-quality professional development with reduced costs—due to no travel—as well as greater flexibility in terms of when educators participate. OPEN NH is especially focused on helping educators with students at high-poverty, low-achieving schools.

Incentives:

Professional development hours (e.g., 35 hours for a 7-week course), which some districts define as continuing education units. Graduate credit from Plymouth State University in New Hampshire is also available.

Instructional Design Considerations:

Courses run in sessions (7-week period in spring, summer, and winter). Courses have a minimum requirement for participation, since they are discussion-based, and Freeda notes that a group of at least eight participants allows for a richer discussion and better opportunities for facilitating learning.

OPEN NH follows the e-Learning for Educators model for developing courses and training facilitators. They prefer to have participants who have taken or facilitated courses become course developers. They have created their own developer and facilitator courses so they can continue to develop and offer courses if the grant funding goes away. The outcome of participation in these courses is an additional course that can then be offered.

Lessons Learned:

While other states in the e-Learning for Educators offer courses for free, OPEN NH charges a registration fee of $130 per person per course. This helps build commitment and appears to prevent course attrition.

The program offers courses in at least each of the four core content areas each year. They also offer courses in popular topics, such as Web 2.0 tools, differentiated instruction, project-based learning, or working with English language learners, but embed them within the context of a content area. Courses are then facilitated by a content expert (e.g., differentiating instruction in science would be taught by a science teacher). These pedagogy-specific courses are more popular than content-area courses that focus on foundational knowledge, research, and theory in a domain.

OPEN NH has developed a course template in their LMS to make it easier for course developers as well as to provide some consistency across courses.

It has been difficult to promote the use of Web 2.0 tools that are not supported by the LMS. Participants don't want to have to leave the LMS or to have multiple accounts for applications just to participate in a single course. Says Freeda, "There's a fine line between how many logins you can support."

Crafting an engaging discussion question is important. Freeda concurs with other providers that it can be difficult to engage people. OPEN NH wants participants to use the information from the course to support their own ideas, to make the content personally relevant. Discussions may include ways content may have to be modified to meet specific settings, such as for different grade levels or students with different needs.

OPEN NH has been trying to seed districts with people who have taken the courses or who know the program. Successful participants tend to encourage others to take their courses and can also give face-to-face support for those who might need it. They now budget and pay for a 2-hour, face-to-face orientation in four sites throughout the state.

Evaluation:

OPEN NH participated in evaluations from the grant evaluator and used that knowledge to create similar pre/post surveys into an online survey for their own use.

See the book's companion website for more information about the profiled programs. **www.corwin.com/rossonlinepd**

Facilitation Training

Most of the experts I interviewed use a facilitated model for their programs. These may be facilitated courses or learning communities with facilitated activities or short-term programs. Effective self-directed, self-paced learning opportunities can be developed for some outcomes, but I'm not convinced you can reach outcomes at the top of the OPD Decision Matrix for the majority of your learners in a self-directed model. When you're going for those higher level outcomes, you're going to need a facilitator, and he or she will have to be trained.

There's not enough room here to go into all the specifics for training online facilitators. In fact, there are entire books (Collison, Erlbaum, Haavind, & Tinker, 2000; Salmon, 2004), courses, and training programs on the topic.

Several successful programs, including some profiled in this book, offer online professional development to learn both how to facilitate and develop online courses, with trainings ranging in length from 10 to 28 weeks. I can't cover all of that information here in detail. Regardless, most would agree that if you're going to have facilitated interactions, some form of facilitator training is a must. Being an effective facilitator in a face-to-face setting can be a good start, but facilitating online learning requires some additional skills, especially since the interactions are so different.

In reviewing some of the models for online facilitation, most emphasize that online professional development has both a professional and a social context. In fact, this is the first principle posited by Collison and colleagues (2000), who arguably created some of the earliest online professional development through the International Netcourse Teacher Enhancement Coalition (INTEC) that gave rise to the successful Virtual High School cooperative that currently provides both online professional development and high school courses. The influence of social discourse may be even greater now than when the model was first developed, as it was before social networking sites like MySpace or Facebook were even available. With the prevalence of social media, both in professional and personal settings, facilitators must develop skills to capitalize on the familiar technologies but use them for professional learning, something they weren't necessarily designed for. That's just one way online learning can be different from more traditional face-to-face settings.

Hootstein (2002) suggests that online facilitators have to wear four different pairs of shoes when they work with their online learners. An obvious pair is that of *instructor*, in which the online facilitator guides the learning. The concept of guiding the learning, the "guide on the side," is a critical component of the model developed by Collison and his colleagues (2000), as well, and is used by several online providers. Matt Huston, currently director of online learning at Peer-Ed, was a classroom teacher who was one of the first to undergo training with the Concord Consortium that used this style of facilitation, and he continues to incorporate the model in online professional development he develops and delivers. Huston reports being pretty confident of his own teaching skills going into that experience, but seeing how the model placed greater emphasis on learners' directing their own learning was something new to him and made a lasting impact— on- and offline. Huston's experience is not unique, as there are many stories of participants who have learned how to facilitate this type of learning online and then took some of the strategies they learned back to their classrooms. More about Huston's experiences can be found in Box 6.3: "Learning From Experience: Creating Powerful Online Learning." Hootstein further elaborates that in this model, the online facilitator doesn't hold all the answers and the focus is on the learner. Instead of dictating the learning, they help learners connect with prior knowledge, provide information, summarize key ideas, identify misconceptions, and model and promote the use of learning strategies. When adopting a model like this, these are skills that facilitators need to learn and practice online.

A critical component for effective facilitation mentioned time and time again by online providers is the ability to craft discussion prompts and moderate discussions that promote deeper learning. Facilitators often have to help their learners overcome the familiar social uses of some of the technologies used in online professional development and guide them towards the deeper skills of reflection, analysis, and evaluation. Very often, learning prompts occur as questions posted in discussion forums or even as polling questions in synchronous events. In some cases, discussion questions are developed as part of the design process, while others may leave those questions up to facilitators. Most questions have to be tested and tweaked with a real audience, so it's best that they can be edited or revised—even if they have been created during the instructional design process. Despite this, sometimes you create discussion questions that just don't elicit the type of response you're looking for. Sometimes different audiences react to the same questions differently. A good facilitator is trained how to build on those responses and guide the learners towards the learning outcomes intended by the question, no matter how well it fared at first.

Another pair of shoes Hootstein (2002) suggests online facilitators must wear is that of *social director*, once more corroborating the importance of the social component that other online experts identify. But the social components in online professional development should be focused on learning, which requires facilitators to learn how to help others cooperate, collaborate, and reach consensus. They must also allow for a healthy sense of respect for other individuals, their beliefs, and the validity of the experiences they bring to the setting. Online facilitators do this by creating opportunities for learners to collaborate with others in pairs or small groups in addition to guiding individual activities and facilitating whole-group discussions. Online facilitators must also wear *program manager* shoes to keep groups organized and following appropriate procedures, as well as *technical assistant* shoes, in which the facilitator models technology use and makes sure that the technology supports learning. As Hootstein describes it, the facilitator helps to "make the technology transparent."

One model that accurately describes how online communities evolve, at least in my experience, is presented by Salmon (2004). Her five-stage model describes the ways participant interactions can evolve in computer-mediated communications and corresponding ways a facilitator's role can change as the group progresses through these stages. I suggest that it's applicable to online professional development courses, learning communities, and even some workgroups that take a blended approach to using technology (using both online and face-to-face interactions). I'm not sure all groups get through all five stages online, but I hope it's a goal to get to these higher stages. She does an excellent job of describing the changes that occur in the kinds of technical support and facilitation skills—what she refers to as e-Moderating—as the group progresses through the stages. The stages are described briefly below, but I encourage you to investigate her work for more detail and many other helpful ideas.

1. *Access and motivation.* In this stage, the facilitator tries to motivate and encourage the learners, who may feel insecure with the technologies and the entire concept of online professional development. The facilitator may step the learners through basic functionality of the site, much like the online orientation I described earlier, making sure the learners know where to go to get help.

2. *Online socialization.* Norms for participation help the facilitator establish a supportive environment to help the participants feel more comfortable. Facilitators also try to develop a better understanding of the personal learning goals and needs of individuals, including anyone with specific disabilities or learning needs, in order to customize the experience for them. The goal is to help the learners understand how to accomplish social and learning interactions with others so the technology supports rather than hinders learning.

3. *Information exchange.* Facilitators try to strike a balance between presenting new information without reaching the point of information overload. Interactions are focused on the content, and the facilitator may pose prompts or probing questions designed to help develop a deeper understanding of the content as participants share information from course materials, external resources, and personal experiences.

4. *Knowledge construction.* In this stage, the facilitator truly shifts the onus of learning to the learner and avoids giving out "the answers." As Salmon (2004) says, "Be prepared to value every participant's contribution but summarize, summarize, summarize" (p. 174). There may be more opportunities for collaboration through paired or small-group work, and the facilitator has to know when to cut off unproductive interactions and promote new lines of inquiry.

5. *Development.* At this most mature stage, learners are encouraged to expand their learning beyond the group as well as try new roles beyond the more traditional roles they participated in during earlier stages. Learners may take on some opportunities for moderation and supporting each other. Reflection becomes a critical component for the learner as well as for the facilitators, who should reflect on their own facilitation practices while providing opportunities for others to build theirs.

Besides the initial facilitator training, several providers encourage or require their facilitators to receive ongoing or periodic training. Some, like PBS TeacherLine, require facilitators meet annually, such as through faculty meetings or peer observations, to stay certified; and PBS TeacherLine also offers an advanced course for experienced facilitators. They, and others, also encourage facilitators to stay connected with each other using an online network or discussion area. Make sure you include appropriate opportunities to provide initial and ongoing training for potential facilitators, perhaps combining training on new and emerging technologies while also addressing facilitation issues. Nurture them. Melinda George from PBS TeacherLine is convinced that high-quality facilitators are the major factor as to why their completion rate is so high—94%, which is truly a laudable accomplishment. I've had similar completion rates, but only with facilitated classes. She also notes that they don't try to recruit as many facilitators as possible. Instead, they identify their best facilitators and try to get them to become repeaters. It's a model you may want to consider. For more ideas on the roles of facilitators that you might want to address in your training, see Box 6.2: "Take Action: What Online Facilitators Should Know and Be Able to Do."

Box 6.2 Take Action: What Online Facilitators Should Know and Be Able to Do

Whether you plan to train your own facilitators or involve them in external training, the following is a list of topics that are routinely covered in facilitator training before the first class or community event takes off. Online facilitators

- **Create a supportive environment that promotes trust and appropriate risk taking.** Professional growth often requires reflecting on current understandings and practices and considering whether and how to change them. This level of growth is challenging, and effective facilitators will establish a culture where the learners feel comfortable taking risks and trying new things.
- **Set norms and expectations for participation and maintain schedules.** Some people are very literal in terms of their participation and really want to know when, how often, and how much they have to participate. Help facilitators gather examples or develop guidelines to support people with these concerns.
- **Model appropriate communications.** Besides modeling accepted Netiquette standards, facilitators may need training in different expectations for communication and knowing what to do when communication goes off target. In the world of instant messaging and texting, many learners expect immediate responses to questions and may not use appropriate language for an academic setting—at first. Facilitators need to learn how to set expectations, such as replying to e-mails within 24 or 48 hours, and how text can be misinterpreted and what to do when it is. They will need strategies for dealing with inappropriate communications as well as with noncommunication, such as going offline and using the phone to address individuals personally.
- **Facilitate deep communication and interaction.** As mentioned earlier, much facilitator training focuses on how to promote deeper responses to discussions. Facilitators need to participate in online discussions and need examples or models for forming strong prompts. Facilitators may also need strategies for developing different groupings and promoting student reflection.
- **Actively engage participants in appropriate learning opportunities.** Facilitators benefit by having multiple examples of what is considered an acceptable outcome and appropriate behavior. Unfortunately, plagiarism using digital materials is a common concern, and good facilitators can design activities that rely less on copy-and-paste and more on interpretation, evaluation, and justification. A tremendous benefit of a highly skilled facilitator is the ability to differentiate the experience for the learners, whether providing flexible options in terms of activities, products, or technologies used to create them.
- **Direct participants to relevant resources and explain how to use them appropriately.** You don't have to expect your learners to access all information from your course content alone. You can incorporate other materials and technologies routinely used in professional learning, including print-based information. Facilitators need to know what resources are available, including online libraries, research databases, webconferencing software, or other technologies, as well as how learners can access them.

(Continued)

(Continued)

- **Skillfully apply strategies to promote professional learning.** Online professional development is learning foremost, and so effective facilitators will capitalize on what we know about supporting learning by promoting collaboration; creating products of consequence; promoting higher order cognition like solving complex, real-world problems; and modeling inquiry-based strategies to encourage participants to develop self-directed learning strategies that will support a lifetime of learning.
- **Routinely monitor participation and provide prompt feedback.** Because there's less tangible feedback online, learners in these settings often crave more opportunities for feedback. Online learners may check grades or other feedback multiple times, even though they know it's updated only once a week. An effective facilitator should also be able to determine when someone is falling behind and quickly put strategies into place for getting him or her back on target. If someone is routinely late or doesn't participate in the first few weeks, you're likely to lose him or her. A skilled facilitator is your best strategy for preventing this from happening.
- **Follow approved procedures, reporting to administrators when necessary.** Your online facilitators need to know what is and isn't their obligation. Are they supposed to keep learners on task? What do they do if they aren't? What about other issues related to academic integrity, like plagiarism? Let your online facilitators know the expected procedures and consequences for these settings and how to document their efforts. Documentation is critical, but you need to show them how to do it according to your established procedures.
- **Manage responsibilities and time well.** In the beginning, facilitators may spend more time than expected getting used to their role. They'll have to juggle events and obligations to find an appropriate schedule where they are available for the learners and provide relevant and timely feedback. You may want to help online facilitators create virtual "office hours" and provide guidance or actual job aids to help them keep up with the required workload and desired schedule.

Box 6.3 Learning From Experience: Creating Powerful Online Learning

Organization: Created by EdLabGroup, now offered by Peer-Ed

Contact: Matt Huston, Director of Online Learning

URL: www.peer-ed.com

Date First Implemented: 2007

Audience: K–12 educators, most in the Northwest (Washington, Oregon, Montana, Idaho)

Need: *What Was the Initial Trigger?*

Huston reports that in the Northwest region, where he is currently located, there was a growing interest in providing online learning, whether completely online or in a hybrid format. Huston combined his current work with the Microsoft Peer Coaching Program with his knowledge about and experience with developing rigorous online learning to create this 6-week professional development course to address this interest.

Intended Outcomes:

The course is intended to help educators understand how to develop online learning of their own. The vision for the course includes the following four expectations. Participants would

1. learn how to be online learners through participation,

2. learn how to be online designers using a hands-on approach and gain comfort and skill in using an LMS,

3. use web-based resources as they designed their courses, and

4. engage with one another and be encouraged to use the underlying understanding-based course design principles when they built their own courses.

Incentives:

Participants can receive credit in the form of clock hours or, for an additional fee, university credit. Certificates of completion are provided. Participants are also given a course in Moodle to practice with during the class that they can then take with them and load on a different Moodle server after completing the professional development.

Instructional Design Considerations:

The course was developed using Understanding by Design (UBD) and incorporated principles from Teaching for Understanding to develop content and help the participants come to a clearer understanding of their own learning. The use of these principles can help participants subsequently create activities in their own courses that draw upon higher levels of cognition that go beyond recall and identification.

Because of his experience with the Concord Consortium, Huston incorporates facilitated collaboration and considers it a critical component of the course design. Every week in the 6-week course featured one, two, or three significant collaborative activities. Initially, most of these were discussion; towards the end of the course, as participants spend more time building their own courses, the collaboration is more likely to focus around design and content choices, with one or a few trusted colleagues offering feedback.

(Continued)

(Continued)

Lessons Learned:

Based on his experience, Huston offered the following design advice: "Be sure to budget time and resources, and do additional learning on your own part as needed" for each of the following key elements:

1. Assessing your participants' needs carefully

2. Working with clients (or potential participants if there are no formal clients) on the course goals and objectives

3. Writing, testing, revising, and arranging compelling activities that are just-in-time for your participants

4. Designing a simple, consistent, pleasing interface in the LMS you are using

5. Assessing your participants' progress continually

Evaluation:

Each 6-week course concludes with a participant evaluation that asks for qualitative data on their experience in the course. These evaluations have been quite positive, with an 80+% satisfaction rating.

In the winter of 2009–2010, Huston surveyed 30 of the participants who took the course between 2008 and 2009 and asked longer term evaluative questions such as, "Did the course impact your teaching? If no, why not? If yes, how did it impact your teaching, and how do you know the course had that impact?" The results were widely varied but revealed several important findings that both reassured Huston that participants were using material and practices from the course and provided some suggestions for further revising the course to best meet teachers' needs.

See the book's companion website for more information about the profiled programs. **www.corwin.com/rossonlinepd**

Marketing and Registration

Needless to say, if you've waited this long to get the word out, you're not likely to have too many people banging on your virtual door to take your online professional development. Instead, as suggested in Chapter 3, begin your marketing campaign early in the development phase. As you're closing in on your launch, however, your marketing should go into high gear and build up to a bang at your launch. Use course materials, like sample courses or activities, especially if they use the media from your offerings, as they become available to give your potential audience members a better idea of what to expect. Address all the questions about basic system requirements, incentives and compensation, and issues addressed in this section about policies for participation.

After your launch, consider means to gather input from participants. As Barbara Treacy from EDC notes, "The participants are our best marketers." This idea was repeated by several other online providers. It's relatively easy to gather data online through survey software that will allow you to collect participant reactions to your system. Treacy notes that if you can get feedback that the technology didn't get in the way, that your participants really learned, or that they enjoyed the community and the experience, it can go a long way.

You'll also likely need a process in place that allows potential audience members to register for your online professional development. Will they be able to do it online? If fees are required, what payment options will you support? Automating your registration process as much as possible will save you time and money. Some LMS will allow participants to register through your system, including signing up and paying for courses, and perhaps even getting on a waiting list and being notified when a course is ready to be launched. If you plan to make these transactions online, make sure you follow e-commerce protocols for the secure transfer of payment and user information. If you don't plan to automate the registration process, do set up a system that provides *immediate* feedback to your participants. They won't want to wait to hear back from you. At the very least, consider having an auto-responder sent to anyone who registers that indicates when he or she can expect to hear from you—and you really need to respond within one business day. With so many commercial interactions completely web-based now, few people are satisfied with the delay that human interaction imposes.

PUTTING THE PIECES TOGETHER

You've got all the pieces to launch your online professional development system. While it's tempting to start this process by thinking about the technologies, considering your vision and mission, conducting a gap analysis, and knowing the requirements of your content can make your technology selection more effective. And once selected, it will be easier to put into place all the human systems, like training and marketing, that are necessary to make it work. Evaluation, which is the focus of Chapter 7, cannot be emphasized enough, so consider the methods and strategies you will use for checks and balances as you develop your system. Formative evaluation is built into most instructional design models, but also do some reality checks along the way as you develop policies and practices and as you select technologies.

It's at this point that you can make much more reasonable predictions about how much it will cost to implement your online professional development system. Throughout all of the steps of the framework, you've been encouraged to consider the action steps required to be successful and the people and resources necessary to conduct those action steps. For years, I've use the simple matrix at the bottom of Box 6.4: "Take Action: Putting All the Pieces Together" to develop timelines for projects with budgets up to several hundred thousand dollars. It is a simple and effective way to map out a timeline and determine if you have the appropriate resources—people, materials, and money—to meet your goals. Note that the vision and mission are listed on the form, because I think it's important to keep your eyes on your goals.

Box 6.4 Take Action: Putting All the Pieces Together

Vision *(the broad view one to three years from now)*:

Mission *(desired outcomes)*:

| Year 1 | Year 3 | Year 5 |

Development Timeline:

| Gap Analysis | Content OR Content Specifications | Technology Specifications |

Human Resource Issues

(Policies, Training, Marketing and Registration, Formative Evaluation)

Action Step	Persons Responsible	Timeframe	Necessary Resources

You will have personnel costs and material costs—some one-time costs for start-up and some reoccurring. Most organizations have formulas to quickly determine the cost of personnel based on the number of hours or days required for each person involved, plus any required travel. These usually include benefits associated with those salaries and may or may not include a percentage for indirect costs, such as rent, utilities, and support staff. Your total costs will include these personnel costs, as well as material resources and external services. You may need to buy a server or other hardware to get started, or you may use a hosted service, in which case you'll have an annual fee. Don't forget contractors, like SMEs, and instructional designers, media developers, and evaluators. This matrix gives you a place to list all of those components to apply those formulas or otherwise project costs. If the Person Responsible is internal, project the number of hours or days necessary, list that time in the Necessary Resources, and insert it into your formula. Travel costs, if necessary, should be entered separately. If the Person Responsible is external, you're likely to be able to put a total cost for contracted services in the Necessary Resources, which becomes a line item in your budget. When Action Steps include purchasing or licensing equipment or content, those costs go into the Necessary Resources. Depending on how big your project is, you may want to break the matrix down for each component of the development timeline.

CELEBRATION

It's pretty exciting when you flip that switch and your professional development program finally goes online. It's not really as simple as flipping a switch, but try to emphasize the importance of the occasion. Celebration is important. Consider having a launch party with those who have helped to get your system up and running. Send out notices to everyone once everything goes live. Press releases can also be timed to coordinate with some physical event that heightens the interest and awareness of your launch. Even if you haven't gone through all of the steps in the OPD Framework, you're likely to have involved a lot of people and spent a good deal of your own time getting to the point of launching your online professional development. Congratulations!

Unlike the others, this chapter ends with Celebration, not a Conclusion, because you need to take that time to acknowledge a job well done. But you're not through. I hope your program is successful and continues to grow from year to year, but after your launch, you'll need to continue to monitor your program, determine new needs that crop up, and ultimately answer the question, Did it work? I have suggestions on how to do that in Chapter 7.

7 Did It Work?

After all you have to go through to design and deliver online professional development, you want to know if it worked, right? It's certainly a question I'm concerned about, but you have to know what the "it" is before you can answer that question. Hopefully, the framework will help you better determine what your "it" is so you can figure out how well "it" worked. Evaluation is too often addressed last, which makes it seem like an add-on, but evaluation should be embedded throughout your development process. It isn't something that happens just at the end of a project. The OPD Decision Matrix encourages you to focus your online professional development on outcomes and think of the data you'll need to collect to measure them from the outset. Benchmarks or milestones in your timeline will help you to evaluate your progress towards these goals throughout the entire design and development process. Once you're up and running, it can be convenient to focus on the evaluation of your project each year, since schools usually work in year-long cycles. This will help you to determine whether your needs have changed or how your project might change to better accommodate a (hopefully) growing audience.

This chapter explores some evaluation considerations during your development process and also evaluates each of the potential outcomes originally presented in the OPD Decision Matrix, from recording and reporting usage through schoolwide changes in practice (as noted in Figure 7.1). This is not a thorough treatise on how or why to evaluate but, rather, suggestions for evaluating the outcomes you've selected for your online professional development. There are also a few things to consider if you're interested in doing a cost-benefit analysis of your online professional development. Knowing whether you've attained your outcomes is a critical component of determining if it was worth the cost. Finally, this chapter concludes with a story from my experience that I believe is a good example to illustrate the framework in this book. It also shows how data informed that process and helped it to grow and evolve over time.

FORMATIVE EVALUATION

In the Content Development Timeline in Chapter 4, Box 4.7, there's a step to "Evaluate system (revise)." That's a pretty brief mention of what is usually a more involved process. Instructional design models usually include a feedback

Figure 7.1 Data from your evaluations feed into the next iteration of your plan.

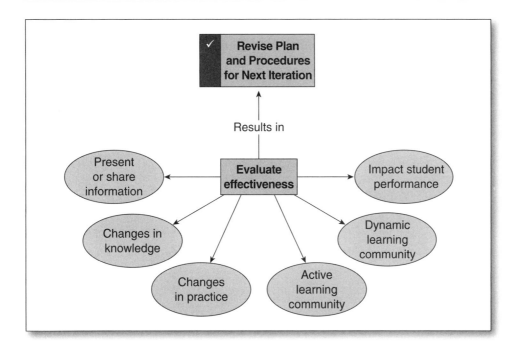

loop that involves evaluation throughout the development process. When evaluation is incorporated in this way, to inform the development process before it's too late to make changes, it's normally referred to as *formative evaluation*. Depending on the instructional design process you use or the quality assurance process you may have to follow, formative evaluation can occur at different times, such as after the initial content is developed, once sample activities are completed, or when media elements are available in a prototype form. The idea, though, is to gather data to make sure the project is on target and is of the highest quality possible so that you don't get to the end and have an inferior product. That's when the dollars can really mount up.

It's become much easier to conduct formative evaluations with online products as you can post parts or entire beta versions of content, activities, videos, animations, or sites for review. It also makes it much easier to obtain feedback from the most critical people concerned—your audience. Having input from experts, like content or media experts, is important, but the most important input comes from the people who are going to use the product. If they don't like it or can't use it, it doesn't matter how accurate or important your content is. Your return on investment will be zero. You really don't need too many people to participate, either. Usability expert Jakob Nielsen (2000) suggests that after five people, you really don't learn much unique information about your product. He recommends running as many small usability tests as you can with no more than five people.

It's helpful to give users a couple of specific tasks to complete and maybe one they come up with on their own. Don't ask them to review *everything*! It can be overwhelming. You have to collect information from them, like what they did, what they found, what they hoped to find, and if there was anything they wanted to do or find that wasn't possible. You can do that through interviews by phone or webconferencing or online surveys. You may want to have people complete a questionnaire or checklist as they are completing their review so you get their immediate impressions.

Don't overlook the opportunity to conduct formative evaluations in person and actually observe people interacting with your content and media and pick up reactions that you can't observe online. It's more costly, but you get better information. You can videotape the session or use screencasting software to actually track what the users interact with on-screen. Another helpful practice is a *think-aloud*, which is similar to the self-reflection process teachers use with students in many classrooms. Basically, the test users describe what they are thinking as they navigate through your user test. With screencasting software and a microphone, perhaps using a headset to block out distractions, you can capture your users' actions and a narrative of what they are thinking all in a single file. Talking out loud about what you're thinking is not something we usually encourage people to do, at least not in public, so if your users have never done a think-aloud before, it's good to have them do a practice run with a warm-up activity first.

While you have access to them, try to gather as much data as possible, as long as it's helpful. The rule in data collection is collect all that you need, but no more. Don't overburden your test audience. You might want to use them again for a different project. You can conduct individual or focus group interviews with your test users after they've completed the test, although you need to be careful once people get into groups, as they can become swayed by dominant personalities. I'm not suggesting people will make things up, but they may not remember their brief interaction with your environment as well as they think they do. Triangulate findings with the actual user test data you collected, whether as a think-aloud or in response to a questionnaire or checklist.

Don't forget to budget for formative evaluation as you're developing your online professional development. Consider what kind of compensation or incentives your test users will require. If you're using teachers, what is the standard compensation they receive outside of the school day? Perhaps they might receive a free copy of materials you have created or access to your online system. Don't wait until the end to evaluate. Within the Content Development Timeline, each of the review steps could be considered opportunities for formative evaluation. You may not need outside expertise at all of these steps, but finding out your product isn't acceptable at what you thought was the end stage of development is far more costly than gathering input along the way.

It was once common to conduct a summative evaluation of a product at the end of the development phase, although with much digital content, there's no reason to consider a final version final. The summative evaluation step is one that was often conducted with standalone products and programs to ensure that the final product met required specifications, but the data collected in this type of evaluation is not used to revise the material. Instead, it's confirmation that you completed all that you set out to complete. That may not be necessary with online professional development. Some elements, like videos and multimedia simulations, may be difficult or costly to revise, but text and graphics may not be. You'll collect information throughout your delivery phase to evaluate your online professional development. That's when you'll really know if it worked or not. And if not, you can use that information to revise it. You'll also need to revise your content and activities over time, as new information is developed, new data is released, or new practices become popular. It can be pretty easy to do this with online content. Later in this chapter are examples of how to collect evaluation data so you can determine if it worked or not.

IS IT BETTER THAN FACE-TO-FACE?

Another great question, right? Well, as someone who works in educational technology, I'm going to take a stand for my fellow tech compatriots and say that while technologists are always being asked whether using technology is better than "the traditional method," it's the wrong question to ask . . . for two reasons. The first is that it's almost impossible to answer definitively. What is online professional development? Is it a series of 1-hour synchronous webinars you had on monitoring school culture? Is it a 10-week asynchronous course on effective math pedagogy? Is it a series of moderated discussions held in an online learning community? There should be enough examples in this book to prove there is no one thing called "online professional development." It's all these things, and more. But there's also no one thing as "the traditional method." What does *that* mean? Is it a full-day, preconference workshop on differentiating instruction? Is it a 2-hour learning community meeting every other week? Or is it the keynote speaker who presents to all of the teachers in a district the week before school starts?

The researcher in me knows that when you want to compare things, you have to be very careful about deciding what to compare and how you do it. You have to isolate the things you want to compare (your treatment) and control the other factors (hopefully through randomization) so you can have some confidence your treatment really did work. There has been a lot of emphasis on implementing more rigorous research studies in education, but we've made limited progress towards that goal, especially when comparing online professional development to the traditional method, whatever those two things mean. Most schools aren't set up to support rigorous research studies, but they can support the collection of evidence to demonstrate how well a chosen method achieved the intended outcomes. The "did it work" question is much more manageable than the "is it better than" question. I remain a member of the school that believes in the statement made by Richard Clark in 1983: "The best current evidence is that media are mere vehicles that deliver instruction but don't influence student achievement any more than the truck that delivers our groceries causes changes in our nutrition" (p. 446). It still sparks some controversy, but it supports the idea that it's not the technology that matters, but how you use it.

We haven't really built much evidence about what works in professional development regardless of the delivery method. And that's my second reason for suggesting the comparison isn't a valid one. How do you know what you're doing now works? In a recent study funded by the U.S. Department of Education (Yoon, Duncan, Lee, Scarloss, & Shapley, 2007), only nine studies about professional development from a pool of more than 1,300 were found to meet the criteria for being a rigorous research study. Nine! Of those selected, none was at the middle or high school level—not because the researchers didn't look at these levels, but because none of the research at these levels made the cut. Neither did anything published between 2004 and 2006. That's *after* No Child Left Behind raised the bar for scientifically based research in education. I suggest that instead of asking if it's better, focus on the "did it work" question, regardless of the format. You can answer that question, no matter what your online (or other) professional development looks like, and it's probably more useful since you've probably gone and developed your system anyway.

Be a Part of the Solution

I know, I know, "If you can't say something nice. . . ." Well, I can. Ironically, when people start to ask me the "is it better than" question, it promotes conversation about how they know what they're doing now works. Very often, they don't. Very few people can point to data that show the effectiveness of their current professional development efforts. Very often, we do things because we've always done them that way and we're already set up for it. We know what to expect and we have the processes in place. Simply by voicing the concern that online professional development must be of some quality provides the opportunity to think about the effectiveness of *all* professional development and to have conversations about what that would look like, regardless of how it's delivered.

For many years now, I've served on teams that visit schools to gather data about different kinds of programs, usually technology integration projects. Very often, it's my job to review school improvement plans, and it's interesting to see how they have changed over the past decade or so. There's much more language about collecting and using data in the planning templates, but the kind of data reported on many school improvement plans is often of little value, especially when it comes to professional development. Repeatedly, the justification for dollars requested for professional development is improved student achievement. And what's the most common data collected to evaluate the effectiveness of that professional development? A sign-in sheet at a workshop. It's a big stretch to think that mere attendance is going to help you improve student achievement. We can do better.

Very often there may be evaluation questionnaires that are distributed at events that focus on whether people did or didn't like the professional development. Sometimes there will be questions that ask whether you thought the presenter was knowledgeable or used appropriate activities, or whether you plan to use what you have learned in your own practice. This is the first critical level of professional development evaluation that Guskey (2000) describes as *participants' reactions*. This type of data is easy to collect and is a step beyond simply signing an attendance sheet. Data of this type that measures satisfaction may be helpful for improving the way you design and deliver future events for similar audiences, but Guskey suggests we need to go further if we want to get to the ultimate outcome of professional development, which is improving student performance.

Guskey's next level is *participants' learning.* You can gather this data in a variety of formats, including objective-based assessments as well as participation in activities that require your participants to demonstrate new knowledge and skills. They can write responses, review and create case studies, participate in a simulation, or document their learning in many other ways. Those assessment activities I encouraged you to develop first in your design process can also be used to evaluate participant learning. Above participants' learning is the level of *organization support and change.* At this level, you want to determine the impact your professional development had on the organizations from which your participants were drawn. You won't be able to determine this level of evaluation without the buy-in from decision makers at those organizations, which is another reason I've encouraged you to get their input from the beginning. In a school, you may need to review documents or interview faculty to determine if policies or practices related to your professional development were implemented. Organization support and change can also be measured by changes in resource allocation, including whether teachers or others are given time to work together on implementing and monitoring their new knowledge and skills. This level of evaluation would be especially well suited to organizations adopting a learning community model.

Your participants can demonstrate they've learned new knowledge and skills, and their organizations may provide support for using them, but that doesn't mean they've actually put them into practice. Data collection at this level, which Guskey calls *participants' use of new knowledge and skills,* is more cumbersome to collect than the earlier levels, and is one that few evaluations get to. No group that I've worked with has provided the resources to obtain data at this level beyond self-reported data, but be careful about using self-reported data to make claims of true changes in practice. Participants may truly believe they are using new knowledge and skills by using resources provided during professional development, but they may not realize how rarely they really are doing so or that they're doing it without true fidelity. Generally, if you want to determine this information, someone has to observe your participants, and those observers have to know what to look for. Developing appropriate observation instruments, and training those observers and getting them into schools, can require significant resources.

The top level of Guskey's five critical levels of professional development evaluation is *student learning outcomes,* in which he includes attitudes, skills, and behaviors in addition to cognitive outcomes. There's a lot of this data available in most schools, but it can be difficult to link to your professional development to show direct impact. Still, it's undoubtedly the most common outcome expressed by those wanting to develop professional development, of any type. Guskey and others (e.g., Desimone, 2009) note that professional development that is intended to reach this type of outcome should be focused directly on student learning goals from the outset. Be specific. Most school improvement plans I review set vague goals, like improving student math scores on the state assessment by 5%, or increasing the percentage of students scoring proficient or advanced. These are nebulous goals. You have to determine the critical skills they are not mastering in order to get more of your students scoring higher in math, if that is indeed your goal. If a majority of your students demonstrate difficulty with numbers and operations with fractions, your professional development should be targeted at helping teachers address number and operations with fractions.

MEASURING YOUR OUTCOMES

With those levels in mind, consider how you can obtain some of that data to support the outcomes for your online professional development. You may indeed want to improve student performance, but you might have to focus on outcomes lower on the OPD Decision Matrix first. If you can demonstrate teachers are indeed using pedagogical methods and resources shown to be effective for improving student learning, you've taken a big step towards the ultimate goal. Again, there's not enough room here to describe how to develop your evaluation. There are excellent books on the topic as well as Program Evaluation Standards developed by the Joint Committee on Standards for Educational Evaluation that provide guidance on developing evaluations and using the data from them. There is room, however, to help you determine how you can collect the data you need to support the type of evaluation you have designed based on your desired outcomes. For some examples of how online professional development programs across the country incorporate evaluation in their programs, review Box 7.4: "A Spectrum of Evaluation Data and Practices."

An interesting point to consider is one brought up by Melinda George at PBS. She surmises that with the emphasis on moving from the notion of *highly qualified* to *highly effective* teachers, professional development providers are going to have to collect data that demonstrates their programs help teachers become more effective, "not that they've just finished a course." That's an especially important consideration for your data collection efforts, especially for growing your program. You may still need to start small, with some foundational outcome levels that you can achieve in a year or so, but as you move forward consider how to collect data from outcomes higher up the OPD Decision Matrix and weave them into your plan.

Each outcome level in the OPD Decision Matrix builds upon the previous; therefore, data collection methods for each level can also be used in higher levels. For example, since measuring changes in schoolwide practice can include looking at changes in the behaviors of individuals, you can use similar observation methods described in the earlier outcome.

Did We Get the Word Out?

It may be important for you to launch your online professional development targeting outcomes related to presenting or sharing information. This is a good entry point for some programs, as you develop the infrastructure and participant awareness and skills necessary to get enough buy-in to grow your program. It can also teach you valuable lessons, including feedback about your infrastructure that you can use to reach higher outcome levels in the future. Just be reasonable about the outcomes you can achieve at this level.

Technology is very useful for collecting usage data, as websites and learning management systems (LMS) routinely include analytic software to measure which material on your site is accessed. You can't really determine the effectiveness of this material, but you can identify materials that seem to be the most popular or used. Common analytics include page hits, views, and visitors. Views are more useful than hits, as views imply that someone opened all of the information on a page, including graphics or other media elements. There's no guarantee they read or understood everything, however. Hits are more granular and are usually related to each element on the page. So a page with four images and a movie on it can garner six hits, one for the page, one for the movie, and one for each of the images, but that is considered just one page view. With views and hits, it may take some effort to determine whether each is by a unique visitor to your site. Using cookies, a piece of software code that identifies a person's computer by IP address, can help. However, people can choose to accept or reject cookies, so it's not a foolproof method. You can also usually drill down to statistics on specific pages and media elements, like videos or simulations you might put on your site. This helps you to determine not only what content is most visited, but what kinds of elements seem to be most popular.

Some analytic software can help determine how users found or came to your site, what they did while they were there, and the sites they visited afterwards. They can also determine where your users come from, geographically, again usually based on the IP address of the computer they used. Some will report what kind of search terms visitors used to find your site as well as those they entered while on your site, giving you an idea not only of the type of content your users are looking for, but whether you actually provide it. This also helps you to determine if your visitors use different terms to describe your content, which you can then incorporate into your site so that it's more likely to be found during searches. You can also gather data from any marketing efforts you might use such as online advertisements or sponsored links in search engines.

In addition to use, you can gather affective data, such as satisfaction data, from people who visit or use your site. Online surveys and polls can be embedded in a variety of ways. Visitors can respond to daily or weekly polls that can help you to determine how to improve your site or what new features or content you might want to offer. Polls are quick and easy. Surveys are a bit more intrusive, but they will be tolerated better by participants who are required to visit your site. You can include surveys or questionnaires as part of a sequence of instruction, or link it in several ways, including a persistent site survey available at all times through your site's navigation as well as pop-up ads or rollover surveys that are layered over content. Unless the survey is required to demonstrate attendance or completion, you may want to give users the ability to opt out of surveys.

If you require users to create an account to access some or all of your content, you have a ready means for collecting follow-up data through interviews, focus groups, or additional online surveys. Again, unless participation is required for employment or other reasons, give your users the ability to "opt in" to follow-up evaluation. Don't assume they'll want to hear from you just because they created an account on your site. Focus groups work best in person so that you can gauge people's physical reactions and incorporate relevant probing questions, but you may want to consider using webconferencing software to cut costs. A follow-up survey, administered by phone, e-mail, or online, may be longer than those embedded on your site, but be careful to have reasonable expectations of how long someone will be willing to participate. Tell them how long you think it will take and provide cues during the survey so they can gauge their progress. For any of these options, even those on your site, you may want to provide some sort of incentive for participation. Even the chance to win a gift card can increase participation.

Did Our Participants Learn?

Common online assessment options include forced-choice formats like true-false, multiple choice, matching, fill-in-the-blank, short open-ended responses, and essays. Most of these formats are supported by common LMS, web-based forms, or actual testing applications. But digital technologies provide a wide range of alternative assessment options to draw upon. You may have participants participate in a simulation, either one that is an immersive multimedia element or one in which they role-play with other participants. The media you use for a simulated task really doesn't have to be that complex if you don't have access to a media developer. Participants could follow a series of linked text and media elements, such as listening to or reading a short story about a student and then following a series of branched questions related to identifying appropriate pedagogies designed to help the student. Actions can be tracked and feedback provided along each step. Open-ended or performance-based assessments require some form of human resource in terms of scoring. Just as in classrooms, checklists or rubrics can be used to evaluate these alternative assessment options, but your rater will require training, and you may want to take steps to ensure that different raters score with consistency. See Box 7.1: "Alternative Assessment Options" for some additional ideas.

Box 7.1 Alternative Assessment Options

- Analyzing and proposing a solution to a problem using digital data sets and real-world information
- Conducting reflections on personal learning goals through a journal, blog, or website
- Creating a digital portfolio
- Creating a digital story
- Demonstrating and recording new skills via digital audio or video
- Developing a concept map to show your understanding and how it might have changed

- Giving a presentation with multimedia support
- Labeling, listing, or sequencing information
- Observing others using a protocol of framework
- Participating in an online discussion forum
- Providing teaching examples, such as lesson plans, activities, or student work samples
- Reviewing or creating text or multimedia case studies
- Using a checklist, rating scale, or rubric

Digital technologies provide options, but you may need to make some compromises. I worked with a client whose original goal was to change teacher practice, but they didn't have the funds to visit classrooms to determine if practices actually changed as a result of the professional development. We had to deliver the assessments from the LMS and so were limited primarily to forced-choice responses (because we didn't have the funds to hire someone to score open-ended responses, either). But we were creative and used the medium as best we could. Teachers were learning to use different assessment techniques with students, so we videotaped teachers using the assessment practices with students at different skill levels and had the participants identify the types of assessments and the skills being addressed, and rate student performances in the videos. Their responses were multiple-choice options, but they did demonstrate new knowledge based on *someone* applying the new skill.

Measuring *changes* in knowledge implies that you determine what your participants know and can do before the professional development. Forced-choice pretests and posttests are common methods for doing this, and a pretest, posttest, and delayed-posttest design allows you to measure indications of long-term retention of information. A good objective-based assessment presented in a forced-choice format takes time to develop because the questions have to appropriately address all of the required learning outcomes of the content. You also have to develop credible distracters, hopefully ones that will identify common misconceptions that can be used in a formative manner to guide learners back to necessary instruction. Consider including this type of assessment creation as part of the requirements for your subject-matter expert during content development, as a thorough understanding of the content is required.

Many LMSs include the ability to present pretests and posttests that are automatically scored and reported to individuals, the facilitators, or administrators. They can also support learning, where participants can see responses they got incorrect and are directed back into the content for additional review and practice. A well-designed pretest can help to determine what prior knowledge and skills participants bring to the learning and can place them appropriately in the content sequence, skipping over content they've already mastered. This is a benefit of using learning objects, where each learning object addresses a discrete set of well-defined objectives. Just be sure your pretest addresses all critical information so no one misses the opportunity to learn and practice knowledge and skills necessary down the road. Incorporating this type of branching, though, may need to be approved or supported by policy. Clients looking for courses based on "seat time" may be reluctant to use this kind of a pretest, but it's more respectful of the needs of the learner.

Did Our Participants Change Their Practice?

Collecting evidence of effectiveness at this level can be more difficult. You have a lot of flexibility in the first two outcomes. When determining whether participant practices have changed, you're either at the mercy of questionable data or you have to actually go into the classrooms or schools somehow and observe your learners.

You can use technology to collect a range of self-reported data—data that is questionable in terms of its validity because people often overestimate their use and skills when self-reporting. For example, when conducting research about online practice with a large lecture class during my training, I was able to track how often different features on the class website were used by the students. In a corresponding survey, students in the class reported using some of the website features multiple times every week when the actual usage data clearly showed they did not. Similarly, Al Byers from the National Science Teachers Association (NSTA) reported that every single participant in a study on the use of NSTA's Learning Center reported they found the feature to e-mail a content expert as helpful, but only 15.6% of the participants actually used it. For more about this program, review Box 7.2: "Learning From Experience: The NSTA Learning Center." You can interview participants; have them fill out surveys or questionnaires; or have them keep a journal, website, or blog of their reflections, but without some tangible evidence, you may need to try other means to truly determine changes in participant practice.

The next step up is probably video recordings from participants, such as classroom videos. Teachers familiar with National Board Certification will be used to recording their classrooms, but it can be difficult for individuals to obtain high-quality video in a classroom. And by quality, I'm referring to the actions and reactions of the participants in the video rather than the lighting and audio. It can be difficult to set up a camera to determine if teachers are implementing new practices and materials correctly. If the camera is on a tripod, you often can't see the entire classroom; nor do you get close-ups on what the teacher and students are actually doing—especially the students. You may miss critical features that are off-camera or simply can't tell what's going on. If you can get an outside person to videotape, use a wireless microphone for the teacher and try to capture some of what the students do in reaction to teacher instruction. Also try to include samples of teacher and student work from the lesson as supporting data. There's also a concern that some teachers will practice a lesson in its entirety before they are videotaped and then "put on a show" for the camera, which again calls into question the validity of the data. Honest, I've seen some of these "performances."

To measure changes in practice, there's no substitute for observation. Many teachers are used to being observed throughout the year by principals, lead teachers, academic coaches, or others. If you want to capitalize on existing observation practices, you have to be sure that those people doing the observing are trained and knowledgeable and can correctly identify skills and knowledge that can be attributed to your professional development. So if you plan to have principals look for changes in practice during their walkthroughs, you not only need their buy-in, but you have to make sure they are trained or otherwise have the expertise needed to accurately complete the form. Even if they have the knowledge, they may need to understand your terminology. You have to be able to define and describe what you're looking for, and everyone has to have a similar understanding. You can help by providing sample checklists, observation, or walkthrough forms for those who will conduct the observations and practice them during the professional development to help them collect data accurately.

Depending on the scope of your project, you may want to send in trained observers who are external to the school or district in which your participants are drawn from. This is the most obtrusive and expensive method of data collection, but it provides the highest quality of data. Potential expenses are associated not only with travel and lodging, but the development of high-quality instruments and the training required to ensure the observers are skilled in collecting the data accurately.

If you're developing online professional development for an external funder, have the discussion with them up front about what kind of outcomes they expect and the steps and costs associated with providing that level of data. Evaluation is the component most likely to be cut during budget discussions. This can be, in part, because it's not always apparent what evaluators do or why it can take the time and effort required. Try to educate your funders about what you can provide and why it's important, but if the funds don't follow, be sure to inform them what kind of outcomes they can expect to monitor. If they want to see changes in participant practice, but they'll only pay for forced-choice responses, it's your obligation to let them know the limitations of that data and how it cannot provide adequate evidence for the outcomes they're seeking.

Box 7.2 Learning From Experience: The NSTA Learning Center

Organization: National Science Teachers Association (NSTA)

Contact: Al Byers, Assistant Executive Director, e-Learning and Government Partnerships

URL: http://learningcenter.nsta.org

Date First Implemented: 2008

Audience: K–20 science teachers

Need: *What Was the Initial Trigger?*

The original conception was to address the need for teachers to develop greater science content knowledge, an often reported national need, with a "just enough, just in time, just for me" model. The effort was designed to fill the niche between online summer institutes and the formal moderated online short courses NSTA offers four times a year.

Intended Outcomes:

The goal of the Learning Center is to provide access to numerous on-demand, self-directed, high-impact professional development resources and opportunities catering to educators' individual needs and learning preferences, as well as to provide a level of accountability for district administrators in order to support teachers' long-term professional growth over time. Overarching the Learning

Center's goals is the charge to establish a sustainable and scalable model of professional learning that is accessible to all of the nations' 3 million teachers of science, including content resources and tools to help effectively diagnose, plan, track, and document individual professional growth over time.

Incentives:

Incentives depend on the type of resource or opportunity in which one participates. Incentives may include continuing education units, graduate credits, certificates of completion, pass/fail certificates, release time, and stipends for some experiences.

Instructional Design Considerations:

NSTA employs current research and proven best practices in all the e-learning resources and opportunities it develops in partnership with its sponsors. For example, each Science Object is structured around a learning cycle modified for adult learners in the online environment. These objects are designed to challenge teachers to struggle with questions, observations, and simulations/representations of scientific phenomena and to apply their ideas in an inquiry-based approach espoused by the 1996 National Science Education Standards. The design of simulations is guided by research in the effective use of multimedia for instructional purposes and incorporates emerging research on cognitive load. The Learning Objects also include embedded and final assessments to provide teachers with feedback and a means to track their progress, incorporate research about how people learn, and include known preconceptions or misconceptions common in understanding certain science concepts.

Lessons Learned:

Correlating all the assets available in the Learning Center to the 50 state standards is a challenge. There are some technology means (e.g., crawlers) for tagging resources, but their alignment is not foolproof. At some point, human reviewers have to ensure accurate alignment to the standards.

Byers notes, "You do need a critical mass of learners to support rich and worthwhile online discussions, especially mailing lists, discussion boards, and the like. Having trained moderators to facilitate discourse and increase engagement is paramount to help foster a vibrant professional online learning community."

The success and impact varies with how well the materials are presented and supported in the states and districts that use them. Scheduling and aligning the professional development as part of a district's larger efforts is critical, which has implications for integrating online professional development into school calendars. NSTA has observed that teacher attitudes and learning are greater when the materials are truly incorporated into professional development plans with incentives and measurable milestones and include technical support and administrator buy-in. But, according to Byers, "if the online PD portal is presented simply as a URL that is forwarded via email with a password to a large number of teachers, the impact is less significant."

Evaluation:

NSTA has conducted one quasi-experimental project (Sherman, Byers, & Rapp, 2008) looking at a three-district pilot of self-directed electronic professional development. Teachers were able to access on-demand content that incorporated a high level of interactivity via embedded simulations, questions, and hands-on learning opportunities in a self-contained, 10-hour web module on force and motion. Using an independent pre- and post-assessment developed and administered online by Horizon Research, NSTA found significant gains in teacher content knowledge across all three participating districts and all participants.

An online survey of 41 teachers using the SciPack professional development program indicated significant improvement in confidence levels regarding their ability to teach concepts related to Newtonian force and motion after completing the self-directed web module. In addition, 98% of the teachers found the content relevant to their needs and the embedded simulations worthwhile to their learning. Additionally, 96% said they would recommend the modules to their colleagues.

A third-party evaluation used a two pretest-posttest, delayed-treatment control group design with random assignment involving 56 teachers across Grades 5–8 from a large urban school district who used two web modules. Results found significant gains in teacher learning, self-efficacy, and preparedness to teach the subject matter. Students taught by educators in both the treatment and control group showed significant gains in learning with students taught by teachers in the treatment group showing significantly higher gains than those in the control group.

See the book's companion website for more information about the profiled programs.   **www.corwin.com/rossonlinepd**

Did We Change Schoolwide Practice?

My placing this outcome at the highest level of the OPD Matrix differs somewhat from Guskey's (2000) levels of professional development evaluation. He places organization support and change third, but his levels are based on the evaluation measures. The OPD Decision Matrix is based on desired outcomes and how they are achieved in a technology-supported environment. The lower outcomes on the Matrix can be achieved through commonly available technologies and LMS and can be measured at the individual level. A learning community has a much greater social component, and successful online learning communities can be much more difficult to achieve. You can't be a community of one. I concur that a group of faculty members that increase their skills and knowledge and change their practice can have an impact on an organization, but purposeful and concentrated changes in organizational outcomes are more difficult to measure than changes in knowledge and practices with multiple individuals. All of the individuals in your group could show gains in skills and knowledge, but still have no impact on the organization. It depends on what your desired outcome is.

In an *active* learning community, participants receive significant direction and oversight to achieve goals usually prescribed by external forces. In essence, these are departments, committees, or entire faculties that are supported by online technologies. In some cases, active communities will grow and evolve into *dynamic* learning communities in which the members of the community are more proactive about the focus of the community's work and the methods they use to support it. To me, the key difference between the two is passion. Participation in a dynamic learning community is driven more by passion than compliance. No one's required to be in a dynamic learning community, or at least they shouldn't be. Both types of communities may make suggestions about what is best for the community or those the community serves. I'm not suggesting that active learning communities cannot impact student performance; however, they are more likely to follow prescriptive processes and procedures to conduct their work. Both types of communities may have formal processes they follow, but active learning communities are usually more reactive and dynamic learning communities are proactive.

In schools, online learning communities may conduct lesson plan studies, create and monitor common assessments, or craft components of a school improvement plan. These outcomes generate many different types of artifacts and data you can collect to determine if online learning communities are working, especially if you have developed and organized your online environment well. Active learning communities often create artifacts such as minutes and reports, and their information may be pulled into schoolwide or districtwide documents or plans. Dynamic learning communities are more likely to explore and experiment with new strategies, materials, and methods, and their outcomes may include reflections on practice and experience. In both groups, any type of online interaction, such as discussion lists or archives of audio- or webconferences, provide additional data that can be evaluated for the quality of interaction, relevance to the topic, and level of participation, but this type of qualitative analysis is time-consuming and comes at a higher cost. The community members may also be asked to respond to polls and questionnaires, perhaps reflecting on the quality of the experience, the relevance of the topics discussed, or suggestions for future topics or methods of organization.

Did We Impact Student Performance?

There's no shortage of student data in schools that can be collected to determine impact on student performance, and please do incorporate multiple data sources. Too often, educators focus on a single data point—student performance on a state-based assessment—and ignore the many different kinds of data that can be used to monitor student learning. Depending on the focus of your online professional development, you may not be addressing skills or knowledge specifically addressed on the state-based assessment and therefore can't show a plausible connection between the two. Achievement data is the most common student data collected, but you may be able to collect data related to attendance, behavior, attitudes, and satisfaction. No matter which data you collect, student data is protected under laws such as the Family Educational Rights and Privacy Act (FERPA), and you must follow appropriate guidelines to obtain and use student data. Very often, you will need a process to obtain student data that has been stripped of identification, which can make it difficult to demonstrate the impact of your specific online professional development. If your data is reported at the school level but not all teachers in the school participated in your online professional development, there's not much connection you can make.

When you're collecting achievement data, consider the many other potential sources, such as benchmark tests, teacher-generated assessments, teacher observation forms, formative assessment practices, and student work output from activities, presentations, projects, and writings. These can come in the form of research papers, multimedia presentations, online blogs or journals, lab handbooks, reflections, products created in virtual environments, portfolios, or student performances that can be captured by digital audio or video. You may also want to develop and provide measures of student performance that your participants can incorporate in their classrooms and schools. Again, determine appropriate data collection methods for the formats you use. In order to be compliant with the Children's Internet Protection Act, students under 13 cannot provide personal information on a website without consent from parents or guardians.

When grades or scores are not associated with artifacts, you may need to include some form of checklist or rubric to evaluate the quality of student work. Perhaps these can be incorporated into your online professional development and your participants will develop the skills to adequately score student work during that experience. Using trained external evaluators can increase the quality of the evaluation of the student works, but it obviously increases cost. The additional costs may be acceptable, however, when you're truly seeking the impact of your online professional development on student performance.

There's no reason that you can't take steps to collect data related to student performance regardless of your intended outcomes, but heed the advice from Guskey (2000) and others and ensure your online professional development is clearly focused on specific student learning outcomes and the data you collect is directly linked to those outcomes. It's not that you can't determine impact on student performance in addition to observing changes in practice; in fact, I hope that those changes in practice would be specifically targeted at student learning. Just be sure to collect relevant data and know how your online professional development is specifically linked to those outcomes. Using several different sources of related data—often referred to as multiple measures—will make your case stronger.

Box 7.3 Take Action:
Measuring Your Desired Outcomes

Once you determine your outcomes, you can then consider the data you'll have to collect to determine if your "it" worked. Based on the outcomes you determined earlier, identify data you plan to collect and who is responsible for that data, whether a network administrator who will provide analytic data or guidance counselors or others who provide student data. Identify multiple sources of data to try to get a better idea of how well your online professional development worked.

	Data to Collect	Person Responsible
Impact student performance		
Dynamic learning community		
Active learning community		
Changes in practice		
Changes in knowledge		
Present or share information		

Box 7.4 A Spectrum of Evaluation
Data and Practices

You can collect many different kinds of evaluation data by different methods. Review this short, and by no means complete, list of evaluation methods by online professional development providers across the country to determine a few approaches you might consider.

- Atomic Learning conducts a yearly customer survey of their user base that helps them determine new features and enhancements. They also conduct focus groups in the product development process to provide formative feedback.
- Education Development Center (EDC) uses pre- and post-surveys and conducts annual evaluation reports. EDC recently completed an evaluation report over multiple years of participation in multiple states titled *e-Learning for Educators. Effects of On-line Professional Development on Teachers and Their Students* that is available from the project website.
- In addition to participating in the e-Learning for Educators grant program, eMints has its own evaluation survey that has undergone approval through

an Internal Review Board (IRB). The current model is pre/post and then a follow-up 6 months later. Common questions include, "Did you apply it in your classroom? Did you find it useful? Would you take another course?"

- All participants in LEARN NC courses must complete an end-of-course survey in order to receive their certificates. It is not a survey focused on skills and abilities but dispositions about content and pedagogy. A 6-month follow-up is also administered, and LEARN NC has newly implemented a precourse survey that asks the same questions.

- All PBS TeacherLine courses are project-based, with activities that result in something tangible. Often, the activities will build to a comprehensive whole rather than a series of isolated activities. All courses have performance objectives, and every objective is assessed through the use of a rubric. Multiple-choice assessments are not used.

- Teachers who participate in Escambia County's SLEEC take participation surveys. Second Life offers unique tools to support data collection and evaluation, such as linking to free Google Docs. SLOODLE tools let you send data to the open-source LMS Moodle from Second Life.

- Virtual High School uses external evaluators. Lessons from the original evaluation were compiled in the book *The Virtual High School: Teaching Generation V* (Zucker, Kozma, Yarnall, Marder, & Associates, 2003) and subsequent reports are downloadable from their website. Around 2003, VHS adopted the Quality Benchmark Indicators (QBI) framework internally to evaluate the quality of the teacher training, the quality of the online courses, and the quality of the online program. More about this program can be found in Box 7.5: "Learning From Experience: Virtual High School."

Box 7.5 Learning From Experience: Virtual High School

Organization: VHS, Inc.

Contact: Liz Pape, President

URL: www.govhs.org

Date First Implemented: 1996

Audience: In terms of professional development, Virtual High School's primary audience has been K–12 classroom teachers interested in becoming an online teacher for their cooperative model. Subsequently, Virtual High School has created a series of shorter offerings called 21st Century Teaching Best Practices that are designed to help K–12 classroom teachers incorporate online technologies into their face-to-face classroom.

(Continued)

(Continued)

Need: *What Was the Initial Trigger?*

During a retreat for the Concord Consortium, Dr. Robert Tinker led a brainstorming session for proposal ideas in response to a Technology Innovation Challenge Grant from the U.S. Department of Education. The group built upon a successful online professional development grant from the National Science Foundation with the intent to teach classroom teachers to teach online in the Virtual High School.

Intended Outcomes:

According to Pape, "Training the teachers was the means to the end." The desired end was to create and deliver online courses that would enable *any* student to have access to that course, regardless of where they lived or what resources were available at their school. VHS's foundation is about "modeling the model." The basic model is the teacher becomes a student in an online course that requires them to behave in a way that is very close to the way they are expected to perform.

Incentives:

Teachers can receive professional development points or continuing education units. Graduate credits are also available. Incentives provided at the school level may include a laptop for the teacher's use and/or a stipend for taking online professional development.

Instructional Design Considerations:

Building on previous work at the Concord Consortium, VHS developed their own online design and delivery standards for developing and delivering courses and uses them to help their teachers understand how to take their knowledge of content and working with students and translate that into effective online instructional activities and content presentation.

Lessons Learned:

Something that was hoped to be an incentive but is probably more of an outcome, according to Pape, is that participation in VHS helps teachers improve their classroom instruction. Teachers report that going through the process has given them better classroom discussion leadership skills. Because teachers reported how their teaching has become more effective, VHS developed the 21st Century Teaching Best Practices courses so that other teachers could benefit from the modeling of these skills in their own instruction.

Pape emphasizes, "Always focus on the learning experience for the learners, not on the bells and whistles...I can say with a lot of confidence, where educators have not gotten it around the whole concept of educational technology is they see it as something *separate* and about using the tool instead of saying, 'this is a really cool tool that will enable me to teach in such and such a way.'" It's about the learning, not the technology.

Because of its longevity, VHS had to undergo an LMS change twice. In order to prepare, VHS sent out multiple communications targeted to their audiences (students, teachers, administrators, etc.) of how the process would occur and what it would look like for each audience group. To make the content migration easier from a technical standpoint, VHS uses templates to consistently organize and present content. Since the templates have consistent content-neutral components, they can use scripts to migrate the content from an old template to the new one without disrupting the content.

Evaluation:

VHS used SRI International as an external evaluator for their Technology Innovation Challenge Grant that originally funded VHS and published them in the book *The Virtual High School: Teaching Generation V* by Andrew Zucker et al. (2003). Because of that, VHS has always had an external evaluation, and these reports are downloadable from their website.

Around 2003, VHS adopted the Quality Benchmark Indicators (QBI) framework for internal evaluation efforts. VHS uses this framework to evaluate the quality of the teacher training, the quality of the online courses (for students), and the quality of the online program. The teacher training is evaluated by successful completion rates and the percentage of first-year teachers (to the VHS cooperative) who demonstrate mastery of online teaching skills as defined by the online teaching standards developed by VHS. Pape suggests that if you want to evaluate the effectiveness of your own online learning, start with a list of characteristics of good online teaching.

See the book's companion website for more information about the profiled programs.   **www.corwin.com/rossonlinepd**

WAS IT WORTH IT?

At the end of Chapter 2, I mentioned that I was able to participate on a team that conducted a cost-benefit analysis of one large-scale online professional development project that I helped to design and deliver—one of the few cost-benefit analyses of this type. The analysis (Cavalluzzo, Lopez, Ross, & Larson, 2005) demonstrated that this online professional development was cost-effective and demonstrated an economy of scale. The project consisted of the statewide delivery of a 16-week online professional development course on literacy assessment and instruction delivered in 2004 (see Box 1.1: "Learning From Experience: Comprehensive Literacy Program" in Chapter 1 for more details). Professional economists determined the effectiveness of reaching the outcomes as well as the cost per person as compared to delivering a comparable workshop in a face-to-face setting. Outcomes were measured at the level of changes in teacher knowledge, as funds were not available to conduct classroom observations that would have helped determine whether an outcome of changes in practice occurred. In reviewing pretest and posttest scores for

896 participants from 56 schools across the state, participant scores on the posttest increased significantly, both as a whole and for each of the five individual modules, even when controlling for teachers with additional experience or expertise in literacy.

Determining overall costs required calculating fixed costs and variable costs (see Figure 7.2). *Fixed costs* are those that would be the same for developing a course no matter how many people enroll and in this case were primarily the content and media development costs and the annual software subscription fee. You have to pay fixed costs regardless of whether one person or 100 people enroll. *Variable costs* fluctuate with the number of enrollments and include costs associated with support personnel salaries, training materials, and a per-person licensing fee. You may have salaries for additional staff members that are involved during your development or materials that are also variable costs. These costs can fluctuate over time as the costs of salaries and materials often increase, at least due to inflation. If you plan to do a cost-benefit comparison to your face-to-face professional development, be sure you include all appropriate costs, including hidden costs. Ross White at LEARN NC worked with professional development coordinators in his state to determine current spending on professional development in order to gauge the market value of their course-delivery costs. They found that school districts often underestimate the full cost of professional development. Says White, "If a district brings in a speaker for $5,000, they tend to forget the additional costs associated with substitutes, stipends for time spent outside of school hours, food, facilities rental, maintenance, and other costs make the total much higher."

Figure 7.2 Determining costs per participant

$$\text{Cost per participant} = \frac{\text{Total Fixed Cost} + \text{Total Variable Cost}}{\text{Number of Participants}}$$

Fixed Costs	Variable Costs
• Content development (subject-matter experts, instructional designer, editors, reviewers) • Media development (graphic, animation, video, and web development) • Software licenses or subscription costs	• Costs associated with doing business (salaries for support and maintenance personnel, rent, phones, printing, consumables, etc.) • Training materials (notebooks, paper, CDs/DVDs, others) and refreshments • Facilitation fees • Stipends or other incentives

It was determined that it cost $87.30 per person to deliver the 16-week course to 896 people in the 56 schools across the state. To determine a comparable face-to-face cost, we estimated we could deliver the same course in 5 days with travel required for a facilitator. Note that this doesn't take into question effectiveness at all. We didn't have any data to suggest that the face-to-face delivery would be any more or less effective. We estimated 16 teachers per school, although the number is immaterial since the workshop would have to be presented at all 56 locations regardless of the actual number of teachers per school. The fixed costs remained the same, but the additional burden of salaries, travel, and lodging for facilitators greatly increased the variable costs. Using a standard facilitation rate and estimates for travel and lodging (that were well founded because we had cost data on providing professional development within the same state for more than 40 years), we determined that it would cost $438 per person to deliver the workshop to these 56 schools as compared to our lower cost of $87.30 online. In terms of economy of scale, while the variable costs that make up the smallest part of online delivery would increase with each new participant, the overall cost per person would drop to $50.15 if we doubled our online enrollment to 1,792 participants. It would be as low as $31.38 per person if we delivered it to 3,584 participants. Over time, we far exceeded that number, so yeah, it was worth it!

This is just one example of how online professional development can be cost-effective. Had we delivered that initial training to far fewer persons, it would not have been as cost-effective. Based on your initial investment (your fixed costs), you may need a significant audience to be cost-effective in your training. You may have different outcomes and may choose different methods and technologies to use them. I've continued to experiment with different formats—discussion lists, book studies, webinars, social networking sites—but have not had the luxury to complete such a thorough analysis as the initial study. Some of these opportunities, however, require significantly less initial investment and can be offered to fewer people at a reasonable cost.

ONE STORY: THE FRAMEWORK IN ACTION

The book concludes with a short recounting of a multiyear project I've been involved with, at least up to the time of this book's publication. I believe it serves as a good illustration as to how the OPD Framework can inform the development and delivery of online professional development. It illustrates many key ideas in the book, like how there's no one such thing as online professional development, it's how you use the technology that matters, and the process is a recursive one based on evaluation data.

Year 1

As the director of technology for the Appalachia Regional Comprehensive Center (ARCC) funded by the U.S. Department of Education, my duties included investigating and integrating technologies that could be used to support large-scale technical assistance initiatives in a five-state region. As part of that work, I was asked to attend a meeting with Joanne Marino, Title III Consultant with the North Carolina Department of Public Instruction (DPI), to determine how the ARCC might help support her work with a statewide cadre of coaches whose purpose was to help teachers learn and use strategies from the research-based Sheltered Instruction Observation Protocol (SIOP) to support English language learners (ELLs). North Carolina has one of the fastest growing populations per capita of ELLs in the country, and DPI had identified SIOP as a framework for helping teachers meet the needs of these students. Important to the project is the fact that SIOP already has a coaching component built into it, and Joanne was helping her cadre members become SIOP coaches who could then return to their own schools and districts. She knew what outcomes she wanted to achieve—changes in student performance by changing teacher practice. Her problem was she was too successful! She had very limited staff (she and one other), and the demand for new coaches was tremendous. Her limited resources also prevented her from providing as much follow-up training as she preferred, so it could be years before a cadre member could return for follow-up training, which was insufficient for systemic change and developing deep knowledge and skills. Despite clear expectations, she was challenged to reach them.

When designing the ARCC program, the management team had proposed something we called *eCoaching*, which owes much of its genesis to a talented and visionary educator, Sharon Harsh, who became the director of the program. The idea was to use readily available digital technologies to connect educators with accomplished peers to promote professional growth by building, expanding, or refining skills and knowledge. No specific technologies are dictated; instead, the idea is to use technologies that are available and appropriate that might help educators connect across school or district boundaries when it wasn't reasonable, feasible, or even possible to do it otherwise. eCoaching is not a coaching model, but is intended instead to support existing coaching models, which is why the coaching cadre in North Carolina was a good fit.

Joanne had received much well-intentioned advice about technologies to support her needs, but there seemed to be too much emphasis on the technology and not enough on the outcomes. It was difficult to determine *how* the technology options would be used. We stepped back from the discussion about what technologies to use and instead collected some information to see how they might be used to reach her goals. Following the suggestion in the first step of the OPD Framework, we conducted a needs assessment. Our results were surprising.

An online needs assessment was used to determine what technologies the cadre members had access to and were comfortable with. Data from the needs assessment indicated technology use for school-based activities was low—including uses related to instruction, research to support teaching, professional development, and assessment. Participants who responded indicated they accessed computers both at home and school, but most often (64.6% of the time) at school. And of the fairly long list of technologies we thought they might have available, the technologies they reported as being most comfortable with and had the greatest access to were e-mail (with attachments), taking digital pictures, and searching the Internet. Few reported using social networking, participating in webconferences, or creating or posting to a blog or wiki. This helped us to realize that if we wanted to support this cadre to develop their coaching knowledge and skills, we had to begin with activities similar to sending e-mails and searching the Internet, but I also incorporated my "one-step beyond" philosophy.

During the first year, we developed an 8-week online book study for a pilot group consisting of 20 members from the cadre. The book study used discussion software that was similar to sending an e-mail—one of our audience's proficiencies—that stored the group's messages online. The idea and process was presented to the cadre members at a face-to-face training session to help generate buy-in and seek input. The book study was facilitated but conducted primarily asynchronously with weekly deadlines. A synchronous kick-off webinar introduced the discussion software (providing an opportunity for technology training) and provided an orientation to the topic, including using two classroom videos previously developed by DPI. An archive of the webinar and a help manual with annotated screen shots and step-by-step directions was created. At the end of the book study, the facilitator arranged to have the authors of the book participate in a second synchronous webconference so the participants could ask questions directly to the authors and share their experiences (talk about relevance!). That webinar, too, was archived, and a separate facilitator's manual was created for the book that included all of the activities from the book study as well as audio clips from the interview with the authors. Evaluators for the project conducted an analysis of the quality and quantity of the discussion posts and administered a participant survey online with forced-choice and open-ended questions. That data was used to revise the program.

One thing we learned from the evaluation was that there was a lack of awareness about SIOP with educators outside of the cadre, especially district administrators and building-level principals, and this made it difficult to get buy-in and support from these key stakeholders. This volunteer group also graciously told us that if this had not been a pilot effort, they would have been reluctant to participate for 8 weeks with no incentive or compensation. The facilitator, who was excellent to begin with and a subject-matter expert in working with ELLs, learned additional strategies for focusing the conversation as well as organizing the specific discussion software we used so participants could more easily find where they were supposed to post. We also learned that about half of the school districts blocked all streaming media, so very few could view the videos at school (where most of them completed their computer time), even though we posted them on a separate website. We took all of these lessons into consideration when revising the opportunities for Year 2.

Year 2

To build awareness and generate greater buy-in from key stakeholders at the district and building level, we delivered three 1-hour webinars for superintendents and principals, not the SIOP coaches or teachers, so the language used and examples selected were targeted to administrators. We demonstrated relevance and addressed these adults' needs to know why this was important by providing background on the SIOP process, some of the research and data behind it, figures on the growing ELL population and how that was impacting student achievement across the state, and what to expect if they wanted to implement SIOP in their schools. The third webinar, which was especially successful, featured stories from several districts across the state that had implemented SIOP and were in different stages of implementation. They were able to use local voices and experiences to share information and actual materials with those on the webinar, and it went on 30 minutes longer than originally planned. Attendance was very high, possibly because the webinars were advertised through e-mail news blasts and superintendent meetings sponsored by DPI. All of the webinars were archived along with any related material mentioned in them.

For the second book study, we planned a shorter 4-week study of a book that included a DVD, so we overcame the streaming media problem. We hoped to get 20 participants. Everyone who participated would get the book with the DVD, and recertification credit was offered upon successful completion, with those requirements carefully spelled out. The response was overwhelming. We had to close registration 2 days early because we had more than 200 people register for the book study. We eventually ran three rounds of the book study with two groups of 25 participating per round. Joanne was able to have representatives from every district that had originally registered and really raised the exposure of SIOP across the entire state.

Evaluations were held after all events in the second year, and we learned that even a small, tangible incentive can be effective. We also believe that providing as much structure as possible led to greater success with high completion rates. Several participants reported using the materials from the book study in their own classes both during the discussions and in the evaluations, demonstrating self-reported changes in practice. From that, we developed replicable processes that the state then continued to use on their own to offer their own book studies on these and other books. For Year 3, based on the level of success with the discussion-based technologies, I wanted to push one step further.

Year 3

During Year 3, the team intended to move beyond directed discussions to trying to promote more open-ended interactions using social networking software. Title III staff created a Ning, which supports discussions through forums and blogs, as well as videos, images, a calendar, and many other functions. Two different groups of SIOP cadre members were targeted, one of which was composed entirely of science teachers who attended a face-to-face training in the summer. The other consisted of faculty members at two different schools who met during the same time period but only with other members in their own faculty. We realized that real coaching takes significant training and practice to master, and while we called our process eCoaching, we didn't want our participants to think that just because they had participated in a session or two they would be fully prepared SIOP coaches. So, to help them build community and develop connections with others in their group, Joanne came up with the name "SIOP Soulmates." The idea was that the SIOP Soulmates would focus on three specific components from the SIOP framework during the year and would have conversations about them, not necessarily formal coaching sessions. We provided support in terms of an SIOP subject expert and a technology expert who supported operational issues.

Again, our evaluators helped us to learn several lessons. Incentives are still important, but perhaps more important are facilitation, structure, and buy-in at the local level. The facilitator for one group had little technical training or experience with the Ning and provided no structured activities. The other, who worked with two schools, provided more structured activities using the Ning, but the greatest indicators of success were demonstrated at the school where the assistant principal attended sessions with her faculty, who were provided release time to complete the activities during the school day. On a different note, we also learned that spontaneous collaboration can occur, so you may want to be flexible with your model. A group of five middle school teachers selected to be SIOP Soulmates to each other rather than to just one other individual, and they collaborated fairly often using the Ning.

The Future

The program continues to grow and has reached an exciting stage. In Year 4, we moved from the Ning platform to a closed, online collaborative site developed specifically to support coaching and mentoring in education. It is structured to allow users to upload or download lesson plans, implementation plans, videos, and other artifacts from teaching and learning. The statewide coaching cadre is excitedly developing or repurposing training materials that can now be posted in a single place and accessed anywhere in the state to supplement face-to-face professional development or be used entirely online by individuals or groups. As powerful and promising as this technology appears to be, if it had been available when we started, the cadre would not have been ready for it. That needs assessment was critical for helping us to know what our target audience would accept, and I feel like we pushed them a step at a time until they are now ready for this dynamic social environment. My hope is that this project is at a new beginning, and it will continue to work its way up the level of outcomes to someday be able to point back to efforts from this online professional development that are clearly linked to student performance outcomes.

DESIGN, DELIVER, SUCCEED!

I truly hope you find this information helpful for successfully designing and delivering your own online professional development. My experiences were opportunities for learning that I hope you can benefit from. Perhaps the most rewarding part of this process was meeting and talking with other people who have taken their own journeys towards providing online professional development. There was a remarkable sense of agreement and even overlapping of experiences in those conversations. I appreciate all of the advice I've picked up from those interviews as well as the many excellent educators I've been able to work with across the nation who have helped to shape my own experiences in designing and delivering online professional development. I hope you find their input valuable.

I like situations that are fairly organized, but sometimes I had to venture into areas where no true organization existed. That's why I hope you find the framework in this book helpful. I hope you find answers to questions you may have about designing and delivering online professional development and find it useful in your own work, whether you're going to do it all on your own or purchase parts or entire programs. Although it provides organization, it doesn't dictate any one solution. There really is no one such thing as online professional development, with my eCoaching story in this chapter being one such example of the many shapes and forms it can take. I would love to hear about your own experiences, and I encourage you to share them through the book's website. As my good buddy and former colleague Joy Runyan likes to say, "We're all in this together."

Earlier I noted—like many other people before me—that perhaps the one true constant in technology is change. Who knows where we're going, what technologies will be developed, and how online professional development will grow and change in the years to come? When I started on this journey, I didn't realize that many thousands of teachers would access and use material I helped to put together. I didn't know I'd be hosting webconferences with people across the nation from my home office (but not in my pajamas). Yet the framework in this book should help you work towards your goals while managing the changes in technology tools and practices. It's a guide, like a map is a guide. A map shows you the possibilities, letting you know how you might get from here to there, but it doesn't dictate the road you have to take. But you can still get there successfully.

References

Chapter 1

Birman, B. F., Desimone, L., Porter, A. C., & Garet, M. S. (2000). Designing professional development that works. *Educational Leadership, 57*(8), 28–33.

Dede, C. (Ed.). (2006). *Online professional development for teachers. Emerging models and methods.* Cambridge, MA: Harvard Education Press.

Gall, M. D., & Vojtek, R. O. (1994). *Planning for effective staff development: Six research-based models* (ED372464). Eugene, OR: ERIC Clearinghouse of Educational Management.

Guskey, T. R. (2000). *Evaluating professional development.* Thousand Oaks, CA: Corwin Press.

Guskey, T. R. (2003). What makes professional development effective? *Phi Delta Kappan, 84*(10), 748–750.

Hassel, E. (1999). *Professional development: Learning from the best. A toolkit for schools and districts based on the National Awards Program for Model Professional Development.* Oak Brook, IL: North Central Regional Educational Laboratory.

iNACOL. (2010a). *National standards for quality online teaching. Updated.* Vienna, VA: International Association for K–12 Online Learning.

iNACOL. (2010b). *National standards of quality for online courses. Updated.* Vienna, VA: International Association for K–12 Online Learning.

Joyce, B., & Showers, B. (2002). *Student achievement through staff development* (3rd ed.). Alexandria, VA: Association for Supervision and Curriculum Development.

Keller, J. M. (1987). Strategies for stimulating the motivation to learn. *Performance and Instruction, 26*(8), 1–7.

Larson, M. (2005). *Professional development models: A review of the literature.* Charleston, WV: AEL, Inc.

National Staff Development Council. (2001). *Standards for staff development.* Oxford, OH: Author.

National Staff Development Council. (2004). *E-learning for educators. Implementing the standards for staff development.* Oxford, OH: Author.

Southern Regional Educational Board. (2004). *Standards for online professional development. Guidelines for planning and evaluating online professional development courses.* Atlanta, GA: Author.

Yoon, K. W., Duncan, T., Lee, S. W., Scarloss, B., & Shapley, K. L. (2007). *Reviewing the evidence on how teacher professional development affects student achievement.* Washington, DC: Institute of Education Sciences, U.S. Department of Education.

Chapter 2

DuFour, R., DuFour, R., & Eaker, R. (2008). *Revisiting professional learning communities at work™*. Bloomington, IN: Solution Tree.

Gray, L., Thomas, N., & Lewis, L. (2010). *Educational technology in U.S. public schools: Fall 2008* (NCES 2010-034). Washington, DC: U.S. Government Printing Office.

Guskey, T. R. (2000). See Chapter 1.

O'Dwyer, L. M., Masters, J., Dash, S., De Kramer, R. M., Humez, A., & Russell, M. (2010). *E-learning for educators: Effects of online professional development on teachers and their students*. Chestnut Hill, MA: Boston College.

Wenger, E., McDermott, R., & Snyder, W. M. (2002). *Cultivating communities of practice* (Kindle ed.). Boston, MA: Harvard Business School Press.

Chapter 4

Cennamo, K., & Kalk, D. (2004). *Real world instructional design*. Belmont, CA: Wadsworth.

Dick, W., Carey, L., & Carey, J. O. (2008). *The systematic design of instruction* (7th ed.). Upper Saddle, River, NJ: Pearson.

Edvantia, Inc. (2004). *Assessment and intervention in a comprehensive literacy classroom*. Charleston, WV: Author.

Ertmer, P., York, C. S., & Gedik, N. (2009). Learning from the pros: How experienced designers translate instructional design models into practice. *Educational Technology, 49*(1), 19–27.

Keller, J. M. (1987). See Chapter 1.

Knowles, M. S. (1990). *The adult learner: A neglected species* (4th ed.). Houston, TX: Gulf Publishing.

Marzano, R. J., Pickering, D. J., & Pollock, J. E. (2001). *Classroom instruction that works. Research-based strategies for increasing student achievement*. Alexandria, VA: Association for Supervision and Curriculum Development.

Trowbridge, L. W., & Bybee, R. W. (1990). *Becoming a secondary school science teacher* (5th ed.). Columbus, OH: Merrill.

Wiggins, G., & McTighe, J. (2005). *Understanding by design* (Expanded 2nd ed.) [Electronic resource]. Alexandria, VA: Association for Supervision and Curriculum Development.

Chapter 6

Collison, G., Erlbaum, B., Haavind, S., & Tinker, R. (Eds.). (2000). *Facilitating on-line learning: Effective strategies for moderators*. Madison, WI: Atwood.

Hootstein, E. (2002). Wearing four pairs of shoes: The roles of e-learning facilitators. *Learning Circuits. ASTD Online Magazine*. Alexandria, VA: ASTD. Retrieved from www.astd.org/LC/2002/1002_hootstein.htm

Salmon, G. (2004). *E-moderating: The key to teaching and learning online* (2nd ed.). New York: Routledge Falmer.

Chapter 7

Cavalluzzo, L., Lopez, D., Ross, J. D., & Larson, M. (2005). *A study of the effectiveness and cost of AEL's online professional development program in reading in Tennessee*. Charleston, WV: AEL.

Clark, R. E. (1983). Reconsidering research on learning from media. *Review of Educational Research, 53*(4), 445–459.

Desimone, L. (2009). Improving impact studies of teachers' professional development: Toward better conceptualizations and measures. *Educational Researcher, 38*(3), 181–199.

Guskey, T. R. (2000). See Chapter 1.

Nielsen, J. (2000, March 19). Why you only need to test with 5 users. *Alertbox*. Retrieved from www.useit.com/alertbox/20000319.html

Sherman, G., Byers, A., & Rapp, S. (2008). Evaluation of online, on-demand science professional development material involving two different implementation models. *Journal of Science Education and Technology, 17*(1), 19–31.

Yoon, K. S., Duncan, T., Lee, S. W., Scarloss, B., & Shapley, K. L. (2007). See Chapter 1.

Zucker, A. A., Kozma, R., Yarnall, L., Marder, C., & Associates. (2003). *The virtual high school: Teaching Generation V*. New York, NY: Teachers College Press.

Index

CORWIN
A SAGE Company

The Corwin logo—a raven striding across an open book—represents the union of courage and learning. Corwin is committed to improving education for all learners by publishing books and other professional development resources for those serving the field of PreK–12 education. By providing practical, hands-on materials, Corwin continues to carry out the promise of its motto: **"Helping Educators Do Their Work Better."**

Advancing professional learning for student success

Learning Forward (formerly National Staff Development Council) is an international association of learning educators committed to one purpose in K–12 education: Every educator engages in effective professional learning every day so every student achieves.